THE
HARBOR

Empowering Your Church Through Creativity and Change

LIBRARY OF CHRISTIAN Leadership

Empowering Your Church Through Creativity and Change

30 Strategies to Transform Your Ministry

Marshall Shelley, General Editor

MOORINGS
Nashville, Tennessee
A Division of The Ballantine Publishing Group, Random House, Inc.

Library of Christian Leadership
EMPOWERING YOUR CHURCH THROUGH CREATIVITY AND CHANGE

The material in this book was previously published in *Leadership,* by Christianity Today, Inc.

Scripture quotations marked (KJV) are taken from the Authorized King James version of the Bible.

Scripture quotations marked (NIV) are taken from the HOLY BIBLE, NEW INTERNATIONAL VERSION®. NIV®. Copyright © 1973, 1978, 1984 by International Bible Society. Used by permission of Zondervan Publishing House. All rights reserved.

Scripture quotations marked (NKJV) are from the NEW KING JAMES VERSION. Copyright © 1979, 1980, 1982, Thomas Nelson, Inc., Publishers.

Scripture quotations marked (NASB) are taken from THE NEW AMERICAN STANDARD BIBLE, Copyright © 1960, 1962, 1963, 1968, 1971, 1972, 1973, 1975, 1977 by The Lockman Foundation and are used by permission.

Library of Congress Cataloging-in-Publication Data

Empowering your church through creativity and change : 30 strategies to transform your ministry / Marshall Shelley, general editor.
    p.   cm. — (Library of Christian leadership ; 2)
Includes bibliographical references.
ISBN 0-345-39597-2
    1. Pastoral theology.   2. Christian leadership.   3. Change—Religious aspects—Christianity.   4. Creative ability—Religious aspects—Christianity.
I. Shelley, Marshall.   II. Series.
BV4011.E466   1995
253—dc20   95-40782
                                            CIP

First Edition: October 1995

10 9 8 7 6 5 4 3 2 1

Contents

Part 6
Making Changes

Part 7
Helping People Change

Part 8
Coping with Personal Change

Introduction

Creativity and change often seem to follow closely on the heels of the Spirit.

—David L. Goetz

Besides death and taxes there is one sure thing in life for church leaders: people don't like you messin' with the status quo.

Making changes at church is a little like kicking a sleeping grizzly. Or playing with her cubs. You risk getting mauled.

People say they want change and improvement, but I've never heard a layperson say, "I love our pastor because he is so creative and makes so many wonderful changes."

I don't subscribe to Machiavelli's ethics, but I resonate with his perceptions about the politics of change. In *The Prince* he wrote, "It ought to be remembered there is nothing more difficult to take in hand, more perilous to conduct, or more uncertain in its success, than to take the lead in the introduction of a new order of things. Because the innovator has for enemies all those who have done well under the old conditions, and lukewarm defenders among those who may do well under the new."

It's not that most church people are openly hostile toward creativity and change. No, if you ask any loyal church member, "Do you think creativity and change are vital to the life of this church?" she would most likely say yes. The question is akin to asking the average middle-class person, "Do you think Congress should take steps to reduce the deficit?"

"Of course! But don't raise my taxes."

The rub always comes with the changes of change: unfamiliar faces, different music, scheduling problems, inconvenience. One layperson recently groused to me about her church's decision to go to three Sunday services.

"I love our pastor," she said. "He's so dynamic. But I don't think it's a good idea to move the traditional service to 8:00 Sunday morning. Our older folks like the traditional service. Now it will be too early for them. And besides, who will sing in the choir if they have to come at 7:15 to rehearse? That's just too early."

She had a point. But for the church to reach out, something—someone—had to give. Someone had to sacrifice. She and her colleagues had been asked to give.

Effective church leaders recognize the inherent sacrifice in change.

Empowering Your Church Through Creativity and Change is written by top-notch practitioners in love not with change for change's sake but with the church of Jesus Christ. All believe that innovation is part of a healthy, vibrant church community, and that creativity and change often seem to follow closely on the heels of the Spirit.

Our hope is that you'll discover in the following pages ideas and principles and stories that can feed your creativity and help you guide your church through change. And thus open it up to a fresh outpouring of God's Spirit.

—David L. Goetz
associate editor, *Leadership Journal*

Contributors

Leith Anderson is pastor of Wooddale Church in Eden Prairie, Minnesota, a suburb of Minneapolis. A contributing editor of *Leadership*, he is author of *Dying for Change* and *A Church for the 21st Century*. He is also coauthor of *Mastering Church Management, Who's in Charge?*, and the tape series *The Best Is Yet to Come*.

Raymond Bakke is executive director of International Urban Associates, a network of church and mission leaders seeking to empower Christian leaders in the world's largest cities. From 1959 to 1979, Ray pastored inner-city churches in Seattle and Chicago. He also cofounded the Seminary Consortium for Urban Pastoral Education (SCUPE). He is the author of *The Urban Christian*.

Ray Bowman is a church consultant for the planning of facilities. He was principal in the architectural firms Kobo, Bowman, and Smallwood in Idaho and Bowman and Nicek in Oklahoma City, Oklahoma. He has also taught at Southern Nazarene University, University of Kansas, and Kansas State University. He is the author of *Church Building Source Book, When Not to Build*, and *When Not to Borrow*.

Ed Bratcher is a retired minister living in Durham, North Carolina. The son of missionaries to Brazil, he pastored for four decades, including pastorates in Virginia, Missouri, and Texas. He is the author of *The Walk-on-Water Syndrome* and coauthor of *Mastering Transitions.*

Harold Glen Brown is a retired minister living in Fort Worth, Texas. He served as professor of pastoral ministry at Brite Divinity School. From 1966 to 1978, he was senior minister of Community Church in Kansas City, Missouri, and before that served churches in Oregon and Texas.

Suzan D. Johnson Cook is pastor of the Mariners' Temple Baptist Church in New York City. She has served on the Domestic Policy Council at the White House and is a special consultant for religious initiatives with Housing and Urban Development in Washington, D.C. She also served as an adjunct professor in urban studies and homiletics at Harvard Divinity School.

George Gallup, Jr., is chairman of the George H. Gallup International Institute, cochairman of the Gallup Organization, Inc., and executive director of the Princeton Religion Research Center. His books include *American's Search for Faith, The People's Religion, Varieties of Prayer,* and *The Saints Among Us.*

Donald Gerig is pastor of Huron Hills Baptist Church in Ann Arbor, Michigan. Formerly president of Summit Christian College in Fort Wayne, Indiana, he also served churches in Illinois and Indiana. He is author of *Leadership in Crisis.*

Bill Giovannetti is pastor of Windy City Community Church in Chicago, which he helped plant in 1987.

Gary Gonzales is pastor of Elim Baptist Church in Minneapolis, Minnesota. He also serves as associate faculty member in preaching at Bethel Seminary in St. Paul, Minnesota.

Eddy Hall is a freelance writer and editor living in Goessel, Kansas. His books include *When Not to Build* (coauthored with Ray Bowman), *Praying with the Anabaptists* (coauthored with Marlene Kropf), and *The Lay Ministry Revolution.*

R. Kent Hughes has been pastor of College Church in Wheaton, Illinois, since 1979. He is author of *Disciplines of a Godly Man* and *Liberating Ministry from the Success Syndrome,* and coauthor of *Mastering the Pastoral Role.*

Robert Kemper is minister of the First Congregational Church (UCC) in Western Springs, Illinois. He was founding editor of *The Christian Ministry,* an ecumenical professional journal for clergy, and was associate editor of *Christian Century.* He is coauthor of *Mastering Transitions.*

Craig Brian Larson is an Assemblies of God minister, itinerant speaker, and writer living in Arlington Heights, Illinois. He is contributing editor of *Leadership* and is author of *Running the Midnight Marathon* and coauthor of *Preaching That Connects.*

Knute Larson is pastor of The Chapel, a downtown church in Akron, Ohio. He has also been the executive director for church growth and Christian education for the Grace Brethren churches. He is the author of *Run Steady, Run Straight* and *Growing Adults on Sunday Morning,* and coauthor of *Measuring Up.*

Michael Lewis is minister of Bammel Road Church of Christ in Houston, Texas. Prior to that, he served as pulpit minister for the Minter Lane congregation in Abilene, Texas, and as professor of communications and Bible at Abilene Christian University. He earned a Ph.D. from the University of Oklahoma.

David Mains is director of The Chapel of the Air, a fifteen-minute radio broadcast heard throughout North America. Before that he founded and pastored Circle Church in Chicago. His books include *Full Circle, Healing the Dysfunctional Church Family,* and *Never Too Late to Dream.*

Calvin Miller is professor of communications and ministry studies, and writer-in-residence at Southwestern Baptist Theological Seminary in Fort Worth, Texas. Before that he served as pastor of Westside Church in Omaha, Nebraska, for more than twenty-five years. His many books include *The Singer; A Requiem for Love; Spirit, Word and Story;* and *Empowered Communicator.*

Robert J. Morgan is pastor of Donelson Free Will Baptist Church in Nashville, Tennessee. Before that, he pastored Harris Memorial Church in Greeneville, Tennessee.

John Ortberg is teaching pastor at Willow Creek Community Church. Before that he founded Horizons Community Church in Diamond Bar, California. He has a Ph.D. (in clinical psychology) from Fuller Theological Seminary, Pasadena, California, and is coauthor of *Dangers, Toils, and Snares.*

Larry Osborne is a senior pastor at North Coast Church in Vista, California, a suburb of San Diego. He is author of *The Unity Factor* and coauthor of *Measuring Up.*

Ben Patterson is dean of the chapel at Hope College in Holland, Michigan. Before that he pastored Presbyterian congregations in New Jersey and California. He is contributing editor to *Christianity Today* and *Leadership,* author of *Waiting: Finding Hope When God Seems Silent,* and coauthor of *Mastering the Pastoral Role* and *Who's in Charge?*

James Rose is pastor of Grace Covenant Church in Austin, Texas. Before that he pastored Calvary Baptist Church in New York City. A graduate of Georgia Institute of Technology, he worked in America's aerospace program for five years before entering seminary.

Douglas Rumford is pastor of First Presbyterian Church of Fresno, California. Before that he served as pastor of First Presbyterian Church of Fairfield, Connecticut.

Donald Seibert was chairman and chief executive officer at J. C. Penney for many years. He is an active church leader: a Sunday school teacher, a singer, and an elder and trustee. He also helped lead a small Bible study group of top corporate executives.

Fred Smith is contributing editor of *Leadership* and a board member of *Christianity Today.* From 1966 to 1986, he owned and operated a Dallas-based food-packaging corporation. He was also an executive for Genesco, Powell Valve Company, and Gruen Watch Company, and was awarded the Lawrence Appley

Award by the American Management Association. He is author of *You and Your Network* and *Learning to Lead*.

James Stobaugh is pastor of First Presbyterian Church of Johnstown, Pennsylvania. He was awarded the Merrill Fellowship and joined the Harvard Divinity School faculty for one semester. Before that he pastored Fourth Presbyterian Church in Pittsburgh, Pennsylvania, for seven years.

David Trumble is pastor of Georgetown Christian Church in Georgetown, Texas. He has also served as instructor at Eastern Christian College. He specializes in assisting struggling congregations find practical ministry options.

Lem Tucker was president of Voice of Calvary ministries in Jackson, Mississippi, until his death in 1989.

Philip Yancey is a writer living in Colorado and an editor-at-large for *Christianity Today*. His articles have appeared in *Reader's Digest, The Saturday Evening Post,* and *Christian Century*. He is author of *Disappointment with God,* and coauthor of *Fearfully and Wonderfully Made* and *Pain: The Gift Nobody Wants*.

Section 1:
Empowering Your Church Through Creativity

Invention, strictly speaking, is little more than a new combination of those images which have been previously gathered and deposited in the memory. Nothing can be made of nothing; he who has laid up no materials can produce no combinations.

—JOSHUA REYNOLDS
eighteenth-century portrait painter

PART 1

The Creative Pastor

1

The Well-Fed Imagination

Original thinking is seldom original.
— Robert J. Morgan

For a long time, I didn't consider myself creative. The very term intimidated me. I'm a traditional guy at heart, a little staid and stuffy. I don't bungee-jump or tie-dye. I prefer Bach to rock, and G. F. Handel to M. C. Hammer. I enjoy the doxology on the Lord's Day, and we still have Sunday night services.

But I wasn't always that way.

As a child, my imagination resembled a kitten in a room of windup toys. I chased every idea, scratched every itch, and pounced on every adventure. My secondhand bicycle became alternately a helicopter and a powerboat. I unraveled mysteries and swept starlets off their feet. I composed poems and plays.

When I lurched into adolescence, my imagination followed like a shadow. It questioned boring traditions, dreaming of better ways and better days. It wondered why no one had ever done a thousand doable things. I was an impressionable teen when Bobby Kennedy campaigned for the presidency with his passionate claim, "Some men see things as they are and say 'Why?' I dream things that never were and say 'Why not?'"

Why, then, twenty years later, didn't I consider myself an innovator? What had happened between adolescence and adulthood to silence my imagination? I Think I Can't, I Think I Can't.

Lack of self-confidence is the biggest barrier to creativity, according to the Center for Studies in Creativity at the State University of New York. We become set in our ways, afraid to change, too old to dream—or so we think.

"The way we talk about creativity tends to reinforce the notion that it is some kind of arbitrary gift," echoes John Briggs, author of *Fire in the Crucible: The Alchemy of Creative Genius.* "It's amazing the way 'not having it' becomes wedded to people's self-image. They invariably work up a whole series of rationalizations about why they aren't creative, as if they were damaged goods of some kind." That was me.

But I realized something else: the acceleration of change in our society makes creativity increasingly important. The ancient message requires up-to-date ways and means to stay relevant with contemporary culture.

"Customers came to us and said if we didn't change, they'd go somewhere else," says David Luther, corporate director of quality at Corning.

That's why in the business world nearly one company in three offers creativity training for its employees. That's why dozens of books, tapes, games, and software packages focus on creativity exercises and processes. That's why increasing numbers of universities offer degrees in creativity training. That's why many experts call creativity "the survival skill of the nineties."

I still appreciate the benefits of the traditional, but I don't want to be confined by its liabilities. I want to be "like the owner of a house who brings out of his storeroom new treasures as well as old" (Matt. 13:52). God sowed the seeds of creativity in the furrows of the left side of my brain, and I realize now is the time to cultivate for the harvest.

So I made an irrevocable decision: to once again think of myself as an imagineer. I would guide my staff and church to "dream things that never were, and say 'Why not?' " I've learned to do that by keeping five steps in mind. I call them my M&Ms, and I use them to feed my imagination.

Milk

"I milk a lot of cows, but I churn my own butter," said one preacher. Original thinking is seldom original; it just looks that way. I begin by milking all the ideas I can from others. I read, study, interview, inspect, dissect, and observe. I take classes and endure seminars. I subscribe and ascribe, describe and transcribe, gathering premium ideas wherever possible, for only God can make something from nothing.

Take existing ideas and play with them, turning them upside down and inside out. Challenge them, change them, and channel them in unlikely directions. Churn milk into butter, then press it into different molds.

I worried for a long time about providing adequate pastoral care for my congregation. When I originally came to the Donelson Fellowship, the membership was small enough for me to shepherd. But as the church grew, my availability shrunk. Staff additions didn't help much because their responsibilities weren't always in pastoral areas. Finally I read of a program called the "Family Flock" developed by another denomination. I decided to import it into our church. We divided the congregation into ten groups and with some fanfare assigned our deacons over the groups.

The fanfare didn't last long. Some of the deacons, despite their good intentions, lacked pastoral skills, and others had logistical problems finding their fold. Our family flock ministry sputtered along for a while, then fizzled. I learned the hard way you can't take an idea and slap it up like a piece of wallpaper.

You have to take a lot of them and mix them together like custom-colored paint. We started reading everything we could find about lay-pastoral programs. We attended "Equipping the Laity for Ministry"–type seminars. We visited churches, telephoned pastors, reviewed notebooks, and conducted surveys. We blended colors, used others as enamel highlights, and ended up with our own uniquely designed program. We commissioned our own lay pastors, who are now doing an admirable job.

"An idea is nothing more or less than a new combination of old elements," wrote James Webb Young in his classic treatise on creativity, *A Technique for Producing Ideas*. Young contends that gathering the data is what most people neglect.

> Instead of working systematically at the job of gathering raw material we sit around hoping for inspiration to strike us. Every really good creative person in advertising whom I have ever known has always had two noticeable characteristics. First, there was no subject under the sun in which he could not easily get interested. Every facet of life had fascination for him. Second, he was an extensive browser in all sorts of fields of information. For it is with the advertising man as with the cow: no browsing, no milk.

Meet

Once you've milked all the available cows, the next step is to gather the butter-makers into one room for brainstorming, a time when we gather around the table with our pails of milk and start splashing each other. We suspend criticism and toss around ideas capriciously.

"To have a good idea," said Edison, "have lots of ideas."

Brainstorming provides them. A great time for this is the beginning of our staff meetings before we've exhausted our mental energies on calendars and budgets.

Just today, for example, we took ten minutes at the beginning of our weekly staff meeting to discuss a problem in the previous Sunday night worship service. We had placed a call to a missionary in France, but it didn't channel through our sanctuary audio system.

"What can we do about it?" I asked.

"Well, we could buy the equipment to do it right," one staff member suggested. "It would sound like the call-in shows on the radio or like the 'Phil Donahue Show.' "

"How much would that cost?"

"Six hundred to a thousand dollars."

"That's an awful lot of money for an occasional phone call to France."

"Well, there are other things we could do with that technology."

"Like what?"

"We could call our missionaries during our annual missions conference and let them preach to us via the phone lines."

"We could have them join us for special prayer times."

"They could bring us news flashes live from the field."

"Is there anything nonmissionary we could do with it?"

"We could call our aged, sick, and shut-ins."

"What about calling people who are absent and ask them why!" (*Laughter*)

"We could call disaster areas for live updates from Christian organizations on the scene."

"And we could call noted authors and well-known Christians. Suppose we devoted a service to the disabled. We could call Joni Eareckson Tada. We may never be able to have her at our church in person, but perhaps we could arrange for her to share with us for five minutes during a service. We could project her picture on our screen while she's speaking to us."

"This would appeal to the unchurched visiting our services because they're used to seeing that on television."

"We could involve noted authorities on our panel discussions, and with a wireless mike we could go into the audience for questions."

"Like Oprah."

In only ten minutes, we had generated a set of possibilities and generated enough excitement to carry us through the remaining fifty minutes of our meeting with enthusiasm.

Mist

But there's a problem.

The brainstorming process usually ends in the fabulous frustration of too many ideas. We become too involved to be rational, too hot for cold calculation, too close for objective thinking. A thick mental mist descends.

Solo creative efforts such as sermon preparation also involve this stage of perplexity. After we've exegeted the text, read the commentaries, and gathered the data, the question arises: Now what? What do I do with all this stuff? What direction do I take? What application do I make? What outline do I follow? It's like fighting through a corridor thick with cobwebs.

Earlier this year when our minister of worship resigned, we appointed a large committee to search out a replacement. We collected resumes and ideas from many sources, and we refashioned the job description and salary package. We developed options and brainstormed potentials. But the committee couldn't agree on anyone, not even on the profile we wanted to follow; we had too many options. I began dreading the meetings—not because of discord but because of the confusion of too many ideas coming from too many people.

But as a reborn imagineer, I eventually recognized it as a good sign. It meant we were right in the middle of the creative process, on our way to the fourth phase.

Mull

For the creative, leisure is no luxury. We need time and solitude. Imagineers walk frequently around Walden Pond. They are children of Isaac who "went out to the field one evening to meditate." That's why creative people often appear absent-minded.

I periodically go for a couple of days to a state park an hour's drive from my house with cabins that rent cheap. I think of it as Camp David—my version of the president's weekend stomping grounds. I retreat there to ponder and pray. Our church staff withdraws there annually for the same purpose. Ideas must incubate awhile before they're hatched. They must wander through the chambers of the mind before they're ready for debut. That often happens as I wander through the forests of the Cumberland Mountains.

Failing that, a hammock in the backyard will do. Or a jog around the block. Or a bit of pacing in the family room.

As I hike, sway, jog, or pace, I ask a lot of questions. I visualize. I throw words into the air and see how they land. I squeeze ideas like oranges to see if they render any juice.

In a word, I mull.

The words *mull*, *mill*, and *meal* all come from an Old English root meaning the pulverizing of corn in a grinder. To mull over a subject is to ponder it, to pulverize it in the millstones of the mind.

Mulling is critical for creative problem solving. Last year, my wife and I took an alcohol and cocaine abuser into our home. He became like a member of the family.

Then he relapsed, and for months he flirted with death. I was so distraught over his condition that I couldn't pastor effectively. My wife and I wept for him as though he were our son.

As I mulled over my discouragement in the light of Scripture, I slowly realized that our relationship, which had begun with my friend being dependent on me, had ended with my being dependent on him. My ability to function depended on his ability to stay straight. I had lost my emotional and spiritual well-being.

When I realized what had happened to me, I changed my attitudes. Pondering my problem in the Lord's presence helped me to straighten out my emotions creatively and victoriously.

Two other elements help me mull:

Prayer. For the Christian imagineer, pondering involves praying. My best ideas come when I'm on my knees.

Someone asked Catherine Marshall, "What advice would you give someone seeking to be more creative?"

"That's easy," she replied. "I would tell them to stay intimately attuned to God."

The reason is obvious. He was and is the Creator. And since we are made in his image, I assume that one component of Christlikeness is creativity, or at least a sanctified imagination.

I experienced the relationship between prayer and creative problem solving when our church needed someone to develop a ministry to adults, but we lacked money for staff expansion. I felt pessimistic about our options, and I was out of ideas.

When the man I wanted to hire received a tempting offer from an advertising agency, I knew we needed to act. We knelt in prayer and specifically asked God, if he pleased, to show us how to fund the position.

A few ideas came to us, and we discussed these ideas with others. A few days later, a businessman, hearing about our desires, offered to underwrite a third of the funding. We restudied our budgets and developed a set of creative proposals. Within two months, the Lord had provided our minister of adults.

Seeding the subconscious. My junior year in college, a nearby church asked me to preach. Having recently dissected the first chapter of Jeremiah, I decided to base my message on the weeping prophet's call to ministry.

I began work on my sermon, but I found that I couldn't formulate an outline. I thought about my text day and night, but I had preacher's block. The mist had descended.

One day I took an hour's stroll through the woods around the dormitory. As I rambled, an outline shot into my mind like the sudden blast of a hunter's rifle. It was perfect. It had come from the Lord via my subconscious.

A few years later, I was stumped by another text. I pondered it day and night, but its truths resisted me. I traveled to a denominational meeting, and that night in the motel I dreamed I was preaching from that text. I awoke, jotted down the outline, and preached it the next Sunday.

I've read of the same thing happening to others. In October of 1920, Dr. Frederick Banting was working on his lecture for the following day. His medical practice was too new to be lucrative, so he supplemented his income by teaching. He worked far into the night on the problem of diabetes, but medical science provided scant data on the dreaded disease, and no cure had yet been discovered.

He fell asleep. At two in the morning, he awoke with a start. Grabbing a notebook, he penned three short sentences; then he collapsed again in sleep. But those three sentences later led to the discovery of insulin.

A century earlier, Elias Howe's fertile mind had imagined the sewing machine. He worked and worked on his invention, but its stitches were jagged and uneven. One night, he dreamed that a tribe of savages had kidnapped him. They threatened to kill him if he didn't invent a sewing machine in twenty-four hours. He failed, but as the spears flew at him, he noticed they had holes near their tips. He awoke with an idea: put the eye of the needle near the tip.

He patented his sewing machine in 1846.

"I am supposed to be one of the more fertile inventors of big ideas," said advertiser David Ogilvy, author of *Confessions of an Advertising Man.* "But big ideas come from the unconscious mind. This is true in art, in science, and in advertising. Stuff your conscious mind with information; then unhook your rational thought process. You can help this process by going for a long walk, taking a hot bath, or drinking a glass of claret. Suddenly, if the telephone lines from your unconscious are open, a big idea swells up within you."

"You remember how Sherlock Holmes used to stop right in the middle of a case and drag Watson off to a concert?" asks James Webb Young. "That was a very irritating procedure to the practical and literal-minded Watson. But Conan Doyle was a creator and knew the creative processes."

That's why I almost always stall for time when I'm confronted with a problem, a need, or an aspiration. Sometimes we want to milk another's ideas and jump immediately to implementation. That's almost always a mistake. Sometimes we want to make snap judgments on big issues. That's seldom wise. Instant ideas are usually more futile then fertile, for "a prudent man gives thoughts to his steps" (Prov. 14:15).

Map

After I've worked through the above steps, I usually get my hands on an idea or vision ready to be mapped out in action steps. Perhaps it's a sermon to be preached, a program to be implemented, a technique to try, or an innovation to launch. I have to take my big idea and do the hard work of working out the details of implementation.

Thousands of good ideas have never seen the light of day

because the persons who conceived them didn't have the ability to take what's in their heads and execute a plan. Like Joseph, the expert in dreams who also masterminded the administration of the huge Egyptian food plan, I have to be both a dreamer and a doer, an imagineer and an engineer.

I know there's a price to be paid for creativity. There will be changes and risks. As time goes by, implementing my ideas will require large doses of evaluation and correction. Many will be tried and discarded. But that's all right. I'm ready. The imagineer has returned.

2

Let There Be Wit and Wisdom— Weekly

The preacher's job, finally, is to look at every moment of time, every inch of space, to find there the old, old story and to keep reminding everyone who will listen that the curse shall not have the last word.

—JOHN ORTBERG

There is an old story about a mother who walks in on her six-year-old son and finds him sobbing.

"What's the matter?" she asks.

"I've just figured out how to tie my shoes."

"Well, honey, that's wonderful."

Being a wise mother, she recognizes his victory in the Eriksonian struggle of autonomy versus doubt: "You're growing up, but why are you crying?"

"Because," he says, "now I'll have to do it every day for the rest of my life."

Preaching is like that. Sundays just keep coming. Like the Energizer power bunny. Like death and taxes and Slim Whitman Christmas albums. Some months, every other day is a Sunday.

One of the most celebrated of all *I Love Lucy* episodes features Lucy wrapping candy as it passes on a conveyer belt. In the mistaken belief that Lucy is handling the candy with competence, her supervisor throttles the conveyer belt up to warp speed. An occasional piece of candy gets wrapped, but most of them end up getting stuffed in her mouth or various other places on her person. There just isn't time to handle them properly.

Preaching is like that too.

In a world where Sundays can't be postponed, where they keep coming ready or not (usually not), how is it possible to move from survival mode to creativity?

God in every inch

Books of illustrations are generally the homiletical equivalent of canned sitcom laugh tracks. And television shows are okay once in a while, but if we use them too often in our sermons, people will start wondering what we do with our time. Having preschool children at home is better from a preaching stand-point, but it gets expensive after a while, and it's hard to keep your spouse motivated to continue having them (unless she is unusually committed to the ministry).

Much of what I learned about the possibilities for creative preaching I learned from Ian Pitt-Watson, who teaches preaching at Fuller Seminary. And more important than any techniques was gaining clarity on what preaching is really about.

I had been brought up to think of preaching as teaching bits and illustration bits. You can teach people for a while, but unfortunately, human nature being what it is, people get bored, so you have to throw in illustrations at regular intervals to hold their attention. Illustrations are spoonfuls of regrettably necessary sugar that make the medicine of doctrine go down.

Ian pointed out that the Bible itself does not teach this way. If God were like most preachers, he would have laid out the Bible entirely differently: "My Attributes. Chapter 1: I Am Omni-scient," and so on. Instead, God chose to reveal himself in history, which is to say in stories.

In particular, Jesus taught in stories. This was not a conces-sion to human weakness. To me there's something arrogant about a preacher who boils down the parables to their "basic principles" as if the story is so much fluff that can be analyzed and safely discarded. Jesus was perfectly capable of laying out "Five Principles to Dynamic Praying," and the fact that he didn't should make us reflect.

Abraham Kuyper once wrote, "There is not one square inch of

the entire creation about which Jesus Christ does not cry out, 'This is mine! This belongs to me!' "

The reason for Jesus' creativity and freshness in his proclamation was not that he was really clever at choosing illustrations. It was that he really did live in the kingdom of God, so that for him not an inch of space, not a moment in time, existed that did not speak about the work of God. So he could look at, say, a seed that must die in the ground before it yields life, or a woman turning her house upside down to find a lost coin, or a flower, or a sparrow, or a great party, and say, "Here is God at work. See him in this inch, this moment."

Ian put it like this: "If we really believe that our crucified Carpenter is the agent of all creation . . . we must expect to find anywhere, everywhere, the handwriting of the Author of both the text of Scripture and the text of life—God in Christ revealing himself to us through the power of the Spirit."

The phrase "creative preaching" then, is a redundancy. Preaching is what happens when I faithfully explain the text of Scripture and the text of life, when the world of the Bible and the world of the listeners collide in Christ. So my task is to find those things that will help me see Christ in the world and see my world in the Bible.

Two times alone

Only God can create ex nihilo. If I start with nihilo, I end with nihilo. I need at least a little chaos to hover over. Certain conditions do exist under which I'm more likely to be creative.

The first one is the most painful: I have to be alone a lot.

In a thoughtful book called *Solitude*, an English psychiatrist named Anthony Storr writes that the capacity to create is inseparably connected with the capacity to be alone, that often people who are frequently alone in childhood become supremely creative (C. S. Lewis is a well-known example). He even says, "It is not unknown for creative people, once they have achieved an intimate relationship, to lose some of their imaginative drive." (I sometimes use this quote to explain why it would not be wise for me to spend all day helping shepherd the kindergarten class outing to Knotts Berry Farm.)

Creativity overlaps spirituality when we're alone. Every character of great spiritual development in Scripture is marked by the use of and desire for solitude—particularly Jesus. (Storr speaks of prayer as the capacity to be alone in the presence of God.) Edward Gibbon wrote, "Conversation enlarges the understanding, but solitude is the school of genius."

For me this means I need two kinds of solitude.

Utilitarian solitude is devoted to preparing sermons. I found, over time, this time was eroding to blocks of a few hours here and there, so now I devote one full day a week to being alone to work on the sermon. I may need to give it some other time during the week as well, but I find a day of utilitarian solitude is worth more than the same number of hours broken up during the week.

Perhaps more important, though, is nonutilitarian solitude. This is time alone, but not devoted to sermonizing or anything else related to my job. It is time set aside for praying or reflecting or looking at the ocean. The agenda is not to get inspirations or ideas for the church. In fact, its purpose is to free me from my compulsive need for ideas, to remind me that I am not my job, so that my preaching can be about Christ, not about my own need to succeed as a preacher.

Feeding on doses of joy

Being creative is much more likely to happen when I'm relaxed and joyful. This leads to a Catch-22: I tend to obsess over sermons, and the more I obsess, the less creative I am, which leads me, in turn, to become more anxious and obsessive.

I remember Saturdays when I've actually hoped I would get sick so I wouldn't have to preach that sermon the following morning. (I would have begged off, but I couldn't conjure up a creative enough excuse.)

I've since discovered a helpful insight: Even in a task as significant as preaching, while I have to take the subject matter seriously, playfulness must be part of the process.

Anthony Storr writes that there is always an element of play in creative living: "When this playful element disappears, joy goes with it, and so does any sense of being able to innovate. Creative people not infrequently experience periods of despair in which their ability to create anything new seems to have deserted them. This is often because a particular piece of work has become invested with such overwhelming importance that it is no longer possible to play with it."

I've had days where sermons come with all the speed and spontaneity of Chinese water torture. I've also had days where they seem to write themselves. The most common variant for me is how relaxed and joyful I am when I sit down to write.

There is even some research to back up the joy-creativity link.

Some time ago a group of social psychologists gave people the task of finding a way of attaching a matchbox to a wall with no tools other than the box of matches and a candle. They divided the subjects into two groups: one group was shown a very depressing documentary before being given the task and the other watched Marx Brothers movies. Those in the latter group were something like ten times more likely to discover how to solve the problem. (If you send me a check for $9.99, I'll send you the actual solution.)

What preachers need to be creative, then, may not be a better filing system for illustrations, or even an administrative assistant, but a good jester. For me that means I need to schedule sermon writing when I'm at my freshest. If possible, I try to make sure that I get to do something fun, or at least something that will put me in a relaxed mood, before I get started. Often I'll begin by "mind mapping," a kind of written-down version of free association where you put a word in the middle of a sheet of paper and then write whatever words come to your mind around it.

The freshness of the familiar

My creativity also increases, I've noticed, when I don't pressure myself to be creative.

I had just moved to my first full-time job as a pastor, and our church was planning to host the monthly ministerial association get-together. I sent out invitations with a tongue-in-cheek postscript that both the pope and Robert Schuller would be joining us, but that in the event they canceled, everyone should bring outlines of his two best sermons: at least we could swap messages and not have to crank out new ones all summer.

To my amazement, one member of the group, at the close of the meeting, approached me and demanded to know when the sermon exchange would be made. Not only had he brought two outlines, he had made enough photocopies for everyone to take home!

The pressure to manufacture creativity can produce forced and pretentious preaching at best and tempt us to sheer plagiarism at worst.

In fact, pressuring myself to be creative caused me to miss for a long time one of the most powerful weapons of preaching—the familiar. It is, after all, the old, old story that we long to hear the most and, when told right, is somehow always new. Sometimes my horror of saying the obvious is a curse and not a blessing.

I discovered this, somewhat to my chagrin, after returning from a two-week trip to Ethiopia a few years ago. Not having much time to prepare, I simply told the story of the church in the book of Acts and relayed the story (largely the same one) of the church in Ethiopia. It connected with people at a level far deeper than what I usually experience with much more carefully prepared messages.

Fred Craddock wrote that preachers are called not only to speak to the congregation but also to speak for the congregation.

My job is not to say something no one has ever said before on a text no one has ever preached before. This syndrome Craddock calls "overlooking the treasury of the familiar."

"No one builds a church," he says, "by leaping off the pinnacle of the temple every Sunday. . . . If a minister takes seriously

the role of listeners in preaching, there will be sermons express-
ing for the whole church, and with God as the primary audience,
the faith, the doubt, the fear, the anger, the love, the joy, the
gratitude that is in all of us. The listeners say, 'Yes, that's my
message; that is what I have wanted to say.' "

Or as C. S. Lewis put it, Jesus' command to Peter was, "Feed
my sheep," not, "Try new experiments on my rats."

I'm often tempted to be creative merely for the sake of being
creative. Nothing is more excruciating than the knowledge that
you're boring a roomful of people, except, of course, being one
of those bored people in the room. In one of my first sermons, I
knew how badly things were going in part because one of the
listeners (and it was a small crowd) actually fell asleep. On the
way home, I said to my wife, "Nancy, next Saturday, you've just
got to get to bed sooner."

But it isn't safe to allow people's response to be the ultimate
criterion by which a sermon is judged. G. K. Chesterton wrote
once that God shares with children the capacity to delight in
what appears to be routine to people who are neither children
nor God, but merely adults:

Because children have abounding vitality, because they are in
spirit fierce and free, therefore they want things repeated and un-
changed. They always say, "Do it again"; and the grown-up person
does it again until he is nearly dead. For grown-up people are not
strong enough to exult in monotony.

But perhaps God is strong enough to exult in monotony. It is
possible that God says every morning, "Do it again" to the sun;
and every evening, "Do it again" to the moon. It may not be
automatic necessity that makes all daisies alike; it may be that
God makes every daisy separately, but has never gotten tired of
making them. It may be that he has the eternal appetite of in-
fancy; for we have sinned and grown old, and our Father is
younger than we.

"Say it again," God says. When we say it again, when we get it
right, it's as if our words were being said for the first time. The
old, old story has again become a new song.

Looking for the Prince to come

Preaching is the coming together of two worlds: the world of the Bible and the world of the listener. It is the intersection of two stories—God's and mine.

When my oldest daughter was old enough to give me an excuse for doing so, I took her to her first Disney movie. I remembered vividly going with my own parents to see Snow White; it hardly seemed possible I could be going now with my child.

For Laura it was as if she entered into the world on the screen. She laughed at Dopey and got mad at Grumpy and cringed before the evil queen, with real tears running down her face. She had been transported.

And then Snow White began to sing, "Someday My Prince Will Come," and Laura's eyes shone. She squeezed my hand and said, "Daddy, the prince is coming."

But at one point the story goes all wrong: the bride tastes the fruit, falls under a spell, and then falls asleep. The dwarves cannot wake her. They, too, are waiting for the prince to come.

In this familiar fairy tale, I began to see hints of a deeper story, one that always and everywhere seeks to break through if only we'll have eyes to see and ears to hear.

For we have all tasted the forbidden fruit, all eaten the poisoned apple. We have all fallen under the spell—the curse—and all fallen asleep.

The preacher's job, finally, is not to figure out how to be novel or distinctive or say something no one has ever said before. Ours is a more humble one: to look at every moment of time, every inch of space, to find there the old, old story and to keep reminding everyone who will listen that the curse shall not have the last word. One day the Prince will come for his bride and take her home.

And every once in a while, in the midst of (and often in spite of) the preacher's words, the Prince comes even now and kisses his bride. And somebody, somewhere, wakes up.

3

Raising Your Creativity Quotient

Creativity is far less subjective and ethereal
than some make it sound.

—Gary Gonzales

Someone once asked William Barclay how he had become such a prolific writer. The key, he said, is learning to apply the seat of your pants to the seat of your chair.

Creativity is far less subjective and ethereal than some make it sound. As much a function of our habits as our "genius" or inspiration, creativity takes discipline.

Here are four ways to enhance your creativity.

Know your moods

Perhaps you've heard the old saying about diet: "Mornings are gold, lunch is bronze, and dinner is lead." Well, the same applies to personal energy levels.

A few months ago, a lay leader handed me a newspaper article outlining the body's daily rhythms. It underscored how, for most people, mornings provide peak energy and concentration. Quick recall and analytical reasoning are strongest in the A.M.

Conversely, the infamous "afternoon grogs," the inability to focus, hits from 1:00 to 3:00 P.M., with a short reprieve from 3:00 to 4:00 P.M., especially in recall.

By evening most people are downshifting, except for the late-night geniuses who hit their creative stride from 11:00 P.M. to 1:00 A.M.

Knowing this, I safeguard morning hours for the challenges of praying, studying, writing, and creative thinking. I no longer feel guilty when my engines are revving low. I pace myself, husbanding my energy for creative times.

I've also learned how to improve my energy and lessen the negative rhythms.

Soon after moving to the Twin Cities from southern California, I thought about joining a fitness club. But I wondered, With my mornings scheduled full with message preparation and my evenings already overflowing with meetings and programs, how can I realistically expect to add an exercise regimen?

But I had heard others describe how a workout increased their energy level, so I decided to experiment. I discovered that a sixty-minute workout during my lunch hour or after 3:00 P.M. worked wonders. Regular exercise dramatically increased my endurance, making my low periods less low—and I feel better about myself. As an added bonus, I find thinking and praying easier while on the NordicTrack or between weight-lifting sets.

While getting into shape, I learned another valuable lesson: If I work out on Friday, resting or going easy on Saturday, by Sunday morning I'm primed to preach. A one-day layoff between workouts enables my body to bounce back with renewed vigor. I can't recall a time in my previous fifteen years of ministry when I've been so clearheaded—able to think creatively and spontaneously—in the pulpit.

Write it down

Someone has said, "Opportunity is like a horse that gallops up and then pauses for a moment. If you don't get on, before long you hear the clatter of hoofbeats dying away in the distance."

Great ideas are just such opportunities.

Whenever you hear, see, or think a worthwhile thought, write it down before another moment passes. Experience has taught me to keep a pen and paper handy on my nightstand. I never know when a brainstorm will strike—and quickly vanish!

That's also true of the ideas we learn from others. For several years I've kept a journal handy at my office. Whenever I come across a good quote, I immediately jot it down and document the source. Often, when I'm stymied while preparing sermons, I thumb through this journal to stimulate ideas.

Others' ideas provoke my ideas. While paging through my journal recently, I ran across the statement, "Leaders are to be imitated, not gold-plated." It triggered a thought: I've wanted to do a series on leadership for some time. Why not develop a series of seven messages on leadership principles using one-liners as memory hooks?

I'm now reading and gathering ideas, illustrations, and resources on that theme.

Let it simmer

Most creative ideas mature over time. So, whether I'm planning a sermon series, a special holiday service, or a seminar, I arrange my time to give it as much advance thought as possible. My mind works best when I'm not clawing for ideas at the last minute.

I don't get overstructured too early. A good idea has a ripple effect, soon suggesting other ideas or applications. At first, all I want to do is grasp the big picture—even if only a piece of it.

Useful ideas sometimes come to me after months of simmering.

Several years ago, I heard the story of Larry Walters, a thirty-three-year-old man who decided he wanted to see his neighborhood from a new perspective. He went down to the local army surplus store one morning and bought forty-five used weather balloons. That afternoon he strapped himself into a lawn chair, to which several of his friends tied the now helium-filled balloons. He took along a six-pack of beer, a peanut-butter-and-jelly sandwich, and a gun, figuring he could shoot the balloons one at a time when he was ready to land.

Walters, who assumed the balloons would lift him about 100 feet in the air, was caught off guard when the chair soared more than 11,000 feet into the sky—smack into the middle of the air traffic pattern at Los Angeles International Airport. Too frightened to shoot any of the balloons, he stayed airborne for more than two hours, forcing the airport to shut down its runways for much of the afternoon, causing long delays in flights from across the country.

Soon after he was safely grounded and cited by the police, reporters asked him three questions:

"Were you scared?"

"Yes."

"Would you do it again?"

"No."

"Why did you do it?"

"Because," he said, "you can't just sit there."

His answer caught my interest. I pondered that story and its implications for several months. Then, as I was preparing a sermon, "The Crisis Called Christmas," my thoughts came together. I used the Walters story in the introduction to set the stage for the idea that each of the birth narratives called for a response— or a reaction—from its participants. When it comes to God's intervention in our lives, we can't just sit there.

Talk about it

Creativity is often synergistic, so I cultivate people in formal and informal settings who cultivate my ideas.

When I write an article, for instance, I'll often send it to a writer-friend in San Diego who gives me an honest, professional critique. After he returns the manuscript, I usually get on the phone with him for a late-night, long-distance dialogue about it.

When I'm planning my six-month preaching calendar, I'll frequently gather select groups of thoughtful people for brainstorming sessions. Such conversations help to both generate ideas and refine the ones I already have.

Creativity isn't reserved for the Einsteins, Shakespeares, and Spurgeons of the world. It isn't something we either possess or don't possess. Creativity is encouraged by developing the habits that create an environment where new ideas can germinate and grow.

4

Handing Your Baby to Barbarians

If you twist the arm of someone who doesn't like your idea,
you get an elbow in the chops.

—Craig Brian Larson

"We have to face reality," I announced to the congregation one bright October Sunday morning. "We are not bringing people to Christ."

Before me, seated on stacking chairs in a grade-school gym, were our fifty adults and a few children, appearing as civilized as landed gentry (toddlers excluded).

"The Great Commission is our mission," I continued. "We have to do whatever it takes to become a church that leads people to Christ."

Our church was nine years old, and I had been the pastor for two years. We had grown from thirty-five to eighty on a bang-up Sunday, but I wasn't satisfied: it was transfer growth. We weren't reaching unchurched people.

I took responsibility and resolved to do something about it. I blocked out time in my schedule, prayed intensely about the problem, and birthed an idea—a seven-step strategy for breaking out of our shell.

Confidently and with great expectations, I handed the congregation my baby.

The coming-out party

The first step was prayer, and on this Sunday morning, I was using my sermon to introduce it.

"James 4:2 says, 'You do not have, because you do not ask God,' " I said. "We must base our outreach on prayer." For the next thirty minutes, I introduced three key prayer requests based on three Scriptures.

As we drove home after the service, my gentle wife didn't say anything about my sermon on this watershed day in our church's epic history. Finally, hoping that things had gone better than I had sensed, I asked, "How did it go?"

"Well, it went okay. But maybe you should have focused on just one Scripture and one prayer," she said. "I think people got a little confused."

"Three Scriptures, and they're confused?" I said incredulously. I had felt insecure; now I was burned. I had offered a clearly biblical message, presented it with passion, and the only response was a tepid critique of my sermon structure. I looked at my wife as if she were Attila the Hun holding my firstborn.

In the next few weeks, I discovered my wife's reaction was one of the most positive. My intensely felt vision wasn't immediately celebrated by the rest of the congregation. The reawakening of passionate prayer, the resurgence of evangelism, wasn't ushered in by my introduction of the seven-part strategy. I was crushed.

When we develop a creative idea, it becomes our baby, the most wonderful, beautiful, intelligent, and promising child ever to grace the earth. However, the time soon arrives for proud parents to bring their brainchild into public, and that can be traumatic.

When we present our idea for approval and support, others may frown at our baby. They have the gall to scorn our baby's looks! If we place our baby in their arms, they hand her back without gushing over her. Some actually seem bent on harming our beloved offspring.

Often that's our own fault. Although the people we lead are thoroughly "civilized," we sometimes present creative ideas in ways that provoke what seem like savage reactions. Upon reflection, I realize more members of my congregation would have welcomed my ideas if I had done five things differently.

Keep it simple, sir

I love to analyze. I can multiply points like children spawn excuses for cleaning their bedroom. Give me several weeks to develop a plan, and it can rival a computer chip for microcomplexity. Here was the thumbnail sketch of our evangelism strategy's first step—the prayer plan:

1. We would make three specific requests each day. "Make our church and me fishers of men." "Send us as laborers into the harvest." "Show me the people you want me to share Christ with."

2. We would develop a "Love List" of ten friends, family members, neighbors, and fellow workers and pray for them daily. Those who were willing would turn their list into me, and we would compile a church Love List we all could pray for.

But I wanted us praying more specifically than "Save Aunt Mildred and Becky Sue." So I developed a list of sixteen scriptural prayer requests (two to the fourth power, no less!) for non-Christians. For example, "Convince ——— of sin and righteousness and judgment" based on John 16:8.

In our church meetings, I modeled these prayers, and in newsletters I explained them. After a few weeks I wanted to involve others, so at the close of a meeting I asked anyone who felt prompted to pray our three strategic, evangelistic prayers.

Silence.

Silence that lasted longer than it takes to reach a human being when a voice-mail system answers your call. (There is no deeper silence on our vast planet than that which engulfs a room of people when no one wants to pray.)

Finally, thoroughly frustrated, I prayed.

On another occasion I popped a spontaneous quiz. "What are the three requests I'm asking everyone to pray daily?" Two out of three was the best the congregation could do.

Further removed from my baby, I can now see my plan was

too complex. The people weren't obtuse. The plan simply struck them as so complex, they didn't want to start. And this was only step one!

If Jesus had adopted this plan to evangelize the world, Peter and the Sons of Thunder would have gone home with an industrial-strength headache. If people ever get the idea something is complex or beyond them, many won't even try.

Here's the painful but simple truth: The more complex our brainchild, the more concentration required to understand it, the more others will seem to us like barbarians.

Be realistic about others' commitments

Once I had begun developing my new outreach strategy, it became my bonfire-sized passion. God answers prayer; I knew it would work. Many lives would be changed, and our church would turn into a pulsing evangelistic center.

Naturally I implemented the plan into my life, as best I could. Incorporating the three key prayers into my day was a snap. I did so once or twice daily.

But then I also began praying for the twenty-five people on my Love List. I found if I named each person and made my sixteen specific requests for the whole group in a heartfelt manner rather than just mouthed words and names from a list, it could take twenty minutes. When I prayed for people individually, it was a schedule buster. I had many other things to pray about as well.

I soon found it challenging to keep praying for my personal Love List even every other day, and I only prayed for ten or twenty names from the church's accumulated list of several hundred names once a week. If such difficulty in follow-through beset me, the originator of the plan, the one for whom the whole church enterprise was most dear, it's no surprise church attenders did less. A few implied they used the prayer guide sporadically, but most discreetly avoided the subject.

I still think the prayer program was a great idea for some, but an unrealistic theory for most. Getting adults to do anything out of the ordinary is as difficult as outdueling the American Gladiators; if we ask for significant commitment, we find significantly fewer people ready to respond.

Douglas Hyde, in his book *Dedication and Leadership*, says if you ask for great commitment, you get a great response; ask for Mickey Mouse commitment and you don't even get that. I first read that while ministering to idealistic collegians, and I still subscribe to it. But I've also learned that asking for a significant commitment rarely gets a quick response from the majority of set-in-their-ways adults.

Ask people to baby sit your brainchild for a few minutes, and there's a good chance they'll agree. But ask them to adopt her, support her from their own means, and promise to send her to a private college, and you'll have far fewer volunteers.

Remember you are the adoring parent

I presented the prayer strategy to the church in a way I hoped would seize attention, using the church's desktop publishing program to design a professional-looking handout. I chose a distinguished-looking type font and a large point size for easy reading.

Then, like an artist penciling in the eyelashes of a portrait, I painstakingly enlarged and put in bold the first letter of each prayer request. When it was ready to print, I stood with anticipation watching my 24 pin Epson craft the words line by line onto paper. I took the original to the office, copied it on goldenrod paper, and immediately slipped one copy into a vinyl sheet protector in my desk-size Day-Timer. (Compulsives keep the stockholders of sheet-protector producers rolling in dough.)

The next Sunday, with concealed pride, I nonchalantly handed those precious documents to the ushers to distribute to the congregation, keeping my eye on them lest any be dropped. (I resisted the temptation to put every copy in a sheet protector.)

After my sermon explaining each of the prayer requests, I urged everyone to "take this intercessory guide home, keep it with your Bible, and pray these requests regularly for the people on your Love List. And do a Bible study of each Scripture so you see how it inspires the prayer."

We closed the service in prayer, and I walked to the hallway, ostensibly to greet people, actually to garner rave reviews. After shaking the last hand—no one said much about the sermon—I returned to the gym and found to my dismay a number of the goldenrod prayer guides littering the seats. In shock, I went through the rows picking them up. Some had been scribbled on with crayons, folded into airplanes, or doodled on by adults— desecrated.

To many in the congregation, this was just another handout, church junk mail. To me it was the master key to our church's future, the product of weeks of thought and prayer, something that in my daydreams I could see helping hundreds—perhaps thousands—of people find a relationship with Christ. (The truth is, I saw it on the same scale as Bill Bright's Four Spiritual Laws!) And there it was, left behind like trash in an alley.

No one adores our high concepts—these reflections of our intelligence, personality, and vision that resemble their parents so closely—as much as we do. We usually believe God inspired the idea. We felt the concept grow in the womb; we labored to give her birth; we nursed and cared for her in the middle of the night. We're emotionally, permanently bonded. To others, our baby-powdered idea is just another one of several billion unex- ceptional children born into the world each year. Cute, yes, adorable, maybe, a prodigy, we'll see. Even if they're warm to the idea, they won't fall over themselves to support it, yet.

I needed to present my ideas not like a mother proudly pre- senting her newborn in public but like a pregnant woman who sincerely wants help from a midwife. Church innovations are team efforts.

Give people freedom to choose

Conferences and books are hazardous to a pastor's health. A few months before conceiving my prayer strategy, I read a popu- lar secular book on leadership. With the book's emphasis on communicating vision fresh in my mind, I campaigned for my prayer program through every available means.

I reminded the congregation of our "three prayer requests" in every weekly newsletter. At the end of our church services, I closed in prayer with them.

In my sermons and pastoral comments during services, I told stories of how I had seen those prayers fulfilled in my life during the week, seeing opportunities arise to share Christ and feeling equipped to do so.

I "asked" all church members to sign a form saying they would commit to pray daily. "We need everyone to join in this effort," I emphasized repeatedly from the pulpit. "We have to be a team." A dozen people complied (anything to placate me).

I even asked people one-on-one, "What do you think of our prayer plan? Have you started praying regularly?" In short, for about four weeks I was twisting limbs as relentlessly as a cranky KGB interrogator.

I felt the awkwardness of my putting people on the spot, and I softened it with a laid-back smile and demeanor, but everyone in the church soon knew that there would be no exceptions and no anonymity. No one had the freedom to say no and remain in a comfortable position with me. I hadn't given a challenge; I had set a policy.

I didn't feel guilty about drafting GI's rather than recruiting volunteers. Strong leadership is appropriate for a mission church. We needed a highly committed, special-forces-type platoon to fulfill our reason for being. We might lose a few people, but at least the ones who remained would be fruitful.

That may be true, but I quickly found that the more a leader pressures followers to adopt an innovation, the more resistant and resentful many become. If you twist the arm of someone unmotivated to support an idea, you get an elbow in the chops.

My first inkling of dental trauma was a letter from a woman explaining she planned to leave the church because, for one thing, I was "pulling teeth" to get everyone to support my prayer program.

That startled me. For the first time I realized what I had been doing for the previous month. I don't consider myself a manipu-

lative person. I doubt if anyone from my previous church would
have described me as such. In my previous pastorate, when I
challenged people to commit to deeper involvement, I offered
optional programs, growth tracks for volunteers, and didn't pressure the uninvolved. But my urgency to reach out coupled with
my convictions about the need for strong leadership had
changed my leadership style.

Within weeks nearly a dozen people in the church had become strong opponents of my leadership. I learned that the more
we coerce people to adopt our brainchild, the more they will
seem to us like barbarians.

Give extra attention to "educators"

Church opinion leaders with a clearly defined, albeit unwrit-
ten, philosophy of ministry are as likely to stonewall avant-garde
ideas as Kathy Lee Gifford is to have her mouth wide open in a
magazine photo.

"Alan (name changed), how do you feel about our prayer
plan?" I asked one of our men. "Are you using it to intercede for
others?"

"Not really," he answered. "I try to pray under the leading of
the Spirit, and so I don't use lists or written prayers."

"But the prayers are based directly on Scripture," I responded.
"Isn't it possible that a prayer based on Scripture could be Spirit-
led?"

I continued to argue my case, but our conversation ended
with Alan unconvinced. Deeply committed to prayer and evangelism, he had his own well-established ideas about how both
should be done. He had read a lot of books, and his mind was
sincerely made up on most things related to the Christian life.

Expertise, real or supposed, often causes hardening of the categories. Just as a specialist in early childhood education may test
a girl's intelligence and conclude she belongs in the "slow"
group, only for the world to later discover she's a genius (for
example, as children, both Albert Einstein and Winston Chur-

chill were deemed slow learners), so "experts" in the church often dismiss a brainchild as stupid.

But church opinion leaders can't be bypassed. As I look back, I think one of my biggest mistakes was presenting my prayer strategy to the whole church rather than first going to the opinion leaders one-on-one, inviting their feedback, giving them time to process the idea, and then presenting it to the congregation. People in the know take kindly to being consulted, require extra attention and respect, and need both early in the process.

The people in my church who said "no thanks" to my pink-ribboned baby weren't the Teutonic hordes. If they seemed like it, that was largely my fault.

Frankly, with perspective I see that few of my brainchildren are wunderkinds and many of my ideas are stupid (though I still think these prayers will replace the Four Spiritual Laws, no offense, Mr. Bright). What's more, most good ideas require considerable feedback to truly find "the mind of the Lord."

And so although it never feels like it, I've decided the "barbarians" in my life just may be godparents in disguise.

PART 2

The Creative Church

5

Does Anyone Know What *Creative* Means?

Creativity is not a luxury, it's survival.

—Fred Smith

The word *creative* has become a cliché. People use it whether they can define it or not. Creativity is expected of ministers no less than of advertising copywriters and fashion designers. If you're not certified "creative," your future is in big trouble.

The blunt fact, of course, is that no one is creative. We live in a closed universe; there is nothing new under the sun. What we are instead is *inventive*; we rearrange and reposition things that have already been created.

Throughout this article I will use the words *creative* and *creativity* even though what I am talking about is inventiveness. This will seem more natural to our speech patterns. And I hope the Creator will not be offended.

Creativity has to do with more than just the arts—painting, sculpture, music, architecture. In my view, creativity is survival. When an institution loses its transitional quality in a moving market, a moving culture, a moving world, it doesn't survive. The railroad industry wanted to stay as railroad companies rather than transportation companies. The transition was toward airplanes and private automobiles, but they liked railroading. Many went out of business.

In the parachurch we have some excellent examples of using creative solutions to satisfy spiritual needs: Torrey Johnson saw wandering crowds of World War II soldiers looking for something to do on the streets of Chicago, so he created Youth for Christ. When secularism swept the West Coast campuses in the sixties, Campus Crusade was the creative answer. Bill Glass, all-pro footballer, found prisoners wouldn't come to hear preaching so he started sports clinics for them.

I was depressed when I heard the average tenure of the pastors of a major denomination is eighteen months. When I asked why, the answer was, "Because that's about how many sermons they have." By the end of eighteen months, they've preached to the bottom of the barrel, and the only choice is to move.

Apparently no springs of creativity have been nurtured so that new (or at least repositioned) things are bubbling up from inside. That's why I say that for people in leadership, creativity is not a luxury; it's survival.

Eight essential qualities

Those who may rightly be called creative show the following characteristics:

Wide association. While most new ideas are conceived by a single person sitting alone, such a moment does not tell the whole story. The truly creative people I know stay in touch with other creative people. Bright ideas may hit them at three in the morning, but they come out of an environment of creativity.

You have to set up an almost constant discipline to maintain your vitality through association. Creative people ask you the right kind of questions. They probe you. So you stay in touch with them.

Special areas. Ralph Carmichael, the Christian musician, and I were talking about marketing one day, and he said, "Fred, if you want to talk fast to me, talk music. I can talk music fast, but I have to talk business slow." I know exactly what he meant, because it's the opposite with me! In the area of a person's gift, he can race along. His pores are open; he knows all the nuances and ramifications; problems in this area excite him.

When I find individuals trying to function in an area that threatens them, I usually say, "This must not be your area."

People who battle stage fright shouldn't be public speakers. All good speakers have nervousness, yes, but they are able to use it. It creates energy; it revs up the mind. Christian leaders who are immobilized by the big problems of their lives should question whether they're working in their area of strength.

John R. W. Stott says expository preaching is chewing on a verse like a dog on a bone. I'd advise most ministers not to spend their time in that way because they're not John Stott or G. Campbell Morgan. If you're not creative in finding new meanings in the nooks and corners of Scripture, then put your energy into another area. I'd hate to see a tremendous communicator like Chuck Swindoll spend time gnawing on individual verses. He's far more creative at mixing words and pictures to convey old truth in a new and vital way.

Dissatisfaction. Some people call it noble discontent. Whatever its name, creative people are infested with the idea that the way things are being done today is not the way they can be done best.

Roger Bannister didn't believe a mile run had to take four minutes. Something inside told him that if he'd break down the mile into four separate parts and go to work on each quarter of the mile, he could cut off seconds. Now, of course, four minutes is old and slow.

That spirit of discontent is crucial to creativity. I'm trying to instill it in my grandson, who plays golf with me occasionally. He loves the game, and when he gets off a good drive down the fairway, he'll say, "Perfect."

"No, Greg," I'll say. "It's good, but it's not perfect."

"Well, it went where I wanted it to go."

"Yes, but it didn't go where it could have gone."

We don't have to be negative or critical to be dissatisfied. Van Gogh was both creative and miserable—that's not what I mean. We can believe in a positive way that everything can be better. Every organization can be improved, every formula perfected.

Once I asked George Schweitzer, "Why do scientists revere Einstein?"

"Because he put more formula into one formula than any other scientist."

"Well, what's the aim of all science?" I asked.

"To put everything into one formula."

What a challenge! No wonder great scientists are dissatisfied.

Great preachers and theologians are dissatisfied, too, not because they want to be authors of truth, but because they want to expand it, to understand it more fully, to rearrange it so people can utilize it better.

One minister asked me, "How do I develop creativity?"

I replied, "Pick out a few of your common problems and think of all the various ways to solve them. You'll have to think very hard, but do it anyway." When Robert McNamara was president of Ford, he would assign his associates problems to work out, and when they would come in to report, McNamara would say, "Now I'm sure this isn't the first solution you thought of. What was another one?" It was his way of forcing everyone to think of at least two ways to solve every problem.

Creative people love to have options. They love to drive home a different route each day. They refuse to drop down on the floor like a toddler and start crying, "I can't." They know there are multiple ways to do almost everything.

If you don't give yourself a lot of options to consider, how do you know which one's best? One of the reasons I'm convinced of original sin is that I rarely see anyone accomplish the best the first time. If there weren't some basic problem with humanity, writers wouldn't have to rewrite their material five times, engineers wouldn't have to return to the drawing board, and preachers wouldn't have to rebuild sermon outlines from scratch. It takes awhile, but eventually quality floats to the top if we are dissatisfied long enough.

Awe. An expanding concept of God and his world is another part of creativity. While dissatisfaction moves us toward *change,* awe moves us toward *exploration.* The great astronomers can hardly change what they see in space, but they are moved by awe to explore it, nevertheless.

I'll never forget traveling as a young man from my native Tennessee up to New York City. Standing on the corner of Fifty-seventh Street and Sixth Avenue one day, I suddenly realized the situation was beyond me. There was simply no way to know all those people, as I did back home. I was overwhelmed. The God I had brought along was too small. He had to be bigger than I thought to take in a place like New York.

From that time, I have had an expanding concept of God. This has not intimidated me; rather, it has pulled me along to grow creatively as I see more and more of him.

High physical and mental energy. A lot of people have wonderful ideas but lack the energy to explore them. Einstein once said nature holds almost no secrets that cannot be found out by prolonged concentration and intense study. We only have to bear down.

Some creative people bear down so hard that they burn out early in life. Some of the great musicians died very young, for example, as did some inventors. Others have lived longer but found they couldn't burn the midnight oil like they used to. All of them were—to be honest—unbalanced. They couldn't help it when they became fascinated with an idea.

One of the more fortunate things in life is when a highly creative spirit comes in a highly energetic body. Let others criticize if they will, great things will result.

And when they do, the creative person will supply his or her own strokes. Some of the most creative solutions I have ever found in my business were things only I knew about. The acclaim of others was not necessary; I knew I had solved a problem.

The ability to think in principles. Less than 10 percent of the population can do this, I'm told; most think only in techniques. And I don't really know how to develop this ability. I only know I can recognize it by listening to a person.

If a speaker thinks in principles, he shows it by his breadth of illustration. He draws from many different fields, not just his particular specialty, because he sees the principles that weave throughout. If a speaker always tells stories from one field, or if his illustrations do not extrapolate accurately, then we know he does not understand the principle.

Mathematicians talk about the elegant answer and the grotesque answer. I mentioned to one mathematician that I had never liked math in school. "I can understand that," he said, "because they taught you the grotesqueness of arithmetic instead of the elegance of mathematics." Great mathematicians work through the welter of technique until they come to a marvelous principle; pi, for example, or the discovery of the zero, which happened in India and revolutionized our ability to work with numbers.

This, incidentally, is why many great mathematicians are musicians. They have moved past drudgery and grotesqueness to elegance.

At a university conference on business, I was scheduled to speak after the dean of engineering. He opened his speech by saying, "I am a scientist. I deal only with hard facts—things you can see and feel."

When it was my turn, I said, "I don't mean to be discourteous, but most of life is made up of soft facts. I respect hard facts, but when I take the long view, I notice that the rocks and the riverbank do not control the water that flows in the stream; the water forms the rocks and the bank.

"All matters of the spirit are soft, but they ultimately control. Armies, formulas, and scientific technology do not guarantee that a civilization will survive. That is up to other factors. The soft is just as factual as the hard, but more difficult to deal with."

In the ministry, we are constantly dealing with the power of soft facts. When we see that as a principle, then we can start to think creatively about it.

A style that is uninhibited (but not undisciplined). Creative people cannot let themselves be hemmed in by tradition.

A member of the Tarrytown Group once said, "The world is between trapezes. We're leaving the one we have known and trying to catch one we do not know." I like that metaphor. We often feel that way about our own lives. Maybe life is a series of trapeze jumps; maybe each day is a new trapeze. Certainly the creative person is always leaving one trapeze and hurtling toward the next.

We Christians limit ourselves too much. To me, the Bible has always been a compass. I am not afraid to wander in anybody's woods so long as I have a compass.

I have friends who are nonbelievers, and some of them never

do get out of the woods. Others get out only by chance. But with a compass, you can relax; you can wander far off the paths, because any time you need to get out, you can. You can feel competent to wander in almost any company, any group, any set of ideas, because you have Scripture to guide you out at the necessary moment.

Too many Christians are worried about the wagon instead of the load. If any idea comes in a wagon they don't like, they reject the load without even looking it over. I don't care whether creativity comes from an atheist, an agnostic, a liberal, or whomever—if the idea is good, I want it, and I'm not going to fuss about the mode of transportation.

Being uninhibited, however, does not mean being out of control. A vice president of General Motors once told me, "We want people with disciplined imaginations." A leader, though tremendously creative, cannot be loose in his behavior.

Pastors are sometimes caught in a unique squeeze when their attempts to be free in ministry are read by the congregation in behavioral terms only. Take Sunday morning, for example. Many Christians have gotten to the place that the eleven o'clock service is nothing more than a ritual. There's no spiritual vitality; there is only habit. This problem has to be solved very, very slowly.

A dear friend of mine, pastor of a large church, a man of great integrity, came to the pulpit one Sunday morning and said, "You look to me for God's message. I have struggled all week, and God has given me no message. Therefore, let us stand and be dismissed."

If I had been there, I would have stood and applauded.

But he almost got thrown out of his church. Although he had done the honest thing, people were outraged. Some had brought friends that day—not to hear a message from God but to hear their preacher. And he didn't perform.

He did invite them all back to the evening service, for which he felt he had a message. He delivered it that night as expected.

While such a shock may be dangerous, it is imperative that we work gradually but steadily toward making Sunday morning more than ritual. As a guest speaker, I can tell a dramatic difference in audiences. Some have been trained to listen—really listen—and others have not.

The other day I was invited to do a laymen's service in a church that usually has mediocre preaching. (The reason I know is that the pastor told me he dreads no day like Sunday.) As I spoke that day, I was half through before they started listening. What a contrast with a church like Key Biscayne Presbyterian in Florida, where they hang on every cough. The people are so used to listening intently that a guest is fascinated by the immediate attention his words receive. This kind of discipline takes time.

But it can be built. Most big problems are not solved fast.

A young pastor in Dallas decided to open the floor for ten minutes of questions following his sermon each week. It was most stimulating; he got some hard queries because people have come to believe he wants them. He wasn't opening up the service to be complimented, but to clarify. The problem he was attacking is people going home misunderstanding what the preacher said.

That's creative.

Sunday morning problems must be attacked creatively and diplomatically, but always with an eye toward the ultimate goal of vitality. Our thinking must be uninhibited, even when our behavior is not.

Evaluation. I know brainstorming is supposed to be a marvelous technique for creativity, but I think it is a silly fad. To sit around spouting ideas with no evaluation makes fools of everyone. Disciplined creativity must ask the following questions:

"Is this practical?" Does this solution make enough difference to be worth the time and energy it will cost?

Will Rogers once listened to an admiral describe the menace of German U-boats during the First World War. Eventually, Rogers raised his hand and asked, "Tell me, can those things operate in boiling water?"

"No," the admiral replied, "I'm sure they can't."

"Well, then," said Rogers, "you've got your solution. Just boil the ocean."

The admiral gave him a blank stare and then muttered, "How?"

Rogers smiled. "I gave you the idea—you work out the details."

"Does this violate scriptural principles?" I make a subtle difference between fulfilling the Bible's principles and not violating them. I probably will never understand the Scripture fully enough to meet all that it teaches, but in my motives I can at least keep from being dishonest.

"Is this factual?" Does it coincide with truth, the way the world really is? Christians can live in fantasyland as easily as non-Christians. The love of truth is more of a scholarly trait than a religious trait, and we must all cultivate an absolute dedication to facts.

These are just three of the checkpoints creative people must employ. Most of us are fortunate to have one good idea out of ten, and so we must screen out the nine. We must be willing to submit them to the judgment of other people, who will help us.

I was bouncing a new thought off a lawyer friend one day, and I'll always remember the way he smiled and said, "Fred . . . that's not one of your better ideas." He did me a great service. I've used his line ever since with others who have brought their creative ideas to me for assessment.

Pastors and boards must do this work together. When a pastor or a deacon says, "I know I'm right. Sometimes you have to stand with God though everyone else stands against you," he is flirting with arrogance. Theoretically he's correct, but in most cases he needs to listen to the evaluation of colleagues.

Does God inhibit creativity?

If you were to conduct a street interview on whether Christians or non-Christians are more creative, I have a hunch the majority would vote for non-Christians. That is partly because they think uninhibited behavior is a sign of creativity when actually it is a sign of rebellion.

Christians are constrained in our behavior, but that does not need to transfer to our thinking. If anything, the Scripture equips us to think as widely as possible and still be secure.

I'm always amused after I make a bold statement, that people will comment, "Well, I wouldn't say what you just said."

I smile and say, "God doesn't know your thoughts, does he?"

They're acting as if God knows only what he hears—in English. They're afraid to verbalize their thoughts for fear God won't like it.

God knows our thoughts, good and bad, creative and trite, spoken and silent. He is entirely in favor of our thinking freely about his world and our particular place in it. These flights of imagination are not frivolous. They are essential to survive.

6

Growing Conditions

Programs seldom produce the spiritual dynamic necessary for growth; rather, the right spiritual climate produces programs that enhance growth.

—DONALD GERIG

After many years of attending pastors' conferences, I have heard my share of formulas for church growth, revival, and renewal. I have done the "pastoral drool" while listening to stories of skyrocketing attendance. I, too, have visited other churches hoping to find the key to growth. But the only church growth I had ever experienced was the plodding, gradual growth that no one writes books about.

Then it happened! We started seeing our monthly attendance rates 30 percent ahead of the previous year. Before we could get used to that, we found ourselves with more than seven hundred in worship. How did it happen?

The disconcerting thing was that we really could not put a finger on any single cause. I could not give any glorious stories of personal renewal to account for the growth—God had been good to me throughout my time here. No new programs had been introduced.

Yes, we had moved into a new building, but that was five years before. And yes, some families had transferred in from a troubled church across town, but the significant growth spurt did not start until later.

It began to dawn on me that what attracted these people, more than anything else, was our climate. Realizing how intangible that word is, I began to analyze it, and I discovered we had encouraged the components of a growth climate for several years without even realizing it.

In that reverse way, I learned an important lesson. Programs seldom produce the spiritual dynamic necessary for growth; rather, the right spiritual climate produces programs that enhance growth. That is why you can visit seven growing churches and discover seven different programming emphases. In each case, the right climate already existed and became the fuel for effective programming.

What we need, then, is a clearer understanding of the components of a healthy climate. From our experiences and those of other growing churches, I've identified six atmospheric conditions that contribute to growth. These are the elements common to growing churches regardless of their specific programs.

1. A positive atmosphere

I risk beginning with an overworked topic, but still it is true: Growing churches emphasize what God *can* do, not what we cannot do; what is best in people, not what is worst; how we can build each other up, not tear each other down.

This has to begin at a personal level. Every church has an ample supply of negative people. What is desperately needed to balance these are other individuals who practice a positive faith in their walk with God as well as their relationships with people.

Walking through our sanctuary one Sunday morning while the choir was rehearsing, I overheard the director say, "I refuse to have a bad performance today. We will get this right!" The choir laughed, rehearsed one more time, and did a magnificent job in the service that day. That happened partly because one person decided to expect the best. He chose to have positive expectations.

The runaway bestseller *The One-Minute Manager* reminded us to be eager to catch people doing something right rather than always looking for something wrong. That spirit is catching!

When individuals with that attitude relate to other individuals as well as God, a climate of expectation can begin to build. The emphasis in a church can begin to shift toward what we can do with God's help. Challenges can be dreamed and accepted.

Recently we had a special drive to raise $100,000 toward the building debt. The willingness to accept that challenge was simply the logical extension of a positive spirit that had grown in the church over several years. Had the climate not been right, the challenge could not have been accepted.

By the way, on the last day of the campaign, receipts passed $103,000.

2. Trust

The burden in creating a climate of trust rests on the one wanting to be trusted, not the one being asked to trust. You don't command trust; you earn it. At the risk of sounding trite, it must be said that trust exists when people are trustworthy.

There is no magic to trustworthiness. For church leaders, it means "going by the book." I am sure part of the trust I have earned has come because I have never tried to circumvent the established order for operation. That means presenting proposals to the proper boards or committees before action has begun. It also means being willing to "lose" graciously on an idea and not seek other means of implementing my plan. It means living by the budget and not seeking to get what I want by "special gifts."

Once I proposed an organizational change that involved revising the constitution. It went through the appropriate study committee and the church board before going to the congregation. At the congregational meeting it was increasingly apparent that this revision was being resisted. I could have fought. But I chose to lose gracefully on that issue, and to this day we are using the old system and making it work. We made no backdoor attempts to circumvent the congregation's wishes. And it has paid off with a level of trust among us that makes progress possible.

If I were to lock horns with our lay leadership or congregation on an issue I felt could not be compromised, I would have to openly persuade them to my position or leave. I would never resort to underhanded means of getting my way. Trust is too important to take that lightly.

3. Excellence

Excellence in ministry is not one arbitrary line that measures all situations. If so, we could paint the perfect church and all seek to imitate it. Instead, excellence is each of us, individually and congregationally, doing our best with the unique resources and limitations we have.

Too often we've made peace with mediocrity, rationalizing our substandard efforts. People are not attracted to that. Our goal must always be our *best* in every part of ministry. This emphasis on excellence is nothing more than being consistent with the glory of God (1 Cor. 10:31). God deserves our best—whether in the way bulletins are printed or how sermons are preached—and that level of excellence is a key ingredient in a climate of growth.

For six years in a row, our church has hosted a concert by the Chicago Staff Band of the Salvation Army. This outstanding brass band is built on excellence, fine music, and clear testimony. It has been interesting to watch our crowds grow from year to year. We have not increased our advertising, but people have come to know this band will always be at its best.

That can happen to an entire church. If people know we will be at our best in ministry, methods, and facilities, they respond.

4. Oriented to Outreach

Ingrown never equals *growing*. Many churches establish an antigrowth climate without even realizing it by allowing their predominant focus to become the needs of those already in the church. This, I'll admit, is the easiest path to follow, but it will not produce growth.

The mentality of a growing church is continually one of reaching out to others. Even the personal development of current members will be seen in light of increasing their ability to genuinely care about others and minister to them. The minute we start to plan for others rather than for ourselves we create a climate where we develop and the church will grow.

This, of course, is easier said than done. Every step we take to facilitate ministry to those outside our congregation causes us to struggle past our own comfort. Once we went to two worship services and two Sunday school sessions to make it possible to handle more people in our present facilities. Though there is nothing unique about this plan, we had to rethink our commitment to outreach. As long as our growth demanded no change from us, it was comfortable. But the minute we had to attend at different hours, divide classes, get used to new teachers, and face the recruitment of additional lay staff, the "cost" of outreach became apparent. Because of their commitment to outreach, however, our people made the changes.

The same outreach mentality has spawned new ministries—ministries that attempt to say we care about others, such as support groups for the divorced and for parents of wayward children. When the church climate is one of genuine concern for those outside the church, growth can happen.

5. Flexibility

The willingness to experiment, to innovate, and even to fail is part of flexibility. You cannot program this spirit, nor can you command it, but a few people placed in key positions can model it. By their own flexibility as well as their ability to allow (even encourage) such flexibility in others, the attitude can spread.

Perhaps a strategic time for instilling this spirit is after someone has taken initiative and flubbed.

I felt we started to see this spirit when a holiday outreach activity ended up going very poorly. I'm not proud of that failure, but I was pleased we could fail without its becoming an all-consuming issue. Rather, our attitude was one of appreciation for the willingness of those who planned the program—at least they were doing their best to reach out. We learned some things about outreach events, and more important, we demonstrated love in spite of failure. That encourages true flexibility.

Another element is the ability to adapt. Almost no program is so good that it never needs to be changed. We once tried to identify whether various evangelistic programs are "sowing, cultivating, or reaping" events. That means we must try to understand the people we are trying to reach and plan events to reach them where they are. Ten-year-old programs probably will not work because people have changed in those ten years.

When the climate is right, when risks are allowed and even traditional events can be adapted, it helps develop sensitivity to the changing culture around us, which is essential to effective ministry and church growth.

6. A Serving Spirit

In a sense, the serving spirit is a summary of a growth climate. Where people truly want to serve and minister, they will be positive, trustworthy, devoted to excellence, oriented to outreach, and flexible.

Just about everything in our society, however, militates against this spirit. It takes a conscious effort to serve rather than be served. We are encouraged today to look out for ourselves or be "fulfilled" (whatever that means). Every opportunity ends up being viewed in light of what we can get out of it.

This attitude easily turns our relationship to God around 180 degrees. Instead of asking what we can do for God, we find ourselves wondering what God can do for us. Christians raised on a pop faith that suggests God is little more than a handy twenty-four-hour heavenly banking service find it hard to relate to a word like *service* or, worse yet, *sacrifice*.

Thus in church we catch ourselves asking *if* people want to serve. Put that way, of course, many choose not to, and so dies the growth climate. A better way is to start with the assumption that God's people will serve. That is a given. The question is not *if* people will serve, but *where* and *how* they will serve. That assumption and commitment to service make up the necessary mind-set for growth.

Again, these components of a growth climate cannot be programmed. Rather, they can only be practiced and modeled. They will begin not with action but with attitudes. They will not be limited to certain settings but will be applicable to all situations. Whatever style church growth may take, underneath will be an atmosphere that is positive, trusting and trustworthy, devoted to excellence, oriented to outreach, flexible, and committed to service.

The beauty is that a growth climate does not have to wait for action by the official board. One individual can begin to model the components of this climate and have an incredible influence. Obviously, when church leaders are the models, growth can happen more quickly. But any person can be the first line of influence.

I recall sitting in a restaurant one Christmas Day. I went in expecting the atmosphere to be grim. After all, who wants to work on Christmas? Much to my surprise, it was almost like walking in on a party. One waitress had obviously decided that if she was going to have to work, she would make the best of it. She had bells tied on her shoes and was joking with customers. She was having a great time, and thanks to her, so was everyone else in the restaurant!

Perhaps that is what it takes in each of our churches—one or two people determined to influence the climate of the church. We may not be able to change weather conditions, but when it comes to the church atmosphere, we can not only survive the elements but adjust them to help the harvest.

7

Adapting to Your Church's Environment

We specialized not in prescriptions but in diagnosis.

—RAYMOND BAKKE

John Wooden, the successful basketball coach at UCLA for many years, can teach us something about pastoring.

When Wooden began his "ministry" of coaching, he won a national championship with a team whose tallest member was only six feet five inches. He had a fast-guard offense, a high post, and a lot of backdoor plays and quick screens. Wooden kept his players moving all over the court.

Then he was fortunate enough to recruit a couple of seven-foot centers, so he totally changed his system. He went to a low-post and strong-forward system. And he kept winning championships.

For Wooden, the goal was to win, not to run a particular offense. He changed to incorporate the gifts of his players.

Pastoral ministry demands similar flexibility. If Wooden was a pastor, he wouldn't insist on preaching the same way everywhere. He wouldn't try to run the same church program in every context. Pastors need to understand the environment in which we're called to preach the Word. We need to exegete both the Word and the world.

Exegeting my church

If we don't take time to understand the environment of our ministry, we're in danger of franchising it. Instead, we need to custom-build each ministry—move into a community, exegete the context, exegete the Scripture, and bring the two together.

I pastored ten years in the inner-city Chicago neighborhood of Humboldt Park. To exegete the culture the first thing I did was get to know the loyal core that had kept that church alive over the years. Their urban church was now declining. It was losing touch with its community and prided itself on programs that ran every night whether anybody needed them or not. Meanwhile houses on the block were burning, and the neighborhood was up for grabs.

So I turned away from programs. That wasn't easy for me. I had been associate pastor in three churches during college and seminary and had been a master of programming. I even received the Christian education director-of-the-year award from the local Sunday school association. I knew how to run programs. But if you're going to catch fish, you have to change the bait and go where the fish are.

What really taught me the importance of this was reading the story of Henry Ford in Amitai Etzioni's *Modern Organizations*. Ford made a perfect car, the Model T, that ended the need for any other car. He wanted to fill the world with Model T cars. But when people started saying, "Mr. Ford, we'd like a different color car," he remarked, "You can have any color you want as long as it's black." And that's when the decline started.

Back in Humboldt Park, I saw churches doing the same thing. Pastors were franchising programs rather than doing what an anthropologist does—learn the language and communicate Jesus with concepts people understand.

I had to learn that the hard way. I tried to run youth retreats at out-of-town camps. But when I invited Spanish kids and black kids from the neighborhood, some white parents resisted. The camp retreat program didn't work here.

So I went back to the basics. Eleven people ran the Fairfield Church, the youngest of whom was 54. They provided 90 per-

cent of the funds. I spent an evening with each one and asked
three questions:

1. How did you become a Christian?
2. What is your history with this church?
3. If you could wave a magic wand and bring about a future
for the church, what would it look like?

On the way home, I dictated my responses to those interviews
and later studied the transcriptions.

I was profoundly moved by those eleven people and their
commitment to this church. At the same time I realized they
didn't want to change. Because the world outside their doors was
fluctuating so dramatically, they wanted to grab the church and
say, "I dare you to change it!" It wasn't because they were inflexi-
ble people—as young people they had gone through a dramatic
Swedish-to-English language change. But now, because they
were proud of what their church had been, they were resisting
another major change to make their church more relevant to a
Spanish-speaking neighborhood. They had come full circle; now
they were the group resisting change.

Their expectations of what the church should be were almost
completely different from mine. They wanted a shepherd to feed
the sheep. I was up there saying, "Onward, Christian soldiers!"
That's what you call a conflict of images, of expectations. (Both
are biblical—in fact, there are almost a hundred different images
of the church in the New Testament; the context a church finds
itself in decides which models are most appropriate.) I decided
that if the church were to survive, I needed to disciple one new
board member per year, to replace the ones who would be moving away. It would take at least five years before the board would
commit to change. That's what it took.

We were in effect replacing many of the backward-looking
people with forward-looking ones. But you need both. In pastoral work, this means taking the ethos of a group of people—
the great memories and traditions of the church—and showing
how they can be translated into present-day deeds that best serve
the future.

One way we did this at Fairfield Church was to hold monthly
memory dinners at which we could remember how God had

blessed us. I began to lift up their memory. I had an older Swedish woman tell me stories by the hour of the great acts of God in the church's past. Then, when I was preaching about something contemporary, I could say, "What I'm asking you to do is not new; this church did this back in 1902." I became a broker of their memory rather than somebody trying to take away the church and make them do things they didn't want to do.

Understanding my neighborhood

I also made it a priority to exegete my neighborhood. I spent one day a week "networking." I went to all the pastors in the neighborhood, introduced myself, and asked them, "What is the most important lesson you have learned about being a pastor in this neighborhood?" Some of them took me by the hand and showed me the community—where kids hang out, where drugs are dropped, where things happen.

I also visited all the agencies in the community. At the police station, I asked, "What kinds of arrests do you make in this neighborhood?" I went to the schools and asked the principals, "What kinds of school problems do you have?" I went to the public aid office and the legal aid clinic. I went to forty four agencies the first year.

I also visited businesses. I met presidents and personnel managers. They told me the history of their businesses, the way they related to the community, the problems they had doing business here. The barber, the gas station attendant, the person who runs the fruit market—these people can tell you better than anyone what makes the neighborhood tick.

Such networking, of course, leads to opportunities for ministry. In one case the owner of a little factory with eighty employees told me he needed people who could run machines. Over the years, I sent him a number of people. In another case, someone walked in the office in desperate financial trouble because his social security checks weren't coming. Well, I had been to the social security office and knew whom to call, so I cut through a lot of red tape quickly.

Networking also made me streetwise to the con games people try to play on churches, especially young ministers. I could say to a public-aid mother playing a rip-off game, "I really admire you. You're like a mother in the Bible, Moses' mother. During a hard time she let her baby son float down the river to the princess who eventually hired her to mother her own child. I have a feeling you're a little like that." (There's always a way to affirm a person without getting conned.)

Five distinct groups

To educate myself further about the people I was pastoring, I studied ethnic backgrounds and cultural units. I was a country boy surrounded by strange people. I identified at least five groups I needed to study: youth gangs, Swedes, Appalachians, Puerto Ricans, and Poles.

The youths in the neighborhood all belonged to gangs, so I studied gang structure and how to work with them. I learned these groups miss certain things in the mainline culture, such as a feeling of belonging to something. But when they try to create these things on their own, they sometimes exaggerate them, and the gang becomes deviant.

I came to a church pastored by old Swedes, so I studied Viking history. I learned it took one thousand years for German missionaries to make Swedish Baptists out of violent Vikings. I studied the missions strategy used to bring about that conversion. And I preached about that on a day after two Puerto Rican kids were killed in our neighborhood. I said, "Who better than a Swedish Baptist church to be in the middle of this violent community? We've been through this before—on the other side. Maybe it will only take five hundred years for us to convert Puerto Ricans." That's how I used people's history in my preaching.

I also studied the Appalachians. I had a problem with them: If their kids got too involved in the church, often the parents pulled them out. I couldn't understand what was happening until I learned about clan structure. In the hills of Kentucky, the patriarch of a clan is powerful. But in the inner city he loses much of his power. I realized I was competing with the father, who was feeling emasculated. So I changed the way I dealt with them.

When you pastor a clan culture, the significant events are weddings, funerals, fires, and fishing seasons—these get the clan together. I stopped seeing people as individuals and began ministering to a whole clan as much as possible. Our missionary strategy could no longer be to look around the fringes of a group for some disaffected person being disciplined by the tribe.

I studied the Puerto Ricans and began to understand their feelings of being used. Five European nations conquered Puerto Rico in a period of three hundred years, using it as a military colony while they plundered South American gold. In the first year of their independence in 1898, we became the sixth outside power to occupy them. Now there are more Puerto Ricans on the U.S. mainland than in Puerto Rico. Meanwhile, about 65 percent of the Puerto Rican population is on public aid. Learning this made me far more sensitive to their feelings of disenfranchisement.

Learning their history and telling the great stories of Puerto Rico from the pulpit really affirmed the Puerto Ricans in our church. The same with the Polish and the Irish. It built a great sense of identification with the church.

Clearly we didn't worry too much about homogeneous units —although in some cases it's a useful principle. I had a student named Craig Burton who started a church in Chicago's Loop. Before he started, he asked, "Who is unreached in the Loop?" He profiled a twenty-five- to forty-five-year-old, bar-hopping, wine-and-cheese-party-going, vocationally-identified professional. After getting a feel for these people, he asked himself, "What would a church have to look like to reach them, and how would I have to pastor it?"

That's using the homogeneous principle to good advantage. I have trouble, however, when the principle is misused to resegregate the body of Christ. I've seen pastors work in just the opposite way Craig did. They say, "I'm going to find out what I'm comfortable with and then build a church out of those people."

That cuts the nerve of any sense of mission into the world. This country is internationalizing, and our churches have to deal with that. At such a time we can't afford to cater to a siege mentality.

This has become especially real to me since we adopted a black son. One of my other sons brought him home one day, and Brian stayed. Eventually we went to court and made it legal. It was electric in the Fairfield Avenue Church for the pastor to have a son who was not white. It affirmed a lot of things about our ministry. A church with a racially mixed membership roll can model care in a world of prejudice.

Helping the church understand itself

Another big part of the pastoral task is discovering people's expectations. You must discover them for two reasons: so you can effectively speak to them, and so you can make the people aware of them if they aren't already. You study the church's history, read the annual reports, find out where they spent their money—which may contradict what they say they want to do. You don't have to be in total agreement with those expectations. But that's where you have to start.

If I were pastoring the Loop church Craig Burton started, I might take a group on a retreat and lead them through an exercise of designing a logo for their church. I'd give them four ground rules:

First, the logo must be biblically and theologically sound. We'd see who they were spiritually, what they considered central to their beliefs.

Second, the logo must have some sense of history. As I mentioned before, these people see themselves not as cultural or ethnic groups but as vocational groups. But even then they bring history to any situation, and that will show up in subtle ways. They may have been the protesters of the sixties, or involved with the Jesus people. Those experiences still affect their lives.

Third, the logo must communicate God's concern for people, the pastoral dimension.

Fourth, it must be intelligible to the unchurched as well as to members.

After agreeing on a logo, we would discuss it. "Does this capture who we are?" If the answer is yes, then I would suggest using the logo to identify Loop Church in the future.

Exegeting the culture in this case means studying the tradition not of an ethnic group but of a cultural one.

Missionary calling

Often when we exegete the culture of our church and town, we will come face-to-face with how different we are from the people to whom we feel called to minister. You're called to Poplar Bluff, Missouri, for example, and you're originally from Boston. In such circumstances how much of a chameleon should you be? Should you buy a pickup truck and listen to country music?

These are missionary questions. You have clearly crossed a culture to minister, and you're doing just what a missionary is doing. You're stammering in a new language, trying to understand how people think, and trying to keep from thinking your culture is superior. Yes, you may want to buy a pickup. Try out the culture. You may come to love it.

But you may never love that culture; in fact you may hate it. The ability to be bicultural is a gift, so if you don't have it, that's God's will. But I think it's a more widely distributed gift than people allow for. It's one I covet for myself and others. Pastors need to give a church a good shot before they decide it's not for them.

After ten years at Fairfield Church I felt God telling me to move on. I was gratified by the progress we saw. When I came in 1969, we had about 100 members on the roll, mostly poor families. We had a fairly significant youth group but no middle class and no middle age. Sunday attendance averaged between 110 and 120. The neighborhood was just starting to change; we had a turnover rate of 70 percent on the block that first year. Many of the white people moved away, so the bottom dropped out of our traditional "market."

Still, we managed to survive, even grow a little. When I left, we had about 140 members. We had helped spawn seven Spanish daughter churches. If you added up all the ministries of Fairfield Church, we were touching at least 200 families a week. We had many ways of reaching out and touching people but never tried to pull it all into one building. Our theory was that in a diverse neighborhood, smaller, multiple churches were the way to go.

What enabled us to have such a diverse and, others say, effective ministry was the effort we put into understanding the church and the neighborhood. When we came to Humboldt Park, we specialized not in prescriptions but in diagnosis.

8

Breathing Life into the Traditional Church

I see a strong relationship between creativity and renewal.

—JAMES ROSE

I once preached a first-person sermon on Jonah. I came out barefoot, soaking wet, with seaweed all over me. Ninety percent of the congregation thought it was wonderful. But 10 percent were irate that their pastor had no shoes on. The seaweed wasn't a problem. The wetness wasn't a problem. No shoes was the issue. For that group, what I had done was undignified for a pastor.

Depending on whom you're talking to, the word *creativity* can evoke a positive or negative response.

In the church setting, creativity is the ability to develop forms different from the ones that presently exist—forms that freshly touch the generational and cultural groups around you. Naturally the younger members and artsy group love creativity because it means breaking with traditional forms. An emphasis on creativity invites them to the banquet table. But as the Jonah episode illustrates, some people will never warm up to innovation.

I helped found a church in Clearwater, Florida, in the 1970s with creativity as one of our watchwords. I also pastored Calvary Baptist, a historic, tradition-rich church. Take it from me: Creativity is much easier in a new ministry than in an old one. But creativity may be even more crucial in a historic church; it's the only way to breathe new life into old.

The need

For several reasons, creativity is more important today than it was a hundred years ago.

First, the culture is changing so quickly.

The Bible gives us our functions, which don't change—evangelism and discipleship, for example. We express these functions in our forms—the type of musical instruments used, for example—which *must* change if we're to touch the cultural groups around us. If we're not creative, we wind up freezing in time, locking into 1955 forms. What was creative at one time is institutionalized. People lock in whenever "it happened" for them, their great era. Those raised on fifties music tend to listen to the oldies station. One reason people are listening to the oldies is the instability of our times. The familiar gives security.

While some forms are of lasting benefit, you have to keep going back to your mission or vision statement and asking, "Are our forms helping or hurting us in accomplishing what we've set out to do?" I question whether God is in evangelistic forms that nobody would understand or come to because they're forms out of the forties. We've got to know what kids are tuned in to; it's easy to miss the next generation.

If a church is going to speak to people in a particular setting at a particular time, somebody must have a creative edge. Either the senior pastor must be a creative person, or the pastor must gather creative people around to keep the forms fresh.

Second, creativity is more important today because we're facing greater and greater needs.

We have a generation growing up that doesn't know the Bible, and we have many kids who can't read and write, so we have to be creative in education. At Calvary Church, we ran a rap program on Saturday nights as an outreach that also taught reading and writing.

In New York we couldn't tell the kids to drive down to the youth program on Friday night. People in Manhattan don't own cars. If kids came to a night meeting, they couldn't go home; you couldn't ask fourteen-year-olds to get on the subway after ten o'clock at night and go tooling over to Brooklyn or Queens or the Bronx. They would get beat up. They had to spend the night at the church.

I've also had to be creative in staffing. When I began interviewing people to come on staff, I found it was difficult to get good people to move to New York: "Where are you? New York City? Well, nice to talk to you." The cost of living was so high. We had to learn to distribute creatively our assignments.

Third, leadership today demands creativity. In some measure I need to stay one step ahead of others in the church. I need to know where the culture is going. I don't need to be ahead of everybody; I have people in the church who are ahead of me in various areas, and I rely heavily upon them. But somebody must have an overall vision.

To develop that vision, I read to keep up with the culture. I meet several times a year with people who are creative just to talk about the culture, about fresh ministry, about ideas, about what they're doing. They don't have to be pastors. One person in this group is an ex-advertising man who has a great creative mind. The point is to keep in touch with today's people.

I find the process refreshing. Sometimes when I'm writing an article or a sermon, I'll intentionally start off in directions I've never tried before. I may never use that approach, but drafting it pushes out my mental parameters. On occasion there's value in planning a service that "pushes the envelope," exercises the mind, keeps you from thinking in boxes and corridors, helps you break out.

Creativity run amok

Having emphasized the importance of creativity, however, I must note that innovation can be overdone.

When I pastored in Clearwater in the seventies, we did a lot of creative things but also some weird things just to be different. One memorable mistake was a Sunday morning concert. I had heard an itinerant hard-rock group ministering at high school assemblies and giving their testimony. I suggested to the church leaders we should put together a morning worship service with

the group. One of our leaders said, "Do you really want to do
this?"

"Oh, yeah. It'll be great."

I walked into the auditorium the day of the concert and saw
large banana speakers hanging in front. When the lead guitarist
tuned his electric guitar, he cleared my sinuses. *We're in trouble,* I
thought.

Sure enough, nobody could relate to it as a church form. At
that time most church people hadn't heard much hard rock. That
worship service wasn't creative; it was weird because it didn't
connect. To be creative without getting weird, you must be in
touch with your various groupings, from the old guard to the
teens.

Creativity also gets out of control when you feel you have to
top the efforts of last week. When that happens, as it did on
occasion for us in Clearwater, creativity becomes a tyrant. In
that case, you're into creativity for creativity's sake.

We eventually realized what was happening and made three
"rules": (1) We don't have to do something new every week, (2)
don't do more than one new thing in a service, and (3) if you
find something good, hold onto it for a while.

We found, for instance, that interview videos on the topic
"Sex, Money, and Power" were a success, so we used that format
again. But eventually we needed to ask, "Is that still working?"

Another way creativity can run amok is when a particular
worship service simply has too much diversity. After reading the
first three chapters of one adventure book recently, I was thoroughly confused. Each chapter was a different story that seemed
to have nothing to do with the others. I said to my son, who had
read the book, "I have no idea where the author's going. Is this a
series of short stories?" My mind was struggling to fit all this
together.

"Just wait," he said. "It'll all come together."

People in a worship service often have the same reaction if a
service is too diverse. No matter what the style of music employed, the service needs a dominant theme. If we're going to
use black gospel music in our Sunday evening meeting, it will be
exclusively that. Yet next week we may use jazz. The human

mind fights for unity and cohesiveness, so I resist having a shotgun service. Just as every sermon has to cohere, so does a service.

Hope for the historic

While ministering at Calvary Church, I saw movement toward greater innovation. Several things encouraged that.

Recall the past. I pointed to the history of our congregation to show that they had a history of creativity. We were building on a tradition of adjusting to the opportunities.

Calvary will be 150 years old in 1997. One reason Calvary has survived and prospered is that while being thoroughly biblical, the church has also been creative. For example, in the late 1910s when flatbed trucks first were sold, Calvary bought one and went to lower Manhattan and ran evangelistic programs on the truck. Other churches excoriated them for it, accusing them of selling out the gospel. But they persisted in innovative outreach.

Then, in the 1920s, they began to realize that to survive in midtown Manhattan, they needed an endowment. Few inner-city churches can survive without some form of financial subsidy. Since John D. Rockefeller had left the church to go build Riverside, the church fathers decided to use the church's land to house both a church and a hotel—a creative solution! Since 1931, the Salisbury Hotel has helped underwrite the ministry of the church.

Find like-minded people. I try to identify individuals who are ready to try new things. In a church of any size, you'll always have a few willing to risk. You have to gather a creative team. (Sometimes you have to calm them down, though, because they're ready to blow the place up with bizarre ideas.)

Move at a snail's pace. Change will always be slower in a historic church than in a church plant. In a historic setting, I can't say to those who don't like what I'm doing, "If you don't like this, there's another church down the street." In a church where others have been there thirty years, the pastor is the one who will be going down the street.

In the church I founded in Clearwater, Florida, we received widespread publicity and eventually had pastors and their entire boards coming to see what we were doing. We'd tell them, "Take our principles, but go slow when you implement them back home."

Yet we heard of pastors who went back, tried some of our creative worship forms, and in weeks were literally out of their church. You have to move slowly, though you must still move. You eventually come to a watershed where the church must decide to go forward or stay put.

Preach suitable themes. First, preach on the mission of the church: What are we about? How do we win people?

If you can get people asking, "Why are we doing this?" you've solved the problem. People don't like creativity because they're locked into what's comfortable rather than into the mission of the church.

Second, you deal with Christ's ministry. Jesus was always shattering human assumptions because he focused on God's original intent. The religious establishment resisted Christ because he didn't fit their traditions.

Third, stress God's creativity. While we're singing the same old tired hymns, God says, "Sing unto me a new song."

Choose innovation zones. You have to accept that there are limits to what you can do with those locked into a particular style of ministry. Innovate where you can and accept where you cannot.

I must balance people's need for security and familiarity with their need for the fresh and unexpected. At Calvary Church, the musical forms of our Sunday morning service—which was the biggest issue—never changed much. We were located in the middle of a classical-music mecca, with Carnegie Hall across the street and Lincoln Center just minutes away, so our worship music stayed classical. While maintaining the historical on Sunday morning, we focused most of our creativity on Sunday night and other occasions.

That wasn't a failure in any way. I believe in creativity, but I also believe we need to keep some of our rich history alive. One great problem today is that people don't know anything about history. C. S. Lewis said one thing that disturbed him as he spoke to people about Christ was that not only did they not buy Christianity, they didn't even buy history. They didn't know why things happened, and they didn't care. That's called "chronological snobbery."

Calvary Church was loaded with busters and boomers, young adults who had moved into the city. They told us, "We love your teaching and the discipleship groups, but it's hard for us to connect with your worship."

We couldn't use rock music in worship, but we found hymns that used a traditional melody but with up-to-date words. We also launched a "seeker service" on Sunday nights, once a month. The music was contemporary—jazz, black gospel, American folk.

At Calvary Church we also found ways for the artistically gifted to use their abilities. We ran an "Arts Fest" every year that included an exhibition of graphic arts, painting, and sculpture. We had concerts with various music forms such as a jazz band and a classical ensemble. We also sponsored mime (though we never broke into interpretive dance), and I often preached on the arts and creativity.

*   *   *

Although creativity can be abused and will face some opposition, I'm willing to take the risk. I see a strong relationship between creativity and renewal. Creativity causes people to think about what they're doing. Creative preaching forces people to think about the Bible. Creative worship causes people to think about God. That's why God says to sing to him a new song. If you do the same thing in worship every week, you just settle and die.

I was with Joe Bayly, the author and publishing executive, when he was leading a seminar in Florida. Joe said one of the characteristics of every great revival has been a new form of worship.

To stay fresh, to be renewed, to be where God wants you to be, you need a creative edge.

PART 3

Creative Solutions

9

Leading from a Cramped Position

Being cramped is a part of ministry at every turn, at every level of growth—and probably at every church.

—LARRY OSBORNE

When I first came to North Coast, the walls of the "sanctuary" were not lined with stained glass. They were spotted with the remains of innumerable food fights. While we rented the facility on Sundays, Monday through Friday it served another function: lunchroom for the local high school.

Obviously, it wasn't an ambiance that lent itself to traditional worship. One Sunday, a dog wandered up the aisle in the middle of my sermon, nuzzling and sniffing at the faithful. Another Sunday, a boisterous gang of adolescent skateboarders decided to show off their skills right outside a row of large Plexiglas windows.

On top of that, I had taken a cut in pay from my previous salary as a youth pastor in a large suburban church. As the new pastor of a fledgling church plant, I no longer had at my disposal a secretary, copy machine, or many of the other trappings of civilized ministry. Instead, my new office was a refurbished garage with a beat-up desk that my previous church had given me as an act of charity.

After a quick start (we jumped from 120 to 150 in a few weeks), we leveled off. It soon became obvious that ministry from a cramped position would not be a short-term aberration but a long-term way of life.

As a twenty-eight-year-old rookie pastor, I had two choices:

adjust or quit. I chose to adjust, all the time thinking that if I hung in there long enough, the day would finally come when ministry from a cramped position with significantly limited resources would be a thing of the past.

That day never came. I've since discovered that there is no time in ministry when something doesn't hinder ministry. Today we have more staff and volunteers, and larger facilities than I ever imagined, yet I still often feel cramped. We always need more space, money, and workers to do ministry right.

Being cramped, then, seems to be a part of ministry at every turn, at every level of growth—and probably at every church. We have no choice: if we are going to minister, we're going to have to learn how to do it from a cramped position.

Here are some things that have helped our church succeed in less-than-ideal circumstances.

Ignore some cramps

Pastors commonly—and mistakenly—assume that if something is wrong, we have to fix it. Whether the pressure comes from well-meaning and caring members or from our sense of duty, I've learned that, in many cases, it's a good idea to ignore these pressures and let the problem be.

Yet one of the hardest facts to accept when ministering from a cramped position is that you're not going to have a well-balanced ministry. When you're working under severe budgetary constraints, for example, shoring up one program inevitably means taking away from another.

During a critical stage of our church's growth, we had a lot of young families with small children, and we had some older adults. But we had almost no families with junior high or high school kids. So we poured our limited resources into creating a topnotch children's program. As a result, we attracted more people with young children. But we had a huge demographic gap where youth ministry was supposed to exist.

Still, there were a few families with junior and senior high kids. It was hard to look them in the eye and say, "I'm sorry, but we just can't minister to your kids right now." But that's exactly what I had to say to one man I dearly love, the father of two high school girls. He understood our limitations and continued to support me and the church, and he's one of our elders today. But it was hard for him—and for me—to ignore this area of weakness in our program.

Of course, it's a lot easier to ignore pressures if we offer the congregation a compelling alternative. Peter Drucker calls it building on our islands of strength—which we did by focusing on families with young children.

That's why, when we hired our first full-time staff person, we resisted the powerful temptation to make youth work part of his job description. I went to the board and asked them to make a rule that Mike would not work with youth. I wanted the church officially to declare that we were going to ignore this area of weakness and focus on building our strengths, which at that time were our children's ministry and home groups. The board agreed. Eventually, those islands became so strong and brought in enough new people and new funding that we were able to develop an outstanding youth program. But the key was waiting until the time was ripe rather than trying to fix it at the first sign of brokenness.

This principle continues to guide us today. Right now, for example, our missions effort is anemic at best. Because our church has been growing rapidly, we've put a lot of effort into absorbing and ministering to new people. So our missions emphasis has taken a back seat.

Does this mean that we don't care about the Great Commission? Of course not. We were active in missions during the years when growth was stagnant. I'm confident we'll be a missions church again in the future. But right now, we're expanding the kingdom by focusing on the corner of the kingdom that is bulging our own walls.

"Be what you are—don't try to be what you are not" is a slogan that helps me work effectively within limitations.

Bend with the church's attitude

Before coming to North Coast, all the churches I had worked in had been large churches, where the unspoken questions are about quality: Are things done with excellence? Is the preaching powerful? Is the music polished and professional?

But the unspoken questions in a small church are different. Lyle Schaller suggests there are only three:

1. Do you love me?
2. Do you love me?
3. Do you *really* love me?

In a small church, few care if Aunt Martha's solo is a little off-key; that's Aunt Martha; everybody knows and loves her. But in a large church, everyone squirms if Aunt Martha misses a note. To my harm, I came into the little church and looked and listened with big-church eyes and ears. I focused on excellence and performance. I even canned our Aunt Martha.

If that wasn't insensitive enough, I made a similar mistake with the woman in charge of our newsletter. I was troubled with our newsletter's jokes, puns, and in-house references, like, "The Blond Bomber hit a home run at the church picnic." I thought newcomers reading the newsletter would feel left out. To me, a newsletter should be a vehicle for communicating with those on the inside *and* the fringe of our ministry.

So I sat down with the woman who put it together and explained my concerns. I said it as gently as I knew how, but all I succeeded in doing was crushing her feelings. Three weeks later, she and her family left the church.

Regardless of the size of the church, though, there is often a basic attitude difference between pastor and people that we must recognize and accept. The pastor's mind-set is visionary; he or she sees the future potential and envisions what the church can become. But the mind-set of the congregation is more often static: people have come because they like what the church is. Their vision of the future is "More of the same, please."

I've learned, then, simply to accept these differences in perspective and be more pastoral about any changes I make or challenges I present.

Give volunteers a break

Since I was the church's only paid employee, and there was no funding for support staff, I had to rely heavily on volunteers.

In the beginning, I was frustrated. I had previously relied on an efficient secretarial pool. Volunteers were well-intentioned but often inconsistent, inefficient, and unreliable. They didn't do things the way I wanted them done.

But I've learned how to work from this cramped position. First, I've changed my attitude. I now realize that while a church ministry is my life and my career, it is only a side dish on the volunteer's plate. A volunteer can and will call in sick at the last moment when a paid staff person might drag him or herself to work. That's a pain. But the truth is, many times I would love to do the same but don't only because I'm paid to be there.

Still, volunteers are fabulous, dedicated, committed people. In addition to the demands of their jobs and families, they give hours of time and energy to keep the ministry of our church humming. To begrudge their inherent limitations is to miss out on one of God's special blessings.

Second, I make sure they're given the best tools to do their jobs. Good volunteers may save the church money, but keeping them isn't cheap.

I once observed our volunteers folding bulletins and newsletters by hand, and I thought to myself, *This is boring, lousy grunt work. If these people are going to volunteer their time, they deserve to have the job made as easy as possible.* So even though our church was still small and struggling, we bought the best folding machine available. It's a pattern we follow today. No matter how tight the budget, we try to ensure that our volunteers have reliable copy machines, efficient computers, and trustworthy printers. Quality tools make a big difference in morale and in ministry.

Third, we've taken the pressure off some of our volunteers by making the job as manageable as possible. For instance, we found that our volunteer Sunday school teachers were often ill-prepared when they stepped into the classroom. You know the routine: sometime late Saturday night, the teacher cracks the

David C. Cook lesson book for the first time and ends up reading or stumbling through the lesson on Sunday morning.

There's an old rule of thumb in business: if three people in a row fail at the same job, the problem is not the people; it's the job. In a similar vein, if volunteer after volunteer comes to class underprepared, perhaps the job needs to be redefined.

That's what we did. We got rid of the traditional teacher and class setup and replaced them with storytellers and shepherds, and we began a program called "Kids' Praise." We brought all the kids together for a fast-moving, entertaining, Sesame Street–type program led by a good storyteller. (We've found it's a lot easier to find four or five good storytellers than to recruit eighteen Sunday school teachers.)

These leaders conduct a program of music, humor, and fun; the gathering then breaks into small groups. An adult "shepherd" leads each group of children through a simple, loosely structured craft and discussion time. There's no lesson to teach, nothing to prepare for. While they lead the children in a craft, the shepherds encourage the kids to talk about the lesson presented in the larger group. Their function is not to teach but to be a loving, adult presence—a much easier job description for volunteers.

Look for partners, not helpers

As the church grew, we reached a point where we needed to add support staff. There was enough money to hire a part-time secretary and a part-time ministry assistant. Naturally, I felt I needed a full-time person at each position!

At first, I decided to lessen my load by hiring a part-time assistant to do all the things I hated doing. But before long the relationship soured, and I had to let him go.

Back to cramped square one. This time, though, I took a fresh approach: I decided to ignore my needs for support staff and hire ministry staff.

I pooled the money that would have been spent on a part-time secretary and part-time assistant and hired a full-time associate pastor. Instead of being hired to do what I didn't want to do, he was hired to do what I couldn't do. He brought a set of ministry gifts and skills that complemented mine. My overall workload wasn't reduced, but our ministry was multiplied. He's still with us years later, and he now shares the preaching load. But in those early years, it meant I didn't have a secretary. Still we were capable of doing a lot more for the kingdom.

Frankly, sometimes I found it hard to share ministry with a partner. To have a secretary or ministry assistant would have sometimes been easier on my self-esteem, like the first time someone in our church asked Mike to perform a baptism. Until then, I had done all the baptisms, so Mike told this person, "I'm sure it will be no problem, but let me check with Larry."

He came into my office and asked me about it. I had somewhat of a relationship with the person being baptized, and I remember wondering why this person chose Mike over me. But I said, "Sure, go ahead."

After Mike walked out, another associate, Paul, whom we had later hired, stepped into my office and closed the door. He had overheard the conversation. "That was tough, wasn't it?" he said. "How do you feel?"

"Not so great," I said.

That conversation gave me helpful insights into myself. Yes, it did hurt a little. I should have been happy that someone asked Mike to do this baptism. My goal, after all, was to create a shared ministry. In the long run, such discomfort is worth it.

Improve it

No matter how many ways you adapt a building, it always seems to prove inadequate in one way or another. Figuring out how to minister in a less-than-ideal facility is one of the most challenging aspects of ministry.

A year after I arrived, we moved out of our elegant cafeteria with its spaghetti-bedecked walls, and we rented space in a church that held its meetings on Saturdays. Though it was a definite step up, we still had plenty to complain about: the lighting was terrible, the sound system was inadequate, and we were still squeezed for classroom space. Furthermore, we felt stymied by being renters, not owners. Cramped again.

The temptation was to crank up a building fund to escape, but that would have taken years to accumulate. And the financial drain would have stifled our fledgling ministry.

Then it dawned on us: Why not offer to improve the facility at our expense? Our landlords were pleased to let us invest in their facility, so we fixed the lighting, improved the sound system, and even paid half the expense of a building-expansion program. We couldn't fix our problem, but we sure could improve upon what we had.

As our congregation continued to grow, we ran into a new problem. Our landlords decided we were getting too big for their facility, and they informed us that they were breaking our lease —without notice. In effect, they were kicking a church of eight hundred out in the street!

We could have sued and forced the church to honor the remaining four years of the lease, but we felt it would be unbiblical to take another church to court—and it would have given the local press a religious scandal to run with. So we decided to pack our bags and go.

Our congregation was too large to move into a storefront, we didn't have enough time or money to put up a building, and no other church properties were available. But by God's providence, we found a large building in an industrial complex. It was a retail frontage, with a warehouse and loading docks in the back. It had plenty of parking. And it was the only place in the area that was large enough to permit us to grow.

But many hearts sank when folks first saw their new "church" —half the floor was at ground level, and the other half five feet lower running back to the loading dock. It made some long for the good old days in the cafeteria!

Again we were forced to find a way to improve what we couldn't fix. We angled the cement drop-off and created a ramped floor, which gave us a creative and functional sanctuary space. Ours may be the only retail space in America with such a fabulously sloped floor!

Make lemonade

Cramped quarters can also make discipleship a challenge. All along we've had trouble getting adequate classroom space, especially for adults. Not having adequate facilities for formal or large gatherings can lead to one of two things: you can complain about what isn't or make creative use of what is. We've chosen the latter. If we couldn't meet in Sunday school classes on Sunday morning, we could at least meet in small groups in homes in the evenings.

As a result, home fellowship groups have become the hub of our ministry (and ironically, the most significant contributor to the health of our church). Today more than 70 percent of our Sunday morning worshipers attend one of these groups. They study in greater depth the Scripture passage preached on Sunday, giving everyone a common focus and allowing people to deepen their knowledge of Scripture and relationships with one another.

This is perhaps the best lemonade we've made from the lemons we've been handed. We wouldn't go back to adult Sunday school even if we had the space to do so.

That's ministry

As I write this, the 1900s are commonly being viewed as the decade of consumption and the 1990s as the decade of limits. It may well be that a lot of pastors and churches will have to learn to live within their limitations and find creative ways to minister from a cramped position.

Does that mean we have to trim our idealism and vision for the future? Must we downsize our goal of expanding the kingdom of God? Absolutely not! Limitations don't have to diminish our effectiveness. Limitations just force us to be more creative as God expands his kingdom.

Looking back, I believe my greatest mistake when first confronted with cramped quarters was comparing my situation with others. I began feeling I couldn't do anything because I lacked the resources others had. I periodically slumped into a mood of paralysis and defeat.

But no more. I now look at limitations from a new perspective, tinker with solutions, and try to come up with the most enterprising and inventive answers I can. Our church is not something we've planned or engineered. It has evolved as we've looked for creative solutions to our cramped circumstances.

In fact, I've come to believe that restricted ministry is in some ways part and parcel of ministry: it's a string of cramped positions, where problems and limitations are just disguised opportunities for ministering in new and creative ways.

10

Major Ministry on Modest Means

*The trouble with our church or any church is not lack of
members or money; it is lack of ingenuity, creativity,
and courage.*

—JAMES STOBAUGH

Our collection one week recently was $691.30. We needed
$1,300 to meet budget.

Standing at the front door of our brownstone church, saying
farewell to our eighty congregants, I saw Robert, a street person
in our neighborhood. He asked a member for a quarter. *We
barely have a quarter to give you,* I thought.

It wasn't always this way. In my closet sits a photograph of
our turn-of-the-century congregation. Healthy-looking men and
parasol-laden women encircle a whole block. Written in optimistic white ink is "The Church in Friendship." Pittsburgh was
thriving, and so was the church. It boasted a huge Sunday
school, active youth group, and overflowing morning worship.
The softball team won the all-church league! The church's potential seemed unlimited.

But the steel industry faltered: our armies won two wars but
our businesses lost the import war. Superhighways enticed people to the suburbs. A few stalwart souls continued to commute
to our declining church, but their children yearned for modern
bathrooms and carpeted nurseries. A popular pastor retired. By
1960 we were a shadow of former glory. By the early eighties, we
were only a handful of dazed saints.

By now the community hardly knew we existed. Robert and
his friends had nothing in common with us. Their world was full

of drugs, unemployment, and juvenile delinquency. Our world
was quiet afternoons with a Sunday paper. Except for when this
community mugged us, raped us, or stole our cars, we were
effectively ignoring it. Most of us hoped to escape.

To our credit, we felt conviction. God wasn't pleased with our
negligence. This was our time and our place. These were our
people. Like it or not, God had called us here to represent his
Son. What were we going to do about it?

Conviction, though, is one thing. The fact was, we didn't
know how we could help anyone. We simply didn't have the
resources. We were in a large, older building, and our expenses,
even cut to the minimum, were often double our weekly offering.

Recognize existing resources

Where could we begin?

With what we *did* have.

No, we didn't have a lot of discretionary income. Our budget
was overstrained. But as we assessed our resources, we realized
we have more than we thought we did.

For example, we have a large building. That gave us space to
host a variety of ministries and programs without having to
worry about finding or renting room for them.

Second, we have a church office with a manual typewriter and
a copier. We can handle, slowly, the basic communication and
correspondence needed in any outreach.

Third, though our congregation is small, it's resourceful. Most
of us have learned the hard way how to get the most for our
money.

Most important, we have an omnipotent God. And our community needs an omnipotent God: unemployment is almost 40
percent; 84 percent of community families are led by single parents; most children are born out of wedlock; and crime is as bad
as anywhere in Pittsburgh. But our God is bigger than even these
staggering problems.

Once we had seen all we did have, we could put those resources to use. For example, we were concerned about the mental health of our community, but we couldn't afford a part-time counselor, let alone a full-time one, to address the staggering needs. So we went to a local Christian ministry and offered office space in our building—for free—if they would provide a counselor available to people in the community. They agreed, and we now have a counselor in our church a couple of nights a week. We were able to provide far more counseling help for the community than we could have otherwise. The trick was recognizing the value of an existing resource—our building—and using it.

Network with other groups

That experience illustrates another principle we've learned: When you can't afford to do it by yourself, don't. Work with other groups.

One widespread and growing problem in our church neighborhood is chemical addiction. *Why not ask a chapter of Narcotics Anonymous to come to our church?* we thought. We couldn't afford staff to tackle the problem, and Narcotics Anonymous had expertise in this area. And to be honest, we were new to all this, and we felt more comfortable risking our building than ourselves!

Narcotics Anonymous came, and within a few months we had the largest chapter east of the Mississippi meeting in our church. Every week, from 350 to 700 people flowed through our church. A few came to our worship service. More important, the community supported our efforts because their families benefited. Feeling cocky, our board refused any rent, except a small stipend we immediately returned to another community ministry. "I've never been loved this way," a surprised NA representative told us.

There were problems, like the time some recovering addicts stole furniture and ruined two carpets. But our board had tasted victory for the first time in decades. We still were receiving about

$700 per week and spending more than $1,000, but we were finally doing something that was changing our world.

We looked around for other ways to affect our community. We remembered that each year we paid dues—$100—to East End Cooperative Ministry, a coalition of forty churches that runs a food closet, soup kitchen, meals-on-wheels program, shelter, halfway house, and employment agency. We decided paying dues was not enough. The board and I volunteered to serve in these ministries. Before long our tiny congregation was logging more than one hundred hours in these ministries every week— more than an hour per member! It didn't cost a nickel, but we started receiving rich spiritual returns.

We began to support, along with other churches and groups, a Jubilee housing project. The project buys abandoned houses, refurbishes them, and allows low-income people to live in them at modest rates. The only stipulation is that they must take good care of them. If they do, in twenty or so years they will own their own homes.

Before long, other people on the block painted their houses and cleaned their yards. Tenement owners made needed repairs. A feeling began to spread: This community is worth taking care of! It wouldn't have happened without many groups working together.

Focus on areas of greatest need

One painful realization for any pastor is that you can't do everything. The number of needs in any church and community is simply too great. We feel this acutely. With so much that needs to be done, and so little money, what can we do?

We have decided, by necessity, to focus on the areas of greatest need. In our community right now, one of these is our young people. One of every twenty young men on our block will die before age twenty. Four of every five young women will be pregnant before age fifteen. At least two youths will die of an overdose of drugs during the year.

Neither I nor my predecessor was equipped for this challenge.

We both asked the Lord for a financially affordable way to do something about this dilemma. He sent us Joe.

A few years before I came, a middle-aged Mafia enforcer named Joe Bellante was shot twice by the mob because he owed them $10,000. While in the hospital, Joe committed his life to Christ. Some of our Session members heard about Joe's situation and got to know him. A few of them raised enough money to make a financial settlement with the Mafia, and thus they literally saved Joe's life.

From this amazing beginning, Joe became an assistant to the pastor and took responsibility for youth ministry. We added a line to the budget, and members who could afford to give extra did. It wasn't easy, but if we were going to stretch anywhere, it would be for this area of great need. Joe began youth clubs, and soon our basement was filled with kids on Wednesday nights. His knowledge of the street was invaluable; the police used him to defuse crises; he went to Florida to retrieve runaways; he held junkies all night to keep them from harming themselves.

After a while, we realized Joe's ministry could be even greater if it weren't restricted to our church. Joe formed an independent ministry named Urban Partners, and its budget is now larger than ours. Members of our church continue to be its biggest financial contributors, and some of our members serve on Urban Partners' board.

Again we faced the problem of funding a staff person to reach young people. Returning to our principle of networking, we talked with East Main Presbyterian Church in Grove City, Pennsylvania, outside the city. They got excited about the potential and agreed to fund a staff person who would be responsible for developing new ministries to young people and others.

Avoid dependence

This raises a key question for churches trying to build a major ministry with modest means: How much can you depend on others? To refuse funds is to refuse opportunities for ministry.

But to accept them is to open yourself to an insidious cycle of dependence.

We've tried to resolve the issue by determining what the funds are for. If they're for operating expenses—lights, heat, my salary —we refuse them. That's our responsibility. We are committed to dying as a church before we accept others' money for basic expenses.

On the other hand, we will gladly accept money for ministry and mission. Our vacation Bible school reached almost a hundred kids. We felt fine about Nabisco's giving cookies for the school. The next summer, the city provided free lunches. In a cooperative effort with three other churches, we provided a hot lunch for more than half the children in our 9,200-member community. The difference was that these gifts weren't given to keep Fourth Presbyterian alive; they were given to help children who might not eat as well otherwise. That was why we rejoiced that East Main agreed to fund Cindy Schartner, our new staff member. She's not an associate pastor or director of Christian education. Her primary responsibility is to coordinate ministries directed outward, to the community.

The "avoid dependence" principle works the other way too: we try not to build an unhealthy dependence in the people we serve. A few years ago Bob Lupton, executive director of the Family Consultation Service in Atlanta, introduced me to the idea of "dignity ministries," programs that build not dependence but dignity. I knew these were needed because in our community I'd seen, for example, people receive donated, hand-me-down Christmas toys for their kids. The people were losing their dignity in having to depend on handouts, in not being able to choose and buy toys for their children. So last Christmas we opened a Christmas store. We asked area churches to provide new toys, and we made sure the toys were both nonviolent and appropriate for people in our community. But instead of giving them away, we *sold* them—at 30 percent of retail price. (We also made Bibles available.) For many customers, it was the first time they had been able to buy Christmas toys for their children.

If folks couldn't afford to pay for the toys—and it was surprising how many could—we allowed them to work for them. They joined others from the community who were already working in the store. These weren't empty, made-up jobs, but real ones. People cleaned the store, set up displays, unloaded boxes, priced items. We made people come to work on time. If they didn't work the whole time they were scheduled for, they weren't paid. In all, we employed twenty-five people, and it was exciting to see homeless people and others of varying financial status gain work experience. When we finished the project, we had actually made a little money, which will give us a start on this year's store.

By minimizing dependence, we maximize impact.

Don't settle for second-rate

I'll be the first to admit we've never had enough money to do anything the easy way. For example, we host a drop-in center for homeless people in our basement and we can't afford a separate phone line for it. If a person wants to reach the church office, he or she may have to call twice: once when it's picked up downstairs, and again while the people downstairs let it ring. But in our ministries to the poor and powerless, we endeavor to provide excellence. We think our Lord demands nothing less.

As we seek to rehabilitate the homeless, for example, we draw on the services of East Liberty Family Health Care Center, an independent Christian health ministry. At the same time an orthopedic surgeon and a dentist in our church offer care to needy street people. The church does not have to take a back seat to any organization in America.

Not settling for second-rate means, among other things, that when you enter new areas of ministry, you have to ask for advice. Recently we took over an eleven-unit apartment building in our neighborhood to house elderly and homeless people in our congregation. We recognized that as a small church we didn't have a lot of expertise in housing ministry.

So we formed an advisory committee, a blue-ribbon panel of committed Christians from outside our church who are specialists in various areas. They examined the facility, helped with legal questions, and guided us through a maze of nonprofit matters.

To help with the renovation, a contractor who belongs to East Main Presbyterian has agreed to bring his workers for a week this summer. We'll provide the materials, while he generously provides the labor. Here again, by tapping others' expertise, we're able to make sure the project is done right.

A simple fact

I will never forget the day we invited Robert into our church and handed him a cup of coffee. We and East End Cooperative Ministry had opened a drop-in center for the homeless. Here people come to get warm, to find counsel. Each Monday evening, for example, some of our members lead a Bible study at the center.

A simple fact dawned on us: with no increase of our budget, we had become a powerful church. We were becoming respected, even loved, by people in our community, and some of them started coming to church. Eventually some became officers; gradually we were becoming a community church again. We had no more broken windows or walls defecated on because this was their church.

One day a drop-in person stole our VCR. Frankly, I never expected to keep a VCR in an inner-city church—they were hot commodities on the street market. So I wasn't surprised when it was stolen. But I was surprised when it was returned by another drop-in. "Hey, man," he scolded the thief, "what you doin'? This is our VCR. This is our place. Don't go stealing from our place!"

Our budget is still $72,000 a year, and we still have 79 members. We still receive $691.30 some weeks. But more and more the congregation offers $1,000 or even $1,500. We have begun to meet budget for the first time in years. Last year, we ended up $7.30 in the black!

One glaring weakness of our work over the last few years is that we haven't been able to incorporate the homeless and recovering addicts into our congregation in a substantial way. We are still searching for ways to make them feel welcome upstairs as well as in the basement. Now anything we start has to be connected closely to the church. When we started an aerobics class, four members committed themselves to come every week so people in the class would get to know people in the church.

And we need more money. I certainly haven't preached enough on stewardship. We need to be challenged to be more responsible in our giving.

Meanwhile, much work remains. Unemployment, for example, poisons our community. We hope to start a small business someday that will employ neighborhood people.

I have never been tempted to indulge myself with any sort of prosperity theology, since prosperity is absent from my world, but I believe the only limits are what God does not allow or we are unable to dream. The trouble with our church or any church is not lack of members or money; it is lack of ingenuity, creativity, and courage.

The book of Esther has meant a lot to me over the last few years. Esther had to act decisively, courageously, and quickly, or the nation of Israel would perish. After praying and fasting, she left her apartment, turned the corner, and peered into the face of the greatest, most powerful force for evil in her day. In every community, the church is turning corners and finding itself face-to-face with King Xerxes. Esther risked everything. We have to risk everything too.

We are the church of Jesus Christ, and we have to be more than a good feeling or an attractive building. Our communities are counting on us.

11

Lean Resources, Robust Worship

Whatever resources God had given us were enough to accomplish his will in our place at this time.

—BILL GIOVANNETTI

I didn't choose to become a church pianist. I was in high school, attending Grace Gospel Church in Chicago, when our regular pianist moved away. Since I had endured piano lessons, the mantle fell on me. My skills hovered somewhere between John Thompson Levels II and III. I was hardly ready for prime time.

For the big day, I learned "To God Be the Glory." The leader led, the people sang, and I played. I finished the song about two measures ahead of the congregation (what I lacked in technique I made up in speed). But it didn't matter. They loved me enough to overlook my mistakes, and they loved God enough to worship him anyway.

Each week I practiced one new song, and each Sunday our congregation endured not only my narrow repertoire but also my nervous accelerando. We had heart, and we had spirit, but no one would have accused us of excellence.

I blush a little as I think about it. Still, when I am tempted to envy big-league churches with their drama, orchestra, and professional singers, my mind slips back to those days on the piano. Was our worship any less spiritual or powerful for its modesty? I don't think so.

Since becoming a pastor, though, I have often forgotten that truth. Years after my not-ready-for-prime-time debut, I found myself striving for perfection in worship and giving my small church a lot of headaches in the process.

What I had to relearn was that it is possible to worship God well with modest means. Here are the values that helped us do that.

Authenticity over excellence

Before planting Windy City Community Church, I had been pumped up by speakers inspiring church leaders to excellence. So I committed myself to avoiding sloppiness. Everything we did would be done with excellence.

In pursuit of musical excellence, though, I became oppressive. I pressured our music directors to recruit better singers, to wave a magic baton to make them sing better than their ability. No matter how much pressure I exerted, however, our musical teams could not satisfy me. We were a small church with a limited pool of talent, and I was raising the bar to a height only a large church could clear.

Then I stumbled upon an uncomfortable truth: What I had nobly justified as excellence turned out to be something else—my ugly need to impress. What my church needed to worship God was not Broadway musicals but authenticity—people worshiping God in spirit and in truth. Authenticity, relating honestly to the Lord, was more important than excellence, doing something well.

Authenticity, however, isn't an excuse for laziness. Excellence is a legitimate value within the church. It's tough for the congregation to worship when they're squirming because the worship leader or special musician is embarrassingly flat.

But when we pursue excellence at the cost of authenticity, the church suffers. I've learned to be satisfied if worship leaders possess decent musical skills. And if some of them are exceptionally talented, that's a bonus. But in recruiting worship leaders, we look first for authenticity—and just enough skill not to embarrass the congregation.

This sends an important message to the congregation: a person doesn't have to be spectacular to serve the Lord. If we say that God uses ordinary people, why promote only extraordinary people?

Shifting from excellence to authenticity has changed the songs we sing. Just as a football coach must send in plays the team can run, so the music director must select songs the church can sing. We won't be singing Handel's *Messiah* anytime soon; we enjoy a treasury of hymns and praise songs that are simple, singable, and powerful.

We occasionally tinker with the music to make a song easier to sing. For example, "Great Is the Lord," by Michael W. Smith, contains a big finish with the words "Great is the Lord" repeated five times. On the last repeat, the music instructs us to sing something like "Great is the (*pause four beats*) Lord!" Every time we tried that, people belted out "Lord" during the pause and were embarrassed. What makes a dramatic finale for a performance makes for a confusing flop in congregational singing. So we eliminated that pause.

Putting the stress on authenticity over excellence has also affected my preaching.

For the first five years of my pastoral ministry, I preached from manuscripts. In the writing phase, I labored over every word. On Sundays before church, I made last-minute corrections on the computer and printed out thirteen pages of notes. I brought them into the pulpit and basically read my manuscript to the church. Though I occasionally ad-libbed, I normally stuck close to the notes.

One Sunday disaster struck. Halfway through printing my sermon, a fuse blew and damaged the disk. I could neither access nor print my sermon notes. A week's study was electronically imprisoned. I had to leave for church, so I scribbled my outline on a single sheet of legal paper, dashed out the door, and preached (on the subject of the Holy Spirit). It went surprisingly well.

Why? In part because I was forced to shift from a focus on performance to authenticity. Instead of giving words, I was giving myself. That day authenticity became more important to me than excellence. Through this little calamity, God taught me to quit fussing over my sermons till they were like overcooked eggs.

W. H. Griffith-Thomas advised young preachers:

Think yourself empty
Read yourself full
Write yourself clear
Pray yourself keen
Then enter the pulpit
And let yourself go!

Leadership over musicianship

Pastor Jones needed a music pastor. He contacted Melody Smith, an old friend from seminary days whose musical gifts were beyond question. An excellent pianist, she could sight-read, transpose, arrange, play in a band, and accompany both soloists and the congregation with equal skill. She displayed an obvious love for the Lord; her character was above reproach; she related to others in an authentic way. It seemed she was the ideal choice.

After considerable discussion, Jones invited Melody to join his staff as music pastor. Patting himself on the back, Jones thought, *That's one less ministry to worry about.*

When Melody arrived, she quickly won the hearts of the people. Her solos led them into the presence of God. She radiated godliness.

A few months passed in sweet harmony, but then discordant notes began to be heard from the music ministry. A persistent discontent surfaced among the two dozen music volunteers. They bickered over song selection, solo schedules, even the tempo of the music. Musicians arrived late to rehearsals. Though church attendance was growing, the number of musicians stayed the same.

Morale plummeted into the bass clef. Melody grew increasingly upset and finally asked Pastor Jones to intervene. After all, God had called her to make music for his glory, not to referee fights.

Jones had already noticed other problems in the music ministry. Little things. Week after week during morning worship, the slides that projected song lyrics were out of order. On a regular basis, the soloist began with a dead microphone. Stage lights burned out without replacement. Melody wanted to play music, not worry about details.

But most disturbing to Pastor Jones was that while the quality of music had improved, the congregational singing had deteriorated. They had moved from being worshipers to being observers. The music ministry had become a performance.

For months Pastor Jones spent considerable time troubleshooting the music ministry, wondering what was happening, trying to get to the root of the problem. One day the root problem became clear: at the head of the music department was a musician, not a leader.

It takes a leader to inspire a congregation to enter wholeheartedly into worship. It takes a leader to create a system to care for the details. It takes a leader to resolve conflict and maintain morale. It takes a leader to motivate others to volunteer for service.

Melody's love for God and her musical talent could not compensate for her lack of leadership. The most important strength of a music leader is leadership, especially when the person is working with volunteers.

Your church may not have the resources to attract topnotch musicians, but the best person to lead the music department may be sitting under your nose: a man or woman who loves the Lord, who has decent pitch and tempo, and who can lead people.

Gifts over imitation

Early in the life of Windy City Community Church, we experimented with "seeker sensitive" worship services. We tried drama, Christianity 101 messages, and shorter worship periods.

Attendance dropped. One Sunday, after sitting through a particularly painful skit (I forced the drama group into it before they were ready) and preaching a weak, uninspired message, I knew something had to change. What we had been trying was foreign to us.

I began asking myself questions: Who are we as a church? Who am I as a pastor? Just what is our mission anyway?

Then I did what many pastors do when all else fails: I went to a seminar. I figured that might help me discover my personal mission and the mission of my church. With a dictation recorder in hand, I interviewed dozens of pastors from all over the country, asking one question: "What is the mission of your church?" (I didn't have the answer, so I hoped to borrow someone else's!)

It turned out we were all in the same boat. Some pastors spoke vaguely about the three E's: evangelism, edification, exaltation. Some talked about their church constitution and their mission statement that filled ten pages. Others confessed they didn't know what their mission was. No one answered with a concise, clear sentence. We were like sermons without propositions.

Almost in despair, I approached the seminar speaker. Like me, he pastored the church he had planted. I stuck out my tape recorder: "What is the mission of your church?"

Without hesitation, he replied, "To mobilize an army to fulfill the Great Commission by developing nonreligious people into fully formed followers of Jesus." He explained that fully formed followers of Jesus "love God with their whole hearts, love the body of Christ, and love the world for whom Christ died."

"How can I decide," I pressed, "if my church should be seeker sensitive?"

Without batting an eye, he asked, "What's your passion?"

That question of four years ago still echoes in my mind. God has wired some leaders one way and me another way. My God-given passion is to expound the Word to believers. I'm not a Christianity 101 kind of guy. I get excited about Christianity 201. That's my contribution to the Great Commission. I don't have to do it all.

All of a sudden, like a dog that gets out of the yard, I felt release. Free at last! I could be myself.

I could also let my church be itself. We started to organize our church around our gifts. We planned our worship around the people we had instead of around the people we wished we had. Whatever resources God had given us were enough to accomplish his will in our place at this time.

God expects us to give him only "such as we have."

Small church, great God

We're surrounded by media offering practical help in the Christian life. Publications, seminars, and counselors offer ways to better marriages, relationships, finances, parenting, and self-esteem.

What the church offers that these resources cannot is meaningful corporate worship.

What makes for meaningful corporate worship?

While the list of important qualities is long—biblically true, practical, relevant, sensitive to the culture, visual, focused, and so on—only one rises head and shoulders above the rest: transcendence.

Transcendence means we catch a glimpse of God and his throne and recognize we are in his presence. Transcendence is what makes a worship service meaningful. Our two most significant tools, singing and preaching, must lead people to God.

Transcendence means doing for our people what Elisha did for his servant. When the servant saw the Syrian army surrounding them, he panicked. At that moment Elisha could have talked about confidence and self-esteem. He could have probed the source of the servant's fears. Instead Elisha prayed that God would lift the veil and give his servant a glimpse of heaven's victory.

Elisha gives us a model for meaningful worship. We may not have drama, exceptional music, or even well-crafted sermons, but the quality of transcendence week after week will provide our people with a bedrock foundation for life.

Transcendence, at first glance, seems easier to convey in a large church with high, vaulted ceilings, a powerful sound system, and an aesthetically inspiring sanctuary. How do you get people meeting in a country church or grade-school gym to lift their eyes to the greatness of God?

It's not a matter of money. Transcendence comes from the content of preaching and singing. It's seeing who God is, and leading people to see themselves in light of who God is.

Someone has said that if you want to convey to people how scary a certain road is, you don't tell them that it is scary; you show them what it is about the road that terrifies. Likewise we convey transcendence when we help people see the greatness of the invisible God.

That's done by praying and singing about the glory of Christ in heaven, which a church with modest means can do. What's important is not what people see around them but what we help them see with their imaginations.

Preaching recently on the despair many people feel, I said, "If we could take such people into heaven, where they could stand before the risen Christ, with myriads of angels on their right, millions of saints on their left, gold under their feet, and then help them see what God is doing, their emotions would change."

When Martin Lloyd-Jones, the great Welsh preacher, came to Aberavon, Wales, he came to a bleak, despairing coastal town. The working-class community had suffered economic depression, high unemployment, and low education. Yet Lloyd-Jones was determined to preach God's transcendence. He brought a great vision of God. Not surprisingly, the church flourished under his ministry.

When the church of my youth let me play the piano, I learned a lesson that will last a lifetime. I learned we can worship God meaningfully even if our means are modest.

12

Salvaging a Sinking Ship

It is my job as lookout on the wall to scan for the signs that give clues to what my people need.

—Suzan D. Johnson Cook

Mariners' Temple was, by all definitions, a dying church. People, playing with the name, referred to it as "a sinking ship." The congregation had dwindled to fifteen members in a facility that holds more than a thousand, so it took some unusual circumstances to bring me there as pastor.

During my last semester in seminary, I was working part-time in our local denominational office. I learned about a vacancy in a church in Chinatown on the Lower East Side of New York, the Mariners' Temple Baptist Church. The only contact I had had with this community was my childhood trips to Mott Street for an authentic Chinese meal. And in January I had preached for Mariners's pastor when he was on vacation.

Now that pastor had decided to resign, and the last voice from the pulpit the congregation remembered was mine. They inquired if I would serve as their interim pastor.

The Sinking Ship

The ancient Mariners' must have been some place. It is the oldest Baptist church in Manhattan, a once-grand congregation that formed to serve the seafaring crowd and thrived for decades. But now, it seemed, I was being sent for the final benediction.

"At least," some said, "it will give you an opportunity to pastor a church," no matter how brief.

The rumor in denominational circles was that the congregation could not sustain itself. It was six thousand dollars in the red, and its credit rating was horrible. Action was imminent to dissolve the church. Without extensive repairs, the grand building was about ready to fall down on the members' heads. *Can these bones live?* I wondered as I wandered the facility my first day.

But I made up my mind to look on the opportunity as a blessing rather than a burden.

It rained my first thirteen Sundays at Mariners' Temple. Even Easter Sunday looked more like the day of Crucifixion than the day of Resurrection.

But we brightened it with ten baptisms at the sunrise service. The ten were five children and five adults—all of them excited to be joining the church. They had come to the church and completed the new-members' class under my leadership, so I was excited about them too.

That day turned out to be a day of resurrection for the congregation, and it startled more than a few. The denomination had all but promised our building to a Chinese congregation sharing our facilities, but like a stubborn heart donor, we refused to die.

What was it that helped us not simply to survive but even to return to vitality? There were several factors.

Attitudinal aerobics

From working on a political campaign for my brother, I knew what it was like to get people motivated and believing in a dream. They first had to be excited about themselves, so my initial sermons were esteem-building, faith-building exhortations. It was not enough to simply unfurl those seminary sermons I had produced for preaching class. Now my faith was on trial, and I had to preach what I believed. What a test of faith! It was a time for me to develop my theology.

I began by lifting out all the positive attributes of the church, the community, and the specific people in the church. I told them, "You're going to make it; you are God's people, and God doesn't make junk. Everybody is somebody in the eyes of God. He doesn't care about your past. His question to you is 'Where are you going?' Just think about what this church and what you mean to the community. We can't let ourselves down!"

By focusing on the positive, I hoped to begin to stem the tide of despair and negativism that would wash away any gains I might make through sheer enthusiasm. I am convinced that people want better, transformed lives, and they will work for them. It is my job as lookout on the wall to scan for the signs that give clues to what my people need.

Next I asked members to join me in some fundamental disciplines: prayer, supplication, study, and fasting. We began to pray for growth, asking God to send "more laborers into the harvest." We thanked God for those who'd had the fortitude to hold on while the going was tough, but we were bold to ask for others.

In my frontal assault on attitudes, I wanted my positive feelings about the church to take hold, but I wanted the *I* vocabulary changed to *we*. Then *we* could decide that *we* were going to make it.

I assigned a Scripture passage for memorization each month and quizzed the congregation at all meetings and worship services. One of our favorites became Philippians 4:13—"[We] can do all things through Christ who strengthens [us]" (NKJV).

It's easy to get discouraged in this work, and I found I also had to keep my own attitude in line. I found myself asking God if this were really where he wanted me to be. I had come from an established church where people (including the pastor) knew what they were doing and where a tradition had long been established. At age twenty-six, I found myself thrust into the middle of a challenge I had never dreamed of. What was I doing here?

As I took inventory of my experiences, however, God showed me I *had* been prepared for this call.

First, as a child I had studied in Valencia, Spain, becoming fluent in Spanish. In college I had traveled to West and North Africa, Israel, and the Caribbean. I often wondered how God would use these experiences. Now I found myself in a multiethnic setting, where black, Spanish, and Chinese populations were about equal. I was praying in Spanish with Hispanic residents, trying to communicate through an interpreter to the Chinese community, and ministering to the black population at the same time.

Second, since this was my first pastorate, I was an unknown quantity. People's expectations weren't as demanding. Had I gone into an established church, I would have made inexcusable mistakes, and there would probably have been barriers already in place. But Mariners' Temple and I could grow together.

Third, being a female in this role also helped. Since I was the first black woman elected to a major American Baptist Church in our two-hundred-year history, there were no role models, and no one really knew what to expect of me—including myself. So I dared to be a dreamer, to be different.

Some days I would come back to church from a business luncheon in the community and play basketball with the men of the church. I wondered how that would be received. But they appreciated my being me, and it allowed me to know them in a different way. This nontraditional approach infected our attitude. I'm convinced a positive attitude, one that is willing to go beyond barriers, is essential in reviving a church.

Getting acclimated

One of my first goals was to get close to our fifteen members, who by now were beginning to share my excitement about this church. The members consisted of one Hispanic woman, one white woman, and the rest black.

The Hispanic member was Mother Belen McCray, a petite woman nearly ninety years old who spoke little English but understood it quite well. She had been coming to Mariners' since she moved into the neighborhood forty years ago, and she continually prayed that the doors would not close.

The black members, mostly men and women in their forties and fifties, were largely the deacons and trustees with a vested interest in the church. They had worked so hard to keep it afloat.

Most of them became active when the Alfred E. Smith housing projects (where 90 percent of our current membership resides) were built.

Their children had come to the church for Scouting programs, classes, and social events, so these stalwarts remembered Mariners' Temple when it was thriving. The church had served as a community church where many of their friends and neighbors celebrated weddings or attended funerals. To these people, it was more than a church; it was a personal landmark, an institution.

In a community like ours, local church history is seldom recorded on paper. Ours is an oral culture; our history is etched in the memories of the faithful. As I rummaged through people's memories, I discovered this community was once known as "Little Africa," a settlement where freed black slaves and those who did not go into slavery had arrived in the early 1800s. I made sure these and other historical facts were written down, because we couldn't understand where we want to go without knowing where we had been.

History pointed out to us the evolution of the community along with the church. We could trace the various ethnic patterns and recall the highlights of each era. It helped us see how Mariners' changed from a predominantly white church for European seamen into a self-supporting, mainly black church that helped shape a community. We could trace the change from the early black community of the late 1800s to the large escalation of blacks in the 1950s when the projects went up.

I first went to the church as an interim pastor. Trying to handle that responsibility cautiously yet boldly, I attempted few drastic changes immediately. It was more important to me to learn what had been done before I set out to change it.

I also got to know the people of the church in their home surroundings. I found a people who felt neglected. Many were on public assistance and caught in various social problems. Drug abusers and dropouts were numerous in the community. Because they were in Chinatown, where much of the emphasis was on Asian problems, the blacks often felt left out. They needed self-esteem and ethnic pride.

The church had many blue-collar workers and city employees.

Members not on public assistance began to help those who were. This gave some the chance they needed.

Many in the community were in need of help and attention. Some asked me to accompany them to the bank to open an account, wanting advice on the best investments. When some particularly needy individuals came to our church dinners, I had to gently remind them about such niceties as waiting for their turn to be served. I accompanied some parishioners to court, where their children or other relatives were on trial for various offenses, and others to business lunches, where they taught me a thing or two. In this way, I was soon baptized into the action of the community.

And this also brought people into the church. On many occasions youths and children led their parents to church. This was the case with the first boys' basketball team.

We realized that young black males needed an environment where they could learn discipline while catching the faith and having fun. We entered two teams in our denominational league, and we encouraged the older males to join as their coaches. The church enthusiastically attended their games and cheered them on.

But we tried to give them more than basketball. We worked to build relationship with their homes and school whenever possible. We let them know they had a support community where they could come if their other situations were not tenable. On any given day, I would drive up to the church and find various team members waiting to talk with me. In just a few months, many of their family members began attending, and now many are active members.

Through various efforts like this, I had 150 new members to get to know within the first six months. In that atmosphere of mounting and infectious energy, I was asked to become the permanent pastor. A unanimous vote was cast, and we planned a week-long installation celebration. To our delight, many of my colleagues joined us to welcome me as a pastor, including Dr. Gardner C. Taylor, pastor of the Concord Baptist Church of Christ.

I was even more gratified to learn a bit later that one of the congregation's greatest concerns was that I remain with them for a decent length of time. They were beginning to open up to me and trust me. Enormous healing had to take place, and they didn't want me to destroy their trust. When my brother and his children joined the church along with me, it solidified our covenant.

Hitting the streets with good news

One of my friends, Dr. Johnny Ray Youngblood, pastor of Saint Paul Community Baptist Church in Brooklyn, suggested that I attend an evangelism and discipleship conference in Dallas. When I got home, we began to focus on what evangelism means in a situation like ours.

One of the first ways we emphasized evangelism was by asking members to bring their family and friends to our worship services. To make them comfortable, we designed a "Come as You Are" service so that those who didn't have "church clothes" would feel as at home as everyone else. We regular attenders made a point of dressing casually. I did my part by shedding my clergy robe that day. We ended up holding such a service quarterly because it was so successful.

We also invited the Addicts' Rehabilitation Center Choir, a gospel group of former drug abusers, to share in these services. Seeing people so obviously changed active in the worship service helped newcomers accept their own pasts, and it gave them incentive to transform their lives.

Soon we began a radio ministry to spread the message rapidly in our community. We even used billboards to advertise major crusade services.

I had helped elect my brother to the New York State Assembly, so I was used to door-to-door campaigns. *Why can't the political model be used for evangelistic purposes?* I wondered. So we made some simple fliers describing our worship services and bearing my picture.

I took all age groups with me to canvass the neighborhood, inviting people to our church and asking them, "What can our church do for you?" Many people refused to answer their doors, but those who did remarked that if the pastor would come to their home, then at least they could try to come to the church. When nobody was home, we just left the flier.

That outreach garnered many of the people who later joined our congregation. We had become a known presence in our neighborhood. People were talking about us.

We were thrilled to see families beginning to come together. On several occasions when we asked the first-time visitors to stand, many announced that they had come at the invitation of their spouse or companion because they had seen the change and joy in that person's life.

Many couples who were not married got married after counseling. Now we have families worshiping together regularly. We stressed that we were family—members of one another—and unless all of us made it, then none of us made it. The Latino community liked this family emphasis, and as a result we have several Latino families actively integrated into our church.

By the end of our first year, 250 members had joined our ranks, and by three years we had 500. It looked as if we would survive.

Meeting community needs

I believe a church should supply every person with a meaningful ministry, and one way to do that is to begin to meet the needs outside the church.

The was the reasoning behind our "Lunch Hour of Power" that we launched in January 1985.

We are located near a business and government center, and many workers would eat lunch on our front steps in good weather. Since my office window opened to those steps, I picked up snatches of conversation from the lunching workers. I'd also take out my lunch and join them on occasion.

A common cry I heard was apathy toward work. Many worked for city agencies or the federal court system, and they enjoyed few advancement opportunities. The pervasive feeling was one of counting days to retirement rather than finding satisfaction and enjoyment in a career. We started our lunch-hour worship service to provide inspiration to help workers make it through the week.

To advertise the new venture, teams fanned out to do "subway stops," greeting and handing fliers to people on their way to and from work. I made myself visible in this campaign, and that gave many of the commuters an opportunity to meet the one who would be leading the services.

Our children and young people also helped in this leafleting blitz. It wasn't easy. Many of the children were discouraged that people could be so rude. Hundreds of fliers were just tossed to the ground. I encouraged the kids to be patient, and I told them this could help them learn how not to act when they were older.

The lunch-hour service was a forty-five-minute worship experience with a hymn, prayer, announcements, welcome of visitors, and a sermon lasting no more than twenty minutes. Promptly at 12:45 we would dismiss the congregation and provide a free lunch.

Some in the congregation felt we shouldn't "bribe" the people with food, but once we considered that the people would be forfeiting their lunch hour and they had to be back at work promptly, many began to catch the vision. I even rounded up our senior citizens to fix the sandwiches each week. That ministry has given new meaning and purpose to their lives.

We had no idea how many would show up at our first service. I hoped to get some from our congregation, and when I asked for a show of hands one Sunday, only about twenty-five went up. We prepared for fifty.

Thirty-eight attended. The attendance doubled the next week. Word of the service spread quickly. The service mixes executives and clerks, local residents and commuters. There was a need, we offered ourselves, and God blessed the effort.

Within six months we were fixing more than 150 lunches, and by the one-year mark, we were averaging 200 every Wednesday.

The first two years I preached nearly all the sermons. Later I arranged for guest pastors and civic leaders who are visible within the church community to preach, and I preached no more than two services a month. We purposely did not announce the speakers in advance so the event would not become personality centered. This service was one of the highlights of our church and community, and it provided *my* inspiration as well.

We are family

As we thought and planned big, we also tried to keep our church like a family. Inner-city living is draining, and to provide balance for the serious side of life, we mixed in sports and other fun activities. We had pastor's teams for basketball and softball that played intramurally and challenged other congregations. It was interesting seeing how other churches respond to a female pastor on the basketball court with men.

Yearly our pastor's team challenged the rest of the men to a game of softball. For months prior to the event we bragged and joked about the outcome. The congregation came out to see who would be the winner. This jesting also served a serious purpose: it brought the men and boys together within the fellowship of the church. We found many of the young boys coming to church were from homes without a male figure, so we challenged the men of the church to become their spiritual fathers. Playing to gether helped cement that bond.

Another element of family life came as a by-product of minis-try to our community. The congregation selected education as a priority area to target. They felt that if we worked on this area, many of the grave social problems that plague our community could be dealt with. With that in mind, we instituted a daily after-school tutorial program for elementary school children in our neighborhood.

Our senior citizens now run that program. It was a joy to watch this intergenerational experience. Minority communities were once run by the extended-family concept anyway. We were just returning to our heritage and traditions in a nontraditional way.

To truly become a church family, we started acting like a fam-ily—taking retreats outside the city or "family trips" to visit

churches where my friends pastor. We organized boat rides, pa-
rades, bazaars, and banquets. We attended concerts and other
events.

Like a mother, I've encouraged family members to look out
for one another and stick together as a family. As soon as a
person accepts the invitation to come to Christ, he or she is
assigned a sponsor—a big brother or sister in Christ who is
already a member of the church—and this person is responsible
for showing that person the ropes. It helped to ease the often-felt
discomfort of entering unknown into a large group.

Once when a child who was doing poorly in school came in
with a good report card after passing a tough examination, we
announced it in the middle of worship and had the child come
to the front of the church. The people applauded, and we placed
that child's name on the Pastor's Honor Roll, prominently displayed in the sanctuary.

This kind of recognition has encouraged good scholarship,
and the other children are attempting to do well in school so the
pastor will single them out. Recently we sent four students to
college, three of whom were first-generation college entrants. We
celebrated as though there were a coronation.

God has called us to worship and shown us that we have a
blessed ministry. Indeed, dry bones can live.

PART 4

Creative Perspective

13

Making Creativity Comfortable

Churches marked with traditions and hair-triggered judgments require relentless patience.

—Michael Lewis

Can a multigenerational, multipurposed, multimanaged, mixed-motive, diversely preferenced congregation grow and adapt to a constantly changing culture?

Of course they can. But who would want to suggest it to them?

Not many ministers enjoy tightening the tension of a congregation stretched between frustration (for moving too slowly) and fear (of changing too fast).

Yet, in an age of newly planted, zero-history, purpose-driven, narrowly targeted, seeker-sensitive success stories, the current love of my ministry life is serving an established congregation. My passion is to communicate to these beloved but diverse people that not only is their past worthy of celebration, but their best days are still ahead.

It is a difficult mission. Most established congregations are somewhat frightened by the thought of relating to unchurched people where they are in our culture. If you lead in that direction, being wounded by "friendly fire" is likely. It is kind of like, well, taking up your cross and following Jesus.

When in Athens . . .

The heritage of our congregation is a complicated mix of history and evolving evangelistic mission. It includes complete trust in biblical authority, congregational autonomy, early Christian ideals, and evangelistic preaching. Our church emphasizes that the Bible—book, chapter, and verse—must support every point and subpoint of all public proclamations.

That solid heritage, though, and the Sunday-night seminars we do each spring ("How to Divorce-Proof Your Marriage") are worlds apart. We intentionally designed these seminars to look like anything but a church service. A few modern-day translations of Bible verses are sprinkled between quotations from movies, news magazines, social scientists, and cartoons from *Leadership*. The seminars are advertised in an interlocking campaign of newspaper ads, billboards, radio, and cable television spots.

I've found both worlds in the passages of the New Testament. The public proclamation of the early church was relentlessly redundant in matters of Christ, the Word, the Cross, the Resurrection, and salvation. That focus was maintained whether in Jerusalem, Athens, or Rome.

The presentation varied, however, tailored to the audience and the situation. When Paul spoke to Jews, he cited their history and multiple passages from the Old Testament. In Athens, however, no Scripture was quoted directly; the only source cited was a well-known Cretan poem written to honor Zeus ("For in him we live and move and have our being")!

As a devout group of Scripture-quoters, we have followed the scriptural example of Paul in Athens: we don't quote Scripture to people not yet ready to grasp it. That kind of flexibility is supposed to be impossible in tradition-loving, middle-aged churches.

Impossible, no. Difficult, yes. It requires a special creativity to manage. Here are five suggestions for this wonderfully challenging task:

1. Redline core areas of identity

Older, multigenerational, diverse congregations cannot afford to become extremely anything in a short period of time without damage to their unity. Such congregations do not turn on a dime. If they did, their commitment wouldn't be worth the dime they turned on.

Established congregations turn like ocean liners, so slowly some changes are barely noticeable. Yet they reach their destination eventually.

We make only minor changes, for example, to our Sunday-morning worship style. For better or worse, most of our long-time members' Christian identity is directly tied to Sunday-morning worship. But the membership core is confident there are no intentions to "fiddle" with Sunday mornings. Consequently they find it much easier to give permission to new small-group ministries, new seminars, a new youth seeker service, and other creative ideas.

Some suggest that Sunday morning is the best time to attract outsiders. And if we were a zero-history group, we could well begin with that purely evangelistic mission. But we have a history: It is the difference between Acts and Hebrews. The Great Commission must be weighed with other critical issues involving discipleship: equipping the saints, offering encouragement toward ministry, and maintaining unity.

So we prepare seekers for Sunday mornings through intermediate activities custom-designed for them. We get permission for those activities because we protect the key elements of our traditional congregational identity.

Areas most crucial to the identity of the longtime members need to be "redlined"; they're out of bounds for major change.

2. Preach maturity as shared sacrifice

We once followed the suggestion of one expert, having members identify their favorite radio station. We did this to discover their true musical tastes. Perhaps the staff and I hoped it would reveal the clear preference for the contemporary, providing a rationale to move beyond the strange blend of old-time gospel songs and the contemporary ones we currently do.

The results: 35 percent preferred contemporary, 35 percent preferred oldies, and 30 percent listened to all news and information stations. Our survey revealed we had no consensus.

Many middle-aged congregations are notoriously middle-of-the-road blends of worship styles and outreach techniques. Such hybrids come from generational compromises: the congregation seek to do what they collectively believe God wants; yet they seek to do it in ways that will offend the fewest in the congregational core.

Some growth experts, however, have said those who pursue blended styles merely take turns "insulting different segments of the congregation."

But we believe otherwise: blended styles are the result of shared sacrifice and spiritual maturity. Traditional congregations committed to outreach also must passionately communicate the concept that sacrifice always goes with spiritual maturity. We've found most in our church ready to live that kind of sacrifice in the name of denying themselves, taking up their crosses, and following Jesus.

A great opportunity to teach this shared sacrifice presented itself at a retreat. I preached on the topic several times that weekend, and between my sermons, our song leader led the congregation in an informal time of singing. He would ask participants to suggest their favorite hymns, and then the group would sing the selections.

At one point, when the song leader asked for a new round of suggestions, I popped up and said, "Why don't we apply this principle of shared sacrifice? From this point on, you can only suggest singing a hymn that is *not* one of your favorites but one that you know is valued by others here."

People looked at me as if I had just shown up, uninvited, to their party. "Then let's pass the acid test," I continued, "by singing those songs as passionately as we would our favorites."

Silence, and a profound pause. Then a few, softly spoken, uneasy suggestions were offered. Before the weekend was out, however, the suggestions came easier and faster. Some huddled to ask others about their preferences. The singing was never better.

Several weeks later, long after the points of my sermon were but faint memories (if that), people were still talking about the great worship times during that weekend. I heard comments: "I didn't realize how satisfying worship could be just by demonstrating love for God and others by intentionally refusing to please ourselves." We remembered that we were a part of a different kingdom where there is no greater love than laying down one's life (and even one's musical preferences) for a friend.

3. Let options reflect your mosaic

Although we must sound the call to sacrifice, we must also recognize our diversity by providing options whenever possible.

This fall, for example, we are launching small groups on Sunday evenings, but for those who do not like groups, the more traditional Bible class will still be available. A special sermon series, "How to Share the Gospel with a Friend," doubles as a traditional gospel meeting for those who want to bring friends.

In general, we have discovered different generations of seekers, like different generations of believers, prefer different evangelism styles. To increase our chances of making a connection, we attempt to match up seekers with witnessing believers by generation, religious background, and philosophical orientation.

Such variety broadens our reach into different segments of our world, lessening the "in-house" hassles that naturally come by asking everyone to do the same thing—take it or leave it.

We are not ready to be all things to all people, but we can be a reflection of our congregation's mosaic. We are using our variety to reach similar people in our surrounding community.

4. Keep your enemies close

This is hard to admit, but I learned this principle from Michael Corleone in *The Godfather (Part II)*. In the midst of great trials, he travels to his boyhood home in New York. An old friend asks Michael how he intends to handle all his problems. Michael responds, "Pop taught me many lessons in this house . . . one of them was to keep your friends close and keep your enemies closer."

Everyone who opposes us, of course, is not an enemy, but such people should not be ignored or left to their own devices. That only invites unnecessary conflict.

We make every effort, early in our planning, to incorporate those who may be bothered by a new ministry. They are allowed to voice their objections. If the church leadership can accommodate their complaints and still reach the desired goal, we modify what we initially planned. This way those who could make life harder, we've found, often feel compelled to voice their support once their contribution has been added.

The "Godfather principle" gives creative ideas a better chance to survive.

5. Offer ambiguity

Our church has a strong commitment to congregational a cappella singing, which appears to us to have been the norm among first-century Christians. But even within that tradition, personal convictions run the spectrum.

I've found publicly I can say nothing of substance on the topic without drawing someone's ire. (Of course, Ire and I are old friends, having spent much quality time together.)

Friction can develop between those who believe the way to please God is by the whole congregation singing and those who believe a hymn by a quartet still permits everyone else to participate internally.

The way to deal with this dilemma is very clear—with a healthy dose of ambiguity. We have discovered that those who believe strongly in congregational participation also enjoy gospel quartets and other singing groups at times outside the official "time of public worship." We build on that comfort zone and use occasional singing groups at the beginning or at the end of a worship assembly.

I usually will introduce such music with statements like, "Before we all have the opportunity to worship by singing together, a group is going to help us focus on the theme for this morning's worship with a special song."

Someone, feeling compelled to have all things nailed down, may come up afterward and ask, "Now, did that singing group sing before our public worship began or at the beginning of it? After all, your introduction left both interpretations possible."

"Thank you," I'll reply.

"What do you mean, 'Thank you'?"

"Thank you for noticing how I am trying to respect a wide range of personal convictions. I want to make it possible for those who believe a singing group is all right before the 'official' worship assembly to be at peace with those who do not make that distinction."

I'm not afraid to voice my convictions, but I've found it wise to resist doing so at every opportunity. I try to keep the primary message primary. Christ, the Word, the Cross, the Resurrection, salvation—these are recurring themes for a purpose.

Strategic ambiguity at less critical points allows a diverse congregation to continue doing the important things together.

Churches marked with traditions and hair-triggered judgments require relentless patience. They also demand a creative mind-set, a healthy respect for the stability tradition brings to a group, and the unwavering hope that Christians really do want to please Christ more than themselves.

14

My Greatest Ministry Mistakes

The most important lesson I learned from Circle Church was to change my perception of how to measure success.

—DAVID MAINS with PHILIP YANCEY

When I was first approached to write an article on painful lessons I learned from ten years at Circle Church, my immediate reaction was to review instead all the successes. Pastors easily fall into the success trap that permeates our culture. We laud winning teams, fire coaches of losing teams. And while we read about "the largest Sunday schools in America," we rarely read about struggling or declining churches. They just don't make the news.

I have already had my chance, though. I wrote the book *Full Circle* when our four-year-old church in Chicago was still moving toward its zenith. We had started with a few friends and a dream to establish a church in the infertile inner city. Ultimately, five hundred people piled into a union hall ballroom each Sunday morning to participate in stirring, creative worship experiences. Circle was a beehive of activities: modules met on art, communications, music, outreach, and urban interests. A drama group wrote and produced several full-length plays. Our musicians gave professional-quality concerts. Prayer, social action, evangelism, and small groups were all finding beautiful expression.

Many of our members moved into the Austin community, which then had the second-highest crime rate in Chicago. Our people responded to the urgent needs around us with a legal clinic, a youth program, social workers, counselors, the beginnings of a medical clinic, and dreams of an alternative school program.

In some ways Circle Church was viewed as a model of an inner-city church. We had a full-orbed ministry of creative worship and social outreach with a racially mixed congregation, and all this was accomplished without pouring money into a church building. Soon I was flying around the country to lead seminars on what made Circle Church work. With Larry Richards and Clyde Hoeldtke, I helped to found Step 2, a national organization designed to stimulate meaningful church renewal. About a dozen times a year I spoke to pastors and denomination heads on the principles that fueled the activities at Circle. The book *Full Circle* expresses those principles.

Today I admit to some embarrassment about the attitudes expressed in that book. I still hold to the same principles, but some of my comments seem cocky and presumptuous now. I saw Circle Church as the tip of a new wave that would sweep across evangelical churches. It didn't happen, at least not as I had envisioned it. Circle Church still exists, but in a smaller form and with a more specialized emphasis.

In my last few years there, I saw many of my dreams crumble. Conflicts arose among the staff that split the very foundations of our church experiment. We could not resolve them. Ultimately, one of the areas that had given us the most satisfaction—interracial mixing in the congregation—failed utterly, and all the blacks pulled out. Everyone in the church felt great pain because of those conflicts, and I'm sure mistrust and bitterness remain with some even today.

As pastor, I experienced a profound disappointment. Did these failures invalidate my entire ministry? Was God telling me I was an unfit leader?

Where had I failed him? Questions such as these tormented me. Although the process involves pain, I feel I need to look back at those years and discern what God taught me through my failures. Even as I think of them, I must fight back a desire to rationalize them away, to blame them on sociological factors of the early seventies or on personality quirks of some of the members. But that process is merely a form of pride, trying to align failures so they look less and less like my own failures.

At times, as I have worked on this article, I have felt like a middle-aged man standing naked before a mirror. His receding hairline shows, as well as a paunchy distribution of twenty extra pounds. As he looks over his body, he flinches slightly . . . then suddenly realizes to his shame that a crowd of people is standing behind him, staring at his nakedness. Exposing failure is never easy.

Fortunately God keeps "success charts," though they are entirely unlike ours. On his, a colossal failure in human terms can rank as a spiritual victory if it pushes a person closer toward him. Although I admit my broad goals for Circle Church ultimately failed, God used my experience—all of it—to teach me important lessons about myself and about him. Let me share with you four warnings.

1. While pastoring, I often allowed myself to fixate on issues.

If a church attempts to reduce a pastor's duties to a written job description, it soon discovers it has created a position that demands superhuman abilities. A good pastor must demonstrate public poise, comfortably leading ceremonies and preaching. He must act as a warm and wise counselor, a "people person" whose vulnerability and compassion invite others to open up to him. Yet he must be an efficient, time-conscious manager who can run committees, meet deadlines, and manage employees. Is it any wonder that a high percentage of churches are at least slightly dissatisfied with their pastor's performance?

Of these three areas—the pulpit ministry, counseling, and management—I would rank my strengths as highest in the pulpit and next in counseling. Yet I consistently found myself getting bogged down in management. When an issue arose in our church and I saw it one way, I had trouble if my pastoral staff or the church board viewed it differently. Frequently I would lock onto that issue with bulldog tenacity and not let go until the dissidents came around to my viewpoint. Obviously I felt I had good reasons, backed up by prayer and Bible study, for espousing my position. But as I insisted on aligning the church behind me, unconsciously I let my real areas of strength slip away.

I have since recognized this problem of fixation as a family trait—a great strength, I might add, in business ventures, but often a hindrance to accomplishing God's work in a volunteer organization. I needed to give problems more time to find resolution, to allow personalities more time to reach consensus, and to allow programs more time to gain momentum. The end result was important, yes, but I have learned the style of achieving that end result can be equally important.

Pyramid-type sales organizations have a firm rule: no plan will work unless the idea and motivation come from the seller. You cannot gather a bunch of salesmen in a room and force-feed a fully developed program to them. Somehow you must win them over to the extent that they accept the program as *theirs*, not yours. In churches, built to a large degree on the clergy's leadership skills, we pastors tend to violate that truth about human nature and think our charisma is sufficient to gain the congregation's support.

For example, the issue of leadership by women arose in our church, as it does in most churches in our society. I resolved the issue in my own mind quite early; however, I discovered to my surprise that others in the church did not resolve the issue nearly so neatly, and some absolutely opposed my position. I would fixate on such an issue and not let go.

Reflecting now on my actions, I can sense at least two warning signals that should have alerted me to my problem. First, I talked about the unresolved issue all the time, much more often than it merited. Second, I kept going after the opposition, seeking to remove it to reach consensus. If in an elders' meeting the sympathies were running fifteen to one in favor of a certain position, I would home in on the one stubborn dissident. How could I get him to change his mind?

Normally I did not try to get my way through overt displays of power. But I would concentrate so intensely on reaching consensus that I have heard people begin to describe me as manipulative. I hated that accusation because I did not feel it was deserved. Yet, as I look back, I can see that I was unwilling to let God have the freedom to accomplish his work in his own way. Privately I prayed pushy prayers: "Come on, God, why don't you resolve this now!" I have since learned to practice a prayer of acceptance every night. It says, "God, some things happened today that I don't like. I want you to know that I accept these, and I'm putting them in your hands."

I encountered a situation in the church I now attend (I am not the pastor) that reminded me of what God has taught me. I was serving on a committee to select an assistant pastor, and I was confident that I had God's mind on who should be invited. The other members of the committee did not act on my recommendation. Their action frustrated me because I knew this man better than any of them, and I was certain he could fill the job. As I prayed about it, I sensed the fixation problem rearing its head, and I decided to back off. The committee asked another prospect. He turned them down. Later they asked him again, to no avail. Finally they turned to me and said, "What about that man you recommended some months ago?" As I look back, I truly believe that if this man had been offered the job when I initially presented him, he would have turned it down; in the ensuing months the Lord had prepared him to accept the call.

2. I was overwhelmingly naive about certain social problems.

Circle Church sprang to life in the sixties, and its genes included all the turmoil and idealism of that remarkable decade. I, in my early thirties, was very dissatisfied with what I saw as the disinterest in meaningful change within the traditional church. The group of people who birthed Circle were just awakening to the racial barriers in Chicago, the oppressive side of capitalism, the class barriers, and sexual discriminations that seemed to explode into light during those years.

We deliberately located Circle Church in the hub of a wild mix of neighborhoods. Across the expressway loomed the University of Illinois Circle Campus, one of the world's largest medical centers; to the rear of our building stretched Chicago's famous westside black ghetto; Skid Row was a couple of blocks north; and a small, Greek commercial district thrived eight blocks east.

We wanted to draw from all those people and show that the church of Christ could break down the walls, and all of us could live together in peace before the world. I still think, idealistically perhaps, that such a confluence of cultures and backgrounds can work, although the scriptural examples of fusing different cultures usually point to severe problems.

I confidently assumed that with God on our side, we could move in, and problems that had been hundreds of years in making would softly melt away. Our ideals were good—the same ideals, I believe, so eloquently stated by the Old Testament prophets. But we consistently underestimated the stranglehold of the enemy.

Christians tend to read overstated biographies of great, godly men like William Wilberforce and John Knox and come away with the impression that they single-handedly remade a society in twenty years. Actually, if you study the historical situation, you realize that though they played a key role, those men were just a part of an incredibly long and complex process that God used to advance righteousness. Like Esther, they responded to God in the right place at the right time. The abolition of slavery in England was the culmination of centuries of Christian concepts eroding an institution that had stood firm for all recorded history. Slavery was rooted deep. Although only Christianity was finally able to help topple it, its dissolution took a long time, and the residue of the problem remains with us today.

For a model of a Christian involved in social change, I look at a man like the apostle Paul, who was as wise as a serpent in the ways of the world. He knew that the full effect of the gospel he preached would take years; he had counted the pain and personal cost involved in attacking evil. Unlike Paul, I was naive. Today I read bold statements in *Full Circle* and cringe, because we didn't even scratch the surface. We were one tiny ripple, and those who watched us probably learned more by our failures than by our successes.

In America we tend to write stories about what people have "achieved" for the kingdom rather than trying to write down from God's perspective and mentioning how people fit into his movements. When Paul wrote about his accomplishments, I think his main concern was to communicate the incredible spiritual warfare that was going on and how he was committed to the side of God. At Circle, and in many places where God is advancing his kingdom, the temptation seeps in to throw the spotlight on the neat little experiment that the world can watch unfolding. Human beings do not respond well to spotlights. It's like that law of indeterminacy in physics: as soon as an action of the Holy Spirit is observed, its nature changes.

If I had not been injected with so much of the American success serum, I would have approached the racial problem with this attitude: "I will do what can be done, and maybe others will join me. Someday my son or my son's son will finally see significant change in one small corner of a major metropolitan area." That approach would have been far more realistic and God-honoring, I believe. Instead, with the first flush of success, as blacks and whites achieved real harmony in worship and fellowship, I naively chalked up a huge breakthrough.

The racial area, which we had pointed to with greatest pride, directly led to a dissolution in Circle. We gradually gave the minority element more and more power within the church. Finally they sought to express in absolute terms that the number one priority of the church should be to address social issues, with the minority pastor answerable to no staff leadership. I don't want to describe the conflict in detail, but they demanded a major shift in the emphasis of Circle.

At one point I realized the problem was developing and tried to split off a branch from our church that would accept this new direction. But I spoke up too late—they wanted the racial issue to be the chief focus of Circle Church.

I was shocked by this. I was too naive to understand that oppressed people have a problem with fixation too. We should not have expected the fiery emotions of a minority that had been downtrodden for several centuries to find a comfortable niche in the multifaceted agenda of our church. Before unleashing those emotions we should have been prepared to deal with them. We weren't.

The racial area was not the only one in which I showed naiveté. I now realize that I lacked a balanced appreciation of human depravity along with the marvel of regeneration.

When the Holy Spirit of God comes to live in someone, a tremendous thing happens. Yet, as the Bible graphically illustrates, the depravity of a person still asserts itself. Apart from an unusual walk with God, human beings always tend to move toward lower levels. I did not give credence to that factor as I should have.

Especially with the new believers, I think I should have realistically assumed that these people had a long way to go in their Christian walk, and that they very likely would not be able to come together without strife, especially because of their diverse backgrounds. Indeed, their insecurities surfaced much faster than their new maturity in Christ. I can hardly remember referring to human depravity while at Circle. I just kept preaching the ideal. And I was very surprised when signs of depravity broke out among the congregation. Now I would look at a given group and almost anticipate it.

In America we are bombarded with anti-God philosophies. The tug of the world is very powerful. Combine with that the conflicts and tensions normally present among diverse people— different tastes, prejudices, expectations, needs—and you can guarantee certain problems will arise.

Just the difference in education created tension. We would work for scores of hours on a creative, God-honoring worship service or a beautiful anthem and find it went over the heads of the uneducated people we had worked so hard to bring into church. Or we would gear programs to them and find another segment bored or resentful.

I was also naive about the pastor's role. Circle began with a cluster of people who loved God but were disillusioned by local churches. Starting from scratch, we tried to create the kind of church that we wanted, making adjustments as we grew. As such, it was a unique phenomenon, not at all the typical church ministry situation. We had the fun and the fireworks and the enthusiasm that many churches lack. But much of pastoring is not vision or glamour; it's patching up wounds and desperately trying to hold families together.

I was only thirty years old when Circle started, having never pastored before, meeting in a very different territory with a demanding audience. I managed to ignite the people with my dreams—to some degree. But perhaps I did not carefully enough peel back their skin to fully see and feel their needs.

In a way those years at Circle were a skyrocket. We attracted attention, and yes, I believe we brought honor to God. We tapped an unusual level of commitment—more than one hundred people moved into one community to have closer fellowship as a result of Circle. We affected lives. God can use skyrockets. But perhaps a better metaphor would be to view pastors as the glue of society. I believe a country will rise or fall based on the quality of its pastors. I do not know of a more demanding or fulfilling occupation.

3. In encouraging the gifts of the congregation, I minimized my leadership role.

When Circle Church was born, discussion about the gifts of the congregation was quite new. The body-life movement had not yet reached toddler stage, and I don't know of any books that existed then on how to mobilize the gifts of the congregation. We tried not just to talk about the gifts but to utilize them. We canvassed people so that when they joined our body, they had a clear idea of what the church expected them to contribute. We tried to make everyone in the church feel like an equal, essential part of the body, and I believe we succeeded.

The church, however, is also an organization. Although every part of the body is important, for certain functions, such as decision making, some members are more important (or specialized) than others. It was hard for people at Circle to understand how we could be equal and yet not equal. A deep, holy fellowship can thrive among peers, but the church also includes a structure in which some people are recognized as leaders among those peers. The leaders are set apart by God to instruct and nurture the flock.

As I look back, I can see that my walk with the Lord was further developed than many of the members'. I had led many of them to Christ. They had weak backgrounds in such areas as prayer life, victory over basic temptations, and knowledge of the Bible. But in setting up the climate of leadership in the church, I stressed the equality of all believers almost to the exclusion of the hierarchical gifts of leadership. I discovered that fact too late; I couldn't turn the congregation around. I had put us all on level ground for so long that they couldn't look up anymore.

Whenever one of the three pastors at Circle would preach, he had to submit his sermon to advance critical review by the other staff members. We also held a lively reaction session after church where members responded to the sermon. These practices were healthy; but we did not balance them with proper teaching on the role of leadership and spiritual maturity.

As I hired each staff member I told him or her that we comprised a team, of which I was the leader. I understood the distinction of leadership, but I am not sure all of them did. When a conflict arose, some would say to me, "We're a team," but no one ever said, "But you're the leader, so we'll defer to you."

For example a staff member submitted a sermon to the team to evaluate in advance of his preaching. Because there were doctrinal problems, I could not allow the sermon to be preached. He responded by going over my head to the board of elders, causing a serious rift from which we never fully recovered.

In setting up the church, I had deliberately played down authority structures and invested power in a broadly based board, not in the pastor. Our members came with an antiauthoritarian bias, and I consented to it. And when it finally came to the place where I said, "I'm sorry, but for the sake of the body I must take this action," they could not follow me. They had not been prepared to accept leadership and could not adapt even when it came to the most crucial issues of the church. By not directly exercising leadership for so long, I had forfeited my option to use it.

I believe this problem of minimizing the pastor's leadership is a disease spreading wildly through evangelical churches. Fifteen years ago the opposite problem existed: authoritarian leadership. But when the laity began emerging with a strong excitement about the faith, attention was so focused away from the pastor that this function was perceived to be almost unneeded. Seminaries began teaching the pastor's role as "enabling the congregation," without balancing emphasis on being a spokesman for God and leading by exhorting.

Awakening of the laity is a beautiful thing, a pulsing, vital sign in the history of the church. But I believe in the Old Testament symbol of the mantle; the cloak signifying that God has set aside a leader for certain strengths and skills. Jesus wore the mantle in a beautiful way. Although he was a servant, he also carried authority, and no one questioned who the leader was.

If you push servant leadership too far, you can turn the leader into a doormat and destroy him. Only if a people recognize that a leader holds tremendous invested dignity will they respect him and treat him as a leader. Throughout church history, without strong leaders even outbreaks of church renewal quickly fizzle.

I would express the balance this way: leadership describes the office; servanthood describes the style of exercising that office.

Almost all conflicts I observe between congregations and pastors hinge on matters of opinion rather than absolutes. In such cases, I believe the congregation would be wise to say, "As long as this is an opinion, and not an absolute, we will yield and follow you as the leader." But too often, they fall victim to the human urge to assert themselves and pick at the scabs of the leader. They end up dehumanizing him. Churches have the power to dethrone leaders who stray way off from God's standards, and that is good—but in these peripheral issues I believe they should practice some following.

4. I feared failure so much that I held onto the church too tightly.

My wife, Karen, has said, thankfully, that she has complete trust in me as a husband; she does not fear my unfaithfulness.

But she will also tell you that I had a mistress once—Circle Church. I clung to the church too tightly at the expense of my own family.

In C. S. Lewis's book *The Four Loves*, he illustrates the principle that first something becomes a god and then it becomes a demon. It seems that the higher we reach and the more good we achieve, the greater will be the temptation to cling to those accomplishments and use them to build ourselves up.

If Circle had been another plodding, no-growth, no-excitement church, I would never have become so emotionally involved. But, truthfully, God was in our midst. The worship services abounded with joyful exuberance and creativity. We came together to worship God. We believed he was there, and we tapped all our creative energies to express our love and devotion to him. I don't know how to express this other than in crude human terms, but I think God left some of those Sunday-morning services with a smile and a confidence that "those people love me. They enjoy my presence."

At Circle, a buzzing conversation in the lobby concerned not weather or baseball but the Lord. We could converse comfortably about our faith. We also learned the true meaning of worship—to attribute worth to the Lord.

All of those occasions were wonderful spiritual experiences that honored God. I still rejoice in them. But as I reflect on how I responded personally to the congregation, I now see that I allowed my own identity to merge with the church. I should have been God's man and let the church develop its own personality. But I cared too much. We became one. I have seen this process duplicated often in the lives of leaders of religious organizations. After twenty or thirty years of slaving away, they awake one day and feel burned out. They have made their ministry almost an idol. I did that at Circle.

I ask myself now in what specific ways this tendency expressed itself. The most direct clue I can identify is that I know I never could have left Circle on my own. The Lord himself had to break me. Except for his intervention I would still be there today, because of too great a love for the people, the church, and the potential they represented. God wanted me out of Circle, and he made it impossible for me to stay.

I say those words very academically now, but they represent so much pain. I can now say that the best thing that ever happened in my life was the process of the breaking of my pride. During that time I felt as if I had been rejected by the church that I had poured my life and soul into for ten years. For a brief time I questioned my faith: Do I believe in God? Can I trust him? Once I worked through those initial doubts I still had to wrestle with the serious question of whether I should continue in the ministry.

I fought back waves of shame. Circle Church had been viewed as a model, yet I had failed at leading it. I wondered who would believe in me for the future. There were temptations, of course, to open up festering wounds before the congregation and to defend myself, but I knew that would only spread the pain.

Elisabeth Elliot, in her novel *No Graven Image*, describes the growth of a young, frustrated missionary who suddenly realizes this: God is not the accomplice of our work; he is the work. We are merely his tools in getting it done.

Gradually I went through the process of consciously releasing my dreams and expectations and even my own personhood. I came around to embrace Christ as head of Circle Church. The body was his, not mine. I chose to submit all things to him.

My worth as a person rests solely on my confidence and faith in his redeeming process in my life. By that standard, Circle Church and specifically its failures have been the greatest aids to spiritual growth in my life. The most important lesson I learned from Circle was to change my perception of how to measure success.

After leaving, more than a year passed before I began to feel like a man again. Now I have sensed a new filling of the Holy Spirit that I believe comes only after a complete surrender to God. Some broken people end up resentful and bitter; but in my case the process taught me to put confidence not in myself but in the Lord. As never before I identify with Paul's words that God's strength "is made perfect in weakness."

15

Courage for the Doubting Pastor

*Leadership doesn't equal certainty. True leadership sees the
inevitable ambiguities of ministry, yet has the spiritual sensitivity
and resolve to advance through them.*

—BEN PATTERSON

When she said, "Now, Pastor, nobody wants you to succeed at
this church more than I do," I inwardly groaned. I knew what
was coming.

After a year as pastor, I had felt deeply that the church must
focus on building leadership for the coming years. So at the
previous board meeting I had asked, "I want to find ten men
who'll meet with me for a year to study and pray, on the premise
that they would go and disciple other men in the church. I want
your endorsement for making this my main focus of ministry,
with a goal of discipling fifty men over the next five years." They
approved what came to be called Project Mustard Seed.

But now they were having second thoughts. One Sunday
morning a board member pulled me aside.

"I think Project Mustard Seed is a great idea," she began, "but
maybe if you waited two or three years, the timing would be
better. Right now, since you're new, you really need to spend
time visiting all the groups in the church and making them feel
supported."

I didn't believe that would be a good use of my time. I felt the
time for getting to know the congregation had passed; now it
was time to develop leaders for the future. But that's when I
began to wonder, *How much of Project Mustard Seed is what Ben
Patterson wants, and how much really comes from God?*

Even during a family vacation that year to England, the trip of a lifetime, the inner debate never stopped. Two or three times a day, whenever a quiet moment came, that Sunday morning conversation would bubble to the surface. Then I would agonize, again and again, about whether I had made the right choice: *Was it too late to back out? What about the men I'd already asked to participate and who were excited about the program? Suppose the board withdrew its endorsement?*

From that episode I learned that *leadership* doesn't always equal *certainty*. Naturally, we are able to press ahead when we have no doubts. But we live as imperfect people in an imperfect world. True leadership sees the inevitable ambiguities of ministry, yet has the spiritual sensitivity and resolve to advance through them.

Here's how I've learned to minister despite uncertainty.

Picking your fights

The older I get, I'm more sure of less, and I'm less sure of more! But one thing I've learned is that certitude has a price. The good and wise leader has a clear idea of what issues are worth paying that price (and I suspect it's a fairly short list) and what issues aren't. In my ministry I've found that, though I may have strong convictions about a subject, it doesn't mean it's always necessary or even advisable to express my certitude in public.

Congregations in America today want it both ways. On the one hand, people in the pews want the confidence and certainty of a Churchill or Patton, a leader who provides clear answers for their complex lives. But they are also pulled by the cultural impulse that extols individuality, that says "different strokes for different folks."

The church where I grew up required members to sign a thirty-point doctrinal statement. Most congregations would consider that an intolerable infringement on their rights. American Christians don't have much stomach for a pastor with a long list of certitudes.

So the issue boils down to two questions: When do I want to

be perceived as certain, and when do I want to avoid that perception?

I want to be certain about fundamental doctrines. All but one of Paul's thirteen epistles are written to churches or pastors, and he returns again and again to the theme of preaching a pure gospel: "Then we will no longer be infants, tossed back and forth by the waves, and blown here and there by every wind of teaching and by the cunning and craftiness of men in their deceitful scheming" (Eph. 4:14).

The church in America today is tossed back and forth, so it's vital that we help steady the ship.

Then again, I don't speak *ex cathedra* about programs or policies. The Scriptures contain no doctrine of "pastoral infallibility," no mandate to equate your word with God's. But our stature can tempt us, from time to time, to draw a line in the sand about a particular (and personally heartfelt) program or policy of the church, saying, "This is what God wants, so choose ye this day whom ye shall serve." If any problems arise, however, your credibility suffers. People know better.

I find it helpful to be clear about my expectations. Recently I had an engaged couple in my office for counseling, and as always I asked them, "What are your expectations about the relationship? Things will go smoother after the wedding if you voice your expectations now."

In the same way, I've always approached my church callings as wedding engagements: both parties enter the relationship with expectations, which ought to be expressed up front.

When I was called to New Providence Presbyterian Church, I was candid with the board: "I can't lead this church if you won't let me lead it according to the way I'm put together. If you want Ben Patterson as your pastor, there are certain things that come with the package, things you'll have to live with." I didn't tell them my style of leadership was necessarily right for every church, but it was right for me.

For example, I need time to read and think and pray. I'm not good at tending institutional machinery—I have to delegate that to someone else. I also need the freedom and latitude to take action without tremendous amounts of consensus building. I want to win, and not just keep from losing—even if it means I sometimes shoot from the hip and make mistakes.

"That's what you get with Ben Patterson," I told the board.

I also try to remember the difference between vision and timing. In one church I served, we went through two building programs like clockwork. When a third building project presented itself, my confidence was soaring. We jumped in with both feet, put out brochures, did stewardship meetings, and went whole hog to get the project built in two years.

I was sure about it and talked often and confidently about God's vision for this new building.

But the building didn't get built in two years as predicted. Years later, my successor in that church is just now getting that project together again.

Was my vision wrong? No, but my timing was. Instead of its being built in two years, right now it appears the Lord had five to seven years in mind.

Strategies for straddlers

One season during my high school football days, our coach installed an incredibly high-powered offense—any professional team would have been proud of its complexity. We gave it our best shot, but the complex system was hard for us to learn. Our school was favored to win the opening game, but when the whistle blew, our guys ran around the field not sure where they were supposed to go and who they were supposed to block. It's a game we should have won over a smaller high school, but our squad was beaten.

A few days later we sat down to watch a film of the game. On play after play, you could see everyone hesitating on the line of scrimmage. By this time the coach was screaming at us, "If you're going to make a mistake, at least do it aggressively!" Over the years my coach's words have stuck with me. Sometimes in ministry, we're not sure what we're doing, and we hesitate, letting circumstances control us.

Or worse: in some situations pastors have given up altogether.

I was visiting one church where only 50 people were scattered across a sanctuary that seated 250. The congregational singing was weak and half-hearted. I wondered why the pastor, who was leading the singing, didn't say, "Let's all get up and move closer together."

Yet as I sat through the service, I started noticing other signs that the pastor had simply given up. The board where the hymn numbers are posted was empty, the sanctuary needed fresh paint, and the sign outside didn't list the times of the services—dozen of little things that said, "I'm too tired for this, and what difference does it make anyway?"

It's easy to get discouraged and give up when you're faced with uncertainty. But it's not all that difficult to adopt strategies of leadership that help project the confidence of a Churchill (a confidence church members want and need), even when on the inside you really feel more like Hamlet.

Let us reason together. Few topics are harder to preach than predestination. Even the apostle Paul had to shrug his shoulders on this subject and say, "Who has known the mind of the Lord?" (Rom. 11:34). So once when I preached a sermon on predestination, I began by admitting, "I really don't know if anything I'm going to say is true, but this is a doctrine that believers need to deal with, and I'm going to share with you a progress report about my own current thinking on the subject."

Though the hard-core Calvinists were disappointed with me, most of the congregation were glad somebody admitted the subject was open for discussion. "All I can do is give you my best interpretation for now," I told them, "and I make no promise that if I preach again next year, I won't have a new point of view. But we need to come to grips with this issue because making no decision is in itself a decision."

Throughout my sermon the tone of the message was, "Here's what I see, what I feel. Let me tell you why I believe this way, why I'm excited about it, and why I think you should be excited about it too. Let me try to persuade you, as one Christian to another."

I would never take this approach with fundamental doctrines, but it works with vital doctrines that don't affect salvation. I am forthright about my interpretation, but I give my people the right to disagree with dignity.

At the same time, I'm under no obligation to lay out all the alternatives to my views, being evenhanded with each, suggesting the congregation choose the alternative that best suits them. That's not leadership but an invitation to indecision and paralysis within the church.

I once saw a Christian drama group put on a skit about pastors and their churches called *That's What We Pay You For*. Committee members come to the pastor telling him that they're upset that in a sermon he gave them two or three possibilities for interpreting a passage. They don't care for that; they're looking for guidance: that's what they pay him for.

A sermon is not a lecture but an occasion where I am called to persuade people to make a deeper commitment to Christ.

When the vision gets cloudy. A friend of mine took a pastorate at a small church in California that shared a building with another congregation. He was convinced the church should build some equity so that someday it could construct a sanctuary of its own. My friend was willing to go fifty-fifty with the congregation in buying a home to serve as a parsonage, with a large enough yard for church picnics and a big family room for small meetings and Bible studies. The church would build equity, the congregation would gain a sense of identity and esteem, and later the house could be sold for the down payment on a new sanctuary.

However, just as the people started getting enthusiastic, my friend began to get cold feet. Did he want to live in a home that wasn't really his? What about the financial and tax complications of going fifty-fifty on the deal? What if he left the church someday? Would the financial entanglement make it harder to leave? Would the church find it harder to recruit a new pastor, since he might not want to be tied to a parsonage?

He had boldly brought forth his idea, and now his credibility as a leader might be at stake if he pulled back. "The people would have thought I was just jerking them around," he later said. "They would have been reluctant to follow my other ideas for fear of being let down again."

My friend adopted a strategy of passivity. He just stopped bringing the parsonage up at the monthly board meetings. If the lay leadership wanted to pursue it, he was prepared to go along. Yet nobody was charged enough to press ahead. Soon the matter died, and my friend wiggled off the hook with his credibility untarnished.

You can't use this strategy often or on key decisions that are already in motion (e.g., a building contract has been signed). But once in a while it gets us out of a jam when uncertainty strikes hard and for good reason.

In general, I try to follow this guideline: I don't back out of a decision because it's becoming unpopular and causing me grief. I feel free to change my mind, though, if people are becoming embittered or losing their faith over the issue. That doesn't settle by itself my uncertainties, but it does help me analyze them better.

The realistic cheerleader. I've always hated cheerleaders who, when the score is 48-0 in favor of the other team, still shout, "Hey, hey, what d'ya know, get that ball and go, go, go!" At that point, the players need to hear something like, "We still love you guys!"

Sometimes the church takes a real beating; it looks as if the game is turning into a rout, and as pastors we're not sure whether the team can make a comeback. We're tempted to lead cheers like, "We're looking forward to a great year!" or "God is going to give us the victory!"

What's needed is an honest look at an uncertain situation combined with confidence about what God can do: "I don't know how it'll turn out, but we are looking to God for guidance," or "This has been hard, but we're going to see God's hand in all this." I call it realistic cheerleading.

Writing it down. It's astounding this power God has given us of being able to put feelings into words, of giving names to things so we can understand them better and gain the victory. That's why I keep a personal journal; it's a place to lay out all the confusions I feel, all the uncertainties, the angers, and the fears, to confess them before God in written prayer.

For example, take the night I realized the building project I had been so anxious for was going to grind to an unceremonious halt. When I came home, I began reading the Psalms, and I got to Psalm 132:

> O Lord, remember David
>   and all the hardships he endured.
> He swore an oath to the Lord
>   and made a vow to the Mighty One of Jacob:
> "I will not enter my house
>   or go to my bed—
> I will allow no sleep to my eyes,
>   no slumber to my eyelids,
> till I find a place for the Lord,
>   a dwelling for the Mighty One of Jacob." (vv. 1–5)

It describes David's struggle to find a place for the ark. He won't rest until he gets it done.

I wanted to build a sanctuary for God. Our church had studied the theology of worship. We had studied the theology of space. From that we had developed a wonderful theological document. And then we drew up plans that expressed perfectly what we believed about worship. I was so excited about it, but it wasn't going to happen.

After I read about David's struggle, I started writing in my journal—two pages in which I poured out my feelings and questions: "Lord, why did you bring us so far in this thing? Everything seemed so clear up to now; it was going so well. But it has stopped! I've been here fourteen years, and I wanted this to be an exclamation point to my ministry. Now it looks like an asterisk. Lord, help me—help me to continue pursuing this, or help me let go if I need to let go of it."

In taking up pen and paper, I see the shadows gain shape; I demystify them, give them the human discipline of sentence structure and syntax, and arrive at a way to face the problem.

Sometimes he speaks. We all want to be like Jonah and have God audibly tell us, "Go to Nineveh." No mistake there! Though clear signs don't come as often as we want, I've never been convinced to despair. I am not a deist, who believes God keeps his distance and lets us solve our own problems. Once in a while, especially when we're attentive, God clarifies our uncertainty.

Earlier I mentioned my doubts about Project Mustard Seed, my program to disciple a small group of men in the church. While I was on vacation in England, I continued to stew over the problem: Should I take the one person's advice to slow down and get to know the congregation better? Or should I reach for the future by training new leaders?

On the final day of our vacation, I toured the annual flower festival in the small Welsh village where we had stayed. As an outreach to the community and a surprise to me, the church that hosted our visit had set up a display with my book *Waiting*, which had just been published in England. And there by a stack of my books was a flower pot with mustard seeds sprinkled all over the top. I wept because, for me, it was such a powerful confirmation of what I felt God wanted me to do.

The certainty of presence. Walter Wangerin's *The Book of the Dun Cow* is an allegory set in a barnyard with animals as characters (and perhaps the most vivid description of evil I've ever read). In the story, the Holy Spirit is represented as a dun-colored cow that appears at unexpected moments. As characters gaze into her liquid brown eyes and feel her warm breath, her presence nurtures and reassures. Only occasionally does the cow speak, but most of the time she's just there, quietly grazing and observing you with her deep liquid eyes.

I can't conclude this section without stating the obvious because it is the obvious I have to keep reminding myself of: there are no guarantees in life. My family, my health, my job, can be devastated in a moment. But one thing is certain: God is present. And the most reliable strategy to face the uncertainties of ministry is to trust in the God who is always there, quietly gazing at us with deep liquid eyes. As Psalm 73 puts it:

When my heart was grieved
    and my spirit embittered,
I was senseless and ignorant;
    I was a brute beast before you.

Yet I am always with you;
  you hold me by my right hand.
You guide me with your counsel,
  and afterward you will take me into glory.
Whom have I in heaven but you?
  And earth has nothing I desire besides you. (vv. 21–25)

Over the falls

In discussing the issue of vocation at life's different stages, Karl Barth notes that younger pastors are usually the ones who boldly plunge ahead, while older men often play things close to the vest—they've been through the mill before, or perhaps they have more to lose.

Then Barth asks the rhetorical question, "Does the river slow down as it approaches the falls?"

The answer, of course, is that the river gains speed, rushing fastest at the very moment it plunges over the edge. I want my ministry to pick up speed as I go along. I don't want to be careless and wantonly make mistakes; I want to use the wisdom God has given me to follow the bends that life presents. But as I face uncertainty, I don't want to trickle off into some side stream. I want to be like that river, rushing toward the falls—and when I go over the edge, I look forward to falling into the arms of God.

Section 2:
Empowering Your Church Through Change

The numerically growing congregations and denominations in the first years of the third millenium will be those that are both able and willing to make the changes necessary to respond in a meaningful way to the religious needs of skeptics, seekers, searchers, inquirers, and pilgrims.

—LYLE SCHALLER
21 Bridges to the 21st Century

PART 5

Weighing Changes

16

Before You Risk

*Risk taking is not an option if we want to be effective in
ministry. But it's vital that those risks be prudent.*

—LARRY OSBORNE

Rich had just taken the pastorate of one of the largest churches
in his denomination. He had experienced tremendous success in
his previous church, a church plant that had grown to more than
two thousand under his innovative, risk-taking style of leadership. Rich entered his new ministry assuming a long and bright
future.

To his dismay, he found that a few arbitrary decisions, small
mistakes in judgment, and the launching of a couple of pet projects took on epic proportions. Things that had been ignored in
Tennessee suddenly became a cause for impeachment in Minnesota.

Baffled, he tried to wrestle more and more control from his
opponents. But instead of gaining more authority and freedom,
he gained only more enemies. Within eighteen months he resigned, a crushed and confused pastor, wondering how someone
who had been hailed as an innovative, risk-taking leader in one
setting could be written off as an incompetent, wild-eyed gambler in another.

What causes a leader to succeed in one setting and fail in
another? More to the point, what makes a leader great?

Hoping to get answers, for years I've studied leaders and their
ministries. I've focused on the highly successful, looking for
their secrets, which I could apply to my own life and ministry.

But what I've found has surprised me. Instead of secrets, principles, and patterns that guarantee success, I've found amazing diversity. Although there are certainly some common threads to be found, the most striking thing about highly effective leaders is how little they have in common. What one swears by, another warns against.

Still one trait stands out: the willingness to risk. Highly successful leaders ignore conventional wisdom and take chances. Their stories inevitably include a defining moment or key decision when they took a significant risk and thereby experienced a breakthrough.

But herein lies the rub. My study of leaders and ministries has also focused on another group—those who have failed miserably —and among them I've also found a common trait: the willingness to risk. They, too, ignore conventional wisdom, go against the odds. But in their cases, the results were tragic, not triumphant.

So what gives? What separates a successful risk taker from a bankrupt gambler?

I've come to believe it's the ability to distinguish between a prudent risk and a wild-eyed gamble. To increase my ability to discern the difference, I've learned to ask myself five key questions before taking ministry out on a limb.

Who else has done it?

My first question is always, "Who else has been there?"

Solomon said, "There's nothing new under the sun," and I believe him. So before I set out on a risky venture, I've learned to search out those who've already gone down that path or a similar one.

By asking what went well and what went wrong, I can usually pinpoint where the dangers lie, which takes much of the risk out of a risky situation.

A couple of years ago, without warning, our church, which had been renting facilities from another church, lost its lease. We were forced into an emergency building program, with no lead time and no money. Knowing that time and money are two vital ingredients to a successful program and that any building program is risky in its own right, I was, to say the least, concerned.

Due to our short time frame, purchasing land and building a traditional facility from scratch was not an option. So we hunted for an empty shopping center, industrial building, or warehouse capable of being converted into a church. In addition, we wanted one large enough to allow for future growth.

Finally we found a facility that might work. It was large enough, had adequate parking, and fell within an area zoned for church use. It was also the only facility within fifteen miles to meet those criteria.

Still, we had no margin for error. It would so stretch our finances that even the slightest time delay or cost overrun would break us. I wondered if I shouldn't go for a smaller place, of which there were a number.

Before making any recommendations to the congregation, I decided to talk to other pastors who had already turned a retail or industrial site into a church. To my surprise, I heard the same thing over and over. Their delay and cost overruns could be traced to one of three areas:

1. Architectural plans. To save money, many had used an in-house architect or draftsman to draw up their plans. Inexperience in designing large-occupancy buildings led to long delays as they redrew the plans numerous times to comply with the stricter building codes governing large-occupancy buildings.

2. City approval. I also had heard stories aplenty about the horrors of trying to gain a zoning change or municipal approval to build. One church leader told of waiting two years before receiving a final go-ahead. But in each case where the process had snarled, I found the church had depended upon an inexperienced lay leader or staff member to navigate the bureaucratic maze. The result was a series of wrong turns and dead ends before finally arriving at their destination.

3. Volunteer labor. Everywhere I heard the same story. Many volunteered to help; few actually showed up. Churches depending heavily on volunteer labor spoke of saving money but losing time. In one case, the construction took a year longer than antic-ipated.

I was amazed how similar the stories were. Once I heard their stories, however, I took heart. I now knew where the predictable risks lay, which meant we could devise a plan to minimize them.

I recommended to the board and church that we go for it. We spent a little more money on our architect, hired a professional consultant to guide us through the bureaucratic maze, and counted on little, if any, help from volunteers.

The result was a new facility—finished on time and under budget—capable of handling not only the people we already had but a lot of new folks as well.

How bad can it get?

This question has two parts: "What's the worse thing that can happen here?" and "Can I live with it?"

If I can't live with it, it's seldom a risk worth taking.

Both my theology and my life taught me long ago that what-ever can go wrong will go wrong. It has something to do with what the Bible calls the Fall and the world calls Murphy's Law. By either name it's ignored at great peril.

That was Nick's mistake. Four years after planting a new church, he felt he was at a dead end. No matter what he tried, the church couldn't break the two-hundred barrier. Every growth spurt was followed by an exodus of folks who were upset over some minor issue or were moving out of the area.

To Nick, the major culprit was an inadequate facility. Lacking the people and money to purchase their own site, they had to rent a run-down community hall. From the lingering smell of stale beer to the peeling paint and dim lighting, the facility re-pelled rather than attracted new people.

When the pastor of a small struggling church in the area sug-gested the two churches merge, Nick was intrigued. Though they represented different denominations, the differences were minor, centered on polity, not doctrine. In addition, the other church had a facility and one hundred members. To Nick, it looked like a risk worth taking. If all went well, it would solve his two greatest problems: the lack of a permanent facility and the two hundred barrier.

So he pushed ahead, lobbying his board and congregation until they finally agreed to the merger.

But Nick made a critical mistake. He was so focused on the potential benefits, he failed to seriously consider what might go wrong. To him, trusting God meant focusing only on the upside. Visualizing worst-case scenarios was an exercise for those who lacked faith.

But there were drawbacks. Nick failed to realize successful mergers are rare. More often it means one church will get swallowed by the other, and Nick hadn't asked himself if he could accept being swallowed.

A year later that's exactly what happened. Nick found himself functioning more and more as an assistant to the other pastor. His influence with the board and congregation waned. Finally, feeling bitter and betrayed, he resigned.

The worst thing that could happen had happened, and he couldn't live with it. He now looks back on the good old days when he pastored a church of less than two hundred in a run-down, rented community hall.

There's another advantage to asking, "What can go wrong, and can I live with it?" Sometimes it helps me realize a risk is worth taking but not just yet.

That's what happened when we changed our worship style. When I first came to the church, we were a preaching station. Our services consisted of song, commercial, song, commercial, and then a forty-five-minute sermon. From the beginning I felt if we were going to reach our community, we needed to make worship a higher priority; we also needed to depend less on traditional hymns and more on contemporary musical styles.

There was only one problem. Our 120 people liked it as it was. That's why they came. Only a few wanted to change.

At that point, it would have been foolish to risk a sudden, major shift in worship style. While the upside of such a change was the possibility of reaching more people, the downside was too much to bear: a potential mass exodus at a time when we barely had enough people to pay the bills and keep the place open.

So I waited, making only incremental changes. Four years later we finally reached critical mass. We had enough people in the pews; losing a few wouldn't kill us. And the ones most likely to go were longtime Christians who could quickly find another church with music more to their liking. More important, those likely to go were doing little to help us reach the community. Few of them had brought anyone to church other than an out-of-town relative or a friend who was already a Christian.

So we made the change. We did lose some people. But it was a loss we could live with it. And in our case, we not only lived with it, we flourished.

Can I try it on for size?

A third question I ask myself before taking a risk is, "Can I give it a trial run?"

Obviously that's not always feasible, as when hiring staff or building a facility. But I've found many risky decisions (or at least parts of decisions) can be tried on for size before I commit to them.

A trial run can save heartache. It can turn a stupid decision into nothing more than a popped trial balloon, blunting the impact of what would otherwise be a major failure.

Len was a high-energy, do-it-right-now type. That trait served him well as the new pastor of a small suburban church. Under his leadership it grew from seventy-five to nearly six hundred in four years. But then the growth stopped.

Len had a hard time adjusting. He felt more and more like a failure. Convinced God had more growth in store for the church, he read books and attended conferences about spurring a church on to greater heights. When Len came home from one of those conferences, he was full of enthusiasm and vision for the future. "The key" was a new approach to ministry that had produced phenomenal results at the church hosting the conference.

Len put on a full-court press with his board. The board agreed to follow his lead, and within weeks Len embraced a new preaching style, an aggressive evangelistic outreach program, and a more authoritarian approach to leadership. Len knew the changes would meet some resistance, but he felt sure an influx of new believers would more than make up for the loss of a few opponents.

He was wrong. One year later, attendance logged in at three hundred. What had gone wrong?

An unforeseen cultural clash. Len was emulating a ministry located in a predominantly blue-collar community where a forty-hour workweek was the norm, leaving many members with significant free time for a high-commitment, volunteer ministry. In addition, they were open and responsive to an authoritarian style of leadership.

Len's church was located in an upper-class neighborhood. His parishioners were highly educated, well-compensated professionals who worked fifty to seventy hours a week. They rebelled at even a hint of strong-armed leadership.

By the time Len realized what was going on, it was too late. Even after he shelved new programs and emphases, he couldn't bring back those who had left.

Len's story contrasts sharply with that of another church and pastor I know. There, too, the church had plateaued, leading to a search for new ways to get things moving again.

That pastor also flew home from a week-long conference, ecstatic about a new ministry model. He, too, gathered his board and began to sell them on his new vision. But instead of putting forward his suggested changes as permanent, he suggested a trial period. So, for six months, one Sunday a month, the church experimented with "seeker" services.

It soon became obvious the changes wouldn't turn the church around. No one left over the changes, but only the pastor and a few key leaders were excited about the new direction.

They decided to scrap the idea. Although the leaders were discouraged over their failed experiment, it didn't sink the church.

How much rope do I have?

A fourth question I ask is, "How much room do I have for error?"

When I came to North Coast, I failed to ask this question and nearly hung myself.

I followed a much-loved founding pastor. The tight-knit congregation had not yet finished the grieving process when I arrived and began making changes. Because the changes were small, I figured the risks were minimal.

They weren't. Inconsequential changes in the worship service, bulletin, and church calendar created an uproar. One family said they were leaving because the service no longer ended with a closing hymn. Another because I failed to schedule the annual New Year's Eve party. Still another asked where I intended to send my kids to school and then left when I gave the wrong answer—this despite the fact that my wife and I hadn't yet had any children!

I was left reeling. My stomach churned every time I heard a phone ring, conditioned, like Pavlov's dog, to expect the worst.

Since then, I've learned that the amount of risk in a decision is directly related to the quality of my relationship with the people affected. When the relationships are deep, my margin for error is great. When the relationships are shallow or strained, there may not even be a margin for error.

Frankly, I no longer worry about the effects of my changing the bulletin, an annual program, or how I take the offering. I seldom worry about the fallout from a new ministry or a potential change in direction. After thirteen years, a measure of success, and a couple of major crises successfully navigated, I've acquired enough rope to outlive a few failures or misguided decisions. I'm not cavalier, but I'm aware that as my margin for error has increased, so has my freedom to take risks. Failure doesn't look so bad when I know it won't be fatal.

In some situations, naturally, a newly arrived leader has all the rope he needs from day one. When the church is in a crisis or is looking to the new leader to be a white knight riding to the rescue, the risk of making major changes is often less than the risk of standing pat. Usually, though, it's wise to consider first how much rope you have.

How clearly has God spoken?

The last question I ask before climbing out on a limb is, "How clearly has God spoken?"

The clearer God's direction, the greater the risk I'm willing to take. Like Abraham, mounting his donkey to go sacrifice his son Isaac, or Peter, stepping out on the water to go to Jesus, I want to obey when the Lord speaks clearly, no matter the risk.

The hard part is deciphering whether God has spoken clearly or I've merely baptized my ideas and desires. Sometimes it's hard to tell. That's why I use all the questions we've been looking at. I believe they go a long way in determining God's will for our church. But on top of those questions, I want to be open to a clear word from the Lord.

Sometimes God's leading is so clear, it needs to be followed, regardless of how it matches up with anybody's criteria. One of the best decisions I've ever made (and one of the greatest risks I've ever taken) flew in the face of all my risk questions.

At the time, we were looking to hire our first full-time associate. I wanted the person to preach about 20 percent of our Sunday morning services.

The person I presented to our elder board was a member of our church, in fact, one of the elders. He was also a close friend. He was a godly man, had a Bible degree from a respected Christian college, and had taught a number of home Bible studies over the years.

So far so good. But he'd also just been fired from his post as a Bible teacher and administrator at a local Christian school. He had no seminary education, and he'd never preached a sermon in his life. To top it off, the one time I'd heard him teach a Bible study, it was boring.

On the surface, he was not the most qualified person for the position, and he would enter it with some considerable liabilities. A number of the elders resisted the idea of hiring him. But one night, as I was driving home from a meeting that concerned this decision, I felt God clearly tell me we were to hire him. The message didn't come in an audible voice, but it might as well have: I felt a powerful and deep sense of conviction that this was the man for our church. I couldn't explain it, nor could I explain it away.

When I shared my experience with the elders, they graciously trusted me and acted in faith, and he was hired.

Today, all in our church agree that Mike has been one of God's greatest gifts to our ministry. Along with providing outstanding leadership to a thriving home fellowship ministry, he's become an excellent preacher. He now preaches over 30 percent of the time, and on most of those occasions, I'm in the audience, not on the road.

Risk taking is not an option if we want to be effective in ministry. But it's vital that those risks be prudent. By asking these five questions, I've found it's possible to take risks without risking too much in the process.

17

Getting the Information You Need

*If a pastor wants to nudge people toward changes in their
opinions, I suggest the bottom-up theory. There's tremendous
power to sustain the church if you start with a good nucleus and
move out through groups.*

—George Gallup, Jr.

I majored in religion at Princeton University and intended to go
into the Episcopal clergy. Toward that end I worked one summer
in a church in Galveston, Texas. It was a black church with a
white rector for the first time in nearly one hundred years. My
job was to help him run the summer Bible school, the baseball
team, and similar activities.

It was a great experience. Indeed if I were yet to go into the
ministry—and I sometimes still long for it—I would want to
serve in such a setting. The rector I worked with was instrumen-
tal in breaking down racial barriers in the church.

While weighing the choice of ministry or survey research (my
father's field), I realized that research gave me much of what I
was looking for in ministry: a way to help people. It could give
voice to the voiceless and help churches of all denominations
reach people better.

Some people say religion is a private, internal matter that can't
or shouldn't be scrutinized by research. I disagree, and I conduct
research into religion for three reasons.

One is sociological: The spiritual or religious element in
American life is a key determinant in our behavior—in some
respects more so than education, political affiliation, or age. If
you want to understand society, you need to understand the
religious dynamic.

Second is a practical reason: If ministers want to minister to people, they need to know what the challenges are, what they have to do. Surveys can help them focus their efforts.

Third is the religious reason. If there is a God looking over us, and I believe there is, then to bring us closer to God, we should do everything possible to examine the relationship between God and humankind.

Surveys show pastors and leaders the church's levels of belief, knowledge, and practice, which can help pastors deepen beliefs, raise the level of practice and make it more meaningful, and reach new people.

The shape of American spirituality

Polls reveal at least one thing clearly about Americans' spiritual life: spiritual experiences are very common.

In one survey we found that about 40 percent of Americans have had an unusual, life-changing experience. That brings up questions: What are the common elements of these experiences? What brought them about? How are they changing lives?

Often, emphasis in the church has been on "the day I found Christ." I like to look at the day after—what do you do with this experience?

The early evidence indicates that lives are being changed by these experiences in a more ethical direction. Or for these people, life has more meaning. They are less fearful of death or more eager to reach out to others.

Thus it becomes important to examine this experience and determine how it can be encouraged—not in an artificial way but naturally, in settings that will allow these spiritual experiences to happen.

The polls have surprised me in several ways. I was surprised by the proportion who believe in a living Christ. I thought people would be thinking of Jesus Christ more in a historical perspective, but 64 percent express certainty that Christ rose from the dead and is a living presence. As a Christian, I find this very encouraging.

I'm amazed, however, at the low level of Bible knowledge. It's shocking to see that in 1987 only 42 percent knew that Jesus was the one who delivered the Sermon on the Mount.

I'd have to say that people's stated opinions don't always translate into behavior, since religion does not appear to be creating a more loving society. Something is wrong with the way religion is being practiced. It doesn't seem to be working in the broad sense.

In a survey we did for the Christian Broadcasting Network (CBN) called "Twenty-four Hours in the Spiritual Life of Americans," we concluded that much of religion, unfortunately, is superficial—"feel-goodism." Prayer becomes mostly petition, and the Bible is not approached in a meaningful way. People want the fruits of faith but not the obligations. They're not willing to take up the cross. As Anglican bishop Michael Marshall puts it, "People are following their own agenda and not Christ's."

For example, church attendance is not a reliable predictor of behavior. There's as much pilferage and dishonesty among the churched as among the unchurched. I'm afraid that applies pretty much across the board: religion per se is not really life changing. People cite it as important, for instance, in overcoming depression—but it doesn't have primacy in determining behavior.

For CBN we asked a series of questions on whether people rely more on human reason or on an outside power, such as God, for moral guidance and for planning their future. More opted for human reason than for God, although less so among evangelicals. That shows that whatever people say about their beliefs, when they get right down to it, they are not totally prepared to trust God.

Highly committed Christians

In my research I have tried to learn more about committed Christians. That's where the exciting discoveries are, not with the churchgoers or the people who *say* religion is important. You have to go deeper.

We use a list of ten questions that deeply committed people of all denominations would agree to—the divinity of Christ, believing one's faith should grow, trying to put faith into action on behalf of others. These are the givens, the basics. We have people respond to each of these on a four-point scale: agree strongly, agree somewhat, disagree somewhat, or disagree strongly. Taking all the people who "agree strongly" on the ten questions, we arrive at about 10 percent of the American population. On that basis we have labeled them the *highly spiritually committed.*

Then we looked at those people in terms of how often they volunteer, how happy they are, how tolerant they are, and so on. These highly committed people are much more concerned about the betterment of society. They're more tolerant of other people, more involved in charitable activities. And they're far, far happier than the rest.

These factors are especially interesting sociologically, since these people tend to be in what we call downscale or lower socioeconomic groups.

Downscale people typically are less involved in charitable activities because they have less time, less tolerant because their level of formal education is lower, and less happy for obvious reasons. These highly spiritually committed people, though, go against the grain for their socioeconomic group. They are a breed apart, the truly spiritually mature.

If the numbers of these people can be increased, they will have a disproportionately powerful impact on society.

With people like these, the church will change from the bottom up. It's not primarily going to be pronouncements, conferences, strategies from the top; it's going to be people on the grassroots level bonding together and inspiring the church. I think it will trickle up.

(On the whole, it may be both from the top down and from the bottom up. The most fervently committed persons are generally from the downscale groups, but the influence of these highly committed Christians moves back up into other groups.)

Changes

Since I've been conducting research, I've witnessed a number of major changes in the church. The fifties were a boom period. There was a lot of church building, religious book sales were going up, and church attendance and membership were higher than today. People were placing great importance on religion.

However, it's difficult to comment about commitment levels because only recently have we started to develop scales that measure deep commitment. On the whole, 1950 was far different from now in terms of surface indicators, but commitment is harder to gauge.

In terms of church involvement, there has been measurable change. Back in the late fifties, a much higher proportion of people said religion was very important in their lives—about eight out of ten. In the mid-eighties it was down to five or six in ten. The big drop came mostly in the mid-sixties to the mid-seventies.

Religious interest still seems to be growing. When we polled for CBN in 1987 on the question "Are you more interested in religious and spiritual matters than you were five years ago?" the majority said definitely yes. Bible studies and prayer-fellowship groups have grown. So increased interest is not necessarily seen in attendance or membership—that's been remarkably flat—but it is seen in other religious activity.

The highly publicized evangelical surge of the late seventies was a great surge of interest in and awareness of evangelicals. In terms of numbers, however, there hasn't been any great growth in the proportion of evangelicals as far as we can tell. But evangelicals have been more vocal, more active, more visible, giving the perception that there's been a huge surge in the movement.

Our sense that church life is significantly different now from what it was in the fifties is not just nostalgia. In the fifties the intensity of life was always present—the sorrow and human problems and all—but there's a whole new complex of issues now, such as the drug issue. The pastor is called on for a much more active role in dealing with problems like divorce or alcoholism or pornography or other sex-related problems like disease and unwanted pregnancies.

In addition, people's confidence in the church has changed during the latter part of this period. We started a regular measurement of confidence in religion in 1973. Nothing much changed in fourteen years, but then confidence started to turn down, and it has taken quite a slide since then.

I think part of it—and this is speculation—was the discomfort over the relationship between religion and politics. And then, of course, the trend downward was accelerated by the televangelism scandals of 1987. They gave a black eye to organized religion as a whole. Frankly, all the squabbling and the chastising of one another has not enhanced religion's image one bit. Maybe some of it has been necessary, but it doesn't sit well with the public. The damage may be only short-term, but I suspect it's going to be difficult to recover from fully.

The bottom-up theory

Futurists say change is coming about at an accelerated rate. Things that once took centuries to change now change in a matter of decades or years. Technology certainly seems to be exploding.

But public attitudes usually change much more slowly. Public opinion doesn't change quickly without profound developments or events. For example, the Tet Offensive rapidly turned public opinion against the Vietnam War. People felt the war was unwinnable after that.

If a pastor wants to nudge people toward changes in their opinions, I suggest the bottom-up theory. Certainly pastors are key players in bringing about change—they set the tone—but leadership can also come from people in cell groups who are praying and seeking God's will. Maybe it's naive to say this, but I think change can come quickly if pastors concentrate on getting groups together with good leaders. There's tremendous power to sustain the church if you start with a good nucleus and move out through groups.

Although attitudes normally change very slowly, some changes can be made rather quickly when the Holy Spirit is at work.

The ministry of polling

One way that local pastors can encourage accelerated change in their churches is to formally and informally poll the congregation, even every year, to find out what's happening. What are the priorities? Where do people see improvement made in the church? Is your outreach plan working? Things like these can be monitored.

I first realized that polling can be a ministry when I worked in the Galveston church. I thought, *These are remarkable people, but how do you give them a voice?* One way was through surveys. It's wonderful to give people a voice.

Through formal and informal surveys, people get to talk about their church, their way of life, their country. Giving them that chance says, "I care enough about you to want to know what you think and feel."

Often it will take a pastor years to take a read on the parish: What are people *doing* about their faith? Do they know how to pray? Does the Bible have any meaning for them? Do they share their faith? What do they believe about God?

Finding this information informally consumes time, and you still can't be sure of your conclusions. Maybe mine is too mechanistic an approach, but I want to know *exactly* where people are in these areas, so I would validate my informal reading of the congregation's pulse with a formal poll. Often the pastor is surrounded by active people who are the hard workers, and they may give the impression things are better than they are. Or they spend their time with particularly troubled people and assume things are worse than they are.

Of course, surveys have their limitations. To borrow from the political world, surveys are a good way to inform, but a leader is to *lead*, not follow public opinion. Still, a leader will want to listen carefully; a survey is the parishioners talking to their pas-

tor. A leader would be committing a great error not to be attentive to what people need and want.

Future peering

As I attempt to look into the future, I foresee a host of challenges for the church.

Sex-related issues—artificial insemination, abortion, premari-
tal and extramarital sex, homosexuality—will be enormously
important. The sexual revolution was so profound that I don't
think the pendulum will ever swing back all the way to the
Victorian frame of mind.

We will still need to talk a lot about abstinence. Our society's
emphasis has been that you should be totally free; if you restrict
yourself sexually, you might somehow harm your psyche. Because of this, it's important for churches to emphasize restraint.

Another issue, without question, is the moral dilemma surrounding gene splitting. Other problems are divorce, drug and
alcohol use, and child abuse. In some of these immediate problems, close to the church's door, we can step in and make a big
difference.

The continuing breakdown in ethics and morality worries me.
Materialism is one of our root problems in this country. We're an
addicted society—if not to drugs, then to overeating, to sex, to
money, to cars, to owning. There's far too much emphasis on
having rather than being.

Ironically, surveys show that people's hearts seem to be in the
right place. People say they put personal aspects of their lives
ahead of material aspects. They put the family ahead of possessions and getting ahead of the world, and that's encouraging. But
I think we're overwhelmed with the allurement of and attach-
ment to "the good things of life." The church has a big challenge
in fighting that continuing battle.

But I also see many encouraging trends.

One is the great respect for education. Whether they pursue it
or not, most people seem to put a high premium on education.

Another is our tradition of volunteerism. The proportion of

people involved in volunteerism is growing, and volunteerism is important to the stability of our society.

Third and the most important is the spiritual dimension of Americans. It is seen in volunteerism, much of which is religiously motivated. If somehow the importance of religion were to decline in this country, our country would be badly hurt.

The spiritual resilience of our country—it's still there even though culture seems to be winning out over religion in many ways—gives me hope. I think there are enough people spiritually on fire to bring about change.

My wife and I attended the International Conference for Itinerant Evangelists in Amsterdam, led by Billy Graham. To see those evangelists, ten thousand strong, from all over the globe, joining in praise to God was one of the most moving events in our lives. The courage and commitment of those people are remarkable. In fact we learned that three of the participants were martyred upon returning to their countries—just for having attended the conference.

Based on what I see in those who are highly committed, we have great reason to hope.

18

The Art of the Start

Ministry is an art that emerges from a mysterious alchemy of history, personality, timing and, above all, God's providence— large portions of God's providence.

—Douglas Rumford

During these first six to twelve months, the concrete is still "wet," an elder advised his pastor following the second church board meeting. "This is your chance to make your impression. Soon it will set and be too hard." It sounds like good advice. The new pastor may have an opportunity in the early months to make major changes never again possible.

Yet other wise counselors say, "Don't change anything the first year. Build credibility." Which advice does the newly arrived pastor follow?

As a new pastor I wondered, searching for answers. I decided to contact other pastors who had experienced the awkwardness and opportunities of that inaugural year.

The hare and the tortoise

The first thing I learned is that no one pattern fits every pastor and congregation. Consider these two examples.

Roger Thompson went to Trinity Baptist in Wheat Ridge, Colorado, a two-hundred-member church in decline. Within the first year, they rewrote the church constitution, simplified the administrative structure from fifteen standing committees to four, doubled the attendance, and hired staff. "How could you do all that?" I asked him.

"You have to understand the background," Roger explained. Roger already had been in Denver on the staff of Bear Valley Baptist Church for ten years. The Wheat Ridge church across town knew much about Bear Valley, its staff, and their philosophy of ministry. Their five-month courtship of Roger culminated in a nine-day candidating process. During those nine days, Roger met with every group in the church, discussed the issues, assessed their needs, and explained the style of his ministry.

At the end of the process, Roger sent a letter to the congregation. "I told them my observations: everyone recognized this was no longer the powerful, wealthy church it once had been, but great hope remained. If they wanted me to come, I asked them to be ready to let the leadership lead in the specific areas of constitutional change, structural revision, and the establishment of outside ministries." Then with candor, Roger concluded, "If this scares you, don't vote for me."

"I in no way wanted to manipulate them," he told me, "but I felt it essential to give them an immediate indication of our direction." The results speak for themselves.

On the other hand (you knew that was coming), many pastors and congregations better identify with Gary Fenton, pastor of Dawson Memorial Baptist Church in Birmingham, Alabama, who describes himself as an "evolutionist."

"I'm not talking about Genesis," he clarifies, "but about my sense that churches, especially larger ones, are used to handling change slowly. They desire an energetic, proactive pastor, but not a revolutionary."

Again, Gary's context is important. In one church he followed two thirty-year pastorates in which both pastors retired happy. "When I first met with the pastoral search committee," he said, "they told me they were eager for new direction, but they weren't motivated by anger and discontent. That's a real blessing."

As an evolutionist, the pastor knows things will change and works to channel the results of that process. "But," Gary says, "the pastor leads more than pushes. Any major changes take behind-the-scenes preparation. You don't just make pronounce-ments."

Gary's style is to introduce an idea and notice people's reac-tions. This helps him determine not only if an idea will be ac-cepted, but more important, the schedule for its consideration, refinement, communication, and adoption.

Gary applied this principle in suggesting a reorganization of the deacon board. "My initial suggestion to focus on individual ministries and not bring each decision to the entire board was met with a loud silence," he reports. So he stopped the process to provide an opportunity for dialogue with his board members. He told them he'd like them to visit the sick and call on the inac-tives, and they shared they felt it was important for them as a board to oversee all the ministries. He gave a little, they gave a little, and instead of the all-too-familiar pastor-versus-board sce-nario, they adopted Gary's primary proposals and preserved the board's priorities.

The board assented to viewing their responsibility as a minis-tering group, and Gary didn't insist on streamlining their ac-countability procedures. "I've learned the value of a short list of essentials in doctrine and administration," notes Gary. "This gives us the freedom to change without violating ourselves."

So there are times to move with haste and times to feel one's way cautiously. Yet no matter what the pace, what specific activi-ties lend themselves to the first year? What can one do immedi-ately?

Mirror yourself and your observations

Both Roger's and Gary's experiences highlight the necessity of intensive communication. A healthy relationship has a minimum of unexpressed expectations and hidden agendas. The courage of candor in the opening months removes many of the molehills that can grow into mountains.

One pastor told me he'd listed the mistakes he'd made in his previous church. "At the top of the list was the lack of honest communication," he said. "It wasn't that I deceived or lied, but so often I was too timid to express my real feelings."

Within my first six months at the church I pastored in Fresno, I observed some seeds of misunderstanding and hurt feelings that could have developed into conflict on our Session. My phone was ringing: "Doug, I just don't feel right about some of the proposals coming before the Session. We're moving too fast." And another phone call: "You know, we've got to resolve some of the issues and move forward, or we're going to stall."

So I called a meeting of the elders. We began with singing and prayer. Then I shared from my heart the dynamics I'd observed. "By our failure to process things in a more effective way, we're generating a great deal of anxiety for ourselves and for the congregation," I said. "We've got to begin to respect ourselves as elders and prize the calling to serve on this Session in faithfulness and openness."

I followed the model a school administrator gave me. "When you're aware of problems between people," said Charles Fowler, "one of the best things a leader can do is to hold up a mirror. Try to reflect what you see, so they can become aware of their interactions. This will often be a catalyst for change."

It worked for us. We voiced those unexpressed concerns generating anxiety. "I had no idea you were feeling these pressures, Doug," one elder said. And another said, "If you're being distracted, Doug, then we've got to make some changes." As the meeting continued, we took time to be more honest, to listen more carefully, and to apologize.

In reflecting on this approach, the greatest benefit for me is that having once "held up the mirror," it's not as difficult to do again. (I'd never say it's easy.) Many of the elders have alluded to that meeting as a turning point that brought us together.

In the early months, a pastor brings a unique objectivity that eventually will evaporate. The alert pastor who carefully observes and lovingly communicates will develop healthy, stimulating relationships and provide a valuable service to the congregation.

Establish your patterns

Early on, people are sizing up what they can expect from us. Every member has personal expectations of a pastor, but the list can change when people understand our style and rationale. So we need to reach agreement with the board about days off, study time, office hours, visitation, and so forth, and then inform the congregation through newsletter articles, bulletins, and comments at various gatherings.

While we set the precedent for our preferred pastoral style, we can't escape our most glaring need: to build relationships. And that will consume much of the first year, regardless how many other priorities we have.

Sometimes interpersonal opportunities catch us by surprise. I call these kairos moments. *Kairos* is the Greek word for qualitatively special time, moments when time takes on greater-than-ordinary meaning. Such times of crisis or celebration cannot be anticipated, but I want to recognize and respond to them. Several pastors said tragic funerals had the unexpected blessing of bonding them in a special way with the grieving families and congregation.

But most often, relationship building takes time and work. The pace of change, especially in the first year, is linked to how the people feel about their pastor, to the level of trust between pastor and people. Therefore, we must wrestle with the question of availability. In that precarious scheduling act, time—lots of it—must be allocated just to be with the new flock. I liken it to a front-loaded investment: a premium is paid at first, up front, because of the anticipated higher dividends.

Vic Pentz, pastor of First Presbyterian Church in Houston, Texas, said, "In the church I pastored in Yakima, Washington, I decided to put the people before programs, especially in the first year. This established a relational base for ministry."

One concrete way Vic did this was to invite the entire congregation into his home by parishes, their congregation's subgroupings for pastoral care. The church leaders provided refreshments and hosted in rotation, while Vic introduced his family and shared his personal history and hopes and dreams for the church.

"This was no small task for a congregation of fifteen hundred, but I was pleased with the results. We had 60 to 70 percent of the members attend."

Rich Hansen, pastor of First Presbyterian, Visalia, California, also emphasized the importance of availability, especially to the church officers. "We had two elders' retreats my first year. Before we went on the first retreat, I took every elder to lunch."

Does this generate false expectations of pastoral availability? Conventional wisdom says: Whatever you do the first year will be expected of you from then on. This intimidates many pastors, since time demands normally rise progressively each year.

"I think this anxiety is exaggerated," says Vic. "People appreciate the initial effort. They understand the fact that we cannot maintain that pace." This view was confirmed by most pastors I polled.

Honor the past

No doubt the capacity for present change is rooted in past experience. "We need to be aware," cautioned Vic, "that people may interpret change as a value judgment on all that has preceded. We can't come in and act as if this congregation's ministry is just beginning. When we celebrate and honestly affirm the church's history, people say, 'He loves our past; let's trust him with our future.'"

To practice what he preaches, Vic became an expert on the history of his new church. He read the board minutes and the annual reports. He used what he learned to illustrate points in his sermons.

"I want to recall the great experiences of the church," Vic said, "the way Israel recalled the Exodus. That reminds us that God is faithful and he can lead us again."

One pastor put a roll of newsprint on the walls around the fellowship hall. On it he drew a time line of the congregation's existence and encouraged members to fill in significant events in the life of the church. They scribbled the smallest to the greatest events. It became a tangible expression of God's goodness, which generated new enthusiasm to see God work again. It also communicated that the new pastor respected their history.

"Bless the past," said Gary Fenton, "especially when you follow a beloved pastor. Describe the past in victory." Freely celebrating the past helps free a new pastor from defensiveness about his or her predecessors. As one pastor noted, "When people tell me how things used to be, I try to listen for the value, not for a criticism of me."

Identify what you can do immediately

Some projects can be accomplished in the first year. David Peyton, pastor of Dixon (California) Neighborhood Church, came to a church that needed to be loved. "Churches have a sense of self-esteem, just like individuals," he says. "If a church is down, it cannot grow and change."

David's goals in the first year were to affirm the people and to take a more lighthearted approach to everything. "The ministry is serious business, but it's also joyful. We learned to have more fun together."

The most obvious thermostat is the worship service. One pastor said, "The goal for my first year was to reorient Sunday morning from a duty the people endured to an event they enjoyed."

Pastors take different approaches, though, to first-year preaching. Roger Thompson preached from Ezra and Nehemiah, with the theme of rebuilding the work of God. Vic Pentz preached through the gospel of John: "I wanted the congregation to consider Jesus and see him through my eyes."

Another pastor preached a series on the priorities of the church, touching on topics such as worship, study, fellowship, and service. This helped the church to understand his philosophy of ministry.

The Sunday order of service is one area where most pastors tread lightly. For many members, the conduct of the service is the most concrete expression of a congregation's identity and tradition. Changes can be interpreted as judgments against tradition. Teaching and patience seem to be the tools for change.

Beyond the worship service, the physical facilities communicate the tone of a congregation. When Roger Thompson was pastor of Trinity in Wheat Ridge, Colorado, the church decided to paint the front of the church building, transforming it from a rather dark, foreboding appearance to a clean, welcoming one.

David Peyton felt a church that wanted to grow needed a nursery that visiting parents would appreciate, yet the church's nursery had received little attention for years. "I asked the board for free rein to decorate it right. I wanted to show our visitors we weren't a church that just tries to get by, but one that goes first class." Although other factors contributed, it seems significant that the nursery with one to two children a year ago now handles more than a dozen babies and toddlers.

No guarantees

The more I sought advice, the more it became clear that there is no rigid formula for a successful first year. Good ideas—yes. Guarantees—no.

"There are dynamics you cannot know about before you start," observes Jim Dankhead, pastor of First Presbyterian Church of Opelika, Alabama. "I think of my yard. The soil looks beautiful on the surface. But when you start to till the ground, you don't get far before you hit some big rocks. It's often that way in a church. There's no way to see the problems before you begin, but you can guarantee they'll be there."

Ministry is an art that emerges from a mysterious alchemy of history, personality, timing and, above all, God's providence— large portions of God's providence. Every beginning involves risk, but so does not beginning. And God calls pastors and people to start, and start, and start again.

PART 6

Making Changes

19

The Insider's Guide to
Making Changes

It is vitally important for a minister to know about
his or her predecessors.

—HAROLD GLEN BROWN

The senior minister of a large church asserted that the most trying, heated conflict he had experienced in more than two decades as that church's pastor was about changing the light fixtures in the sanctuary.

That large, vital congregation was not known to be quarrelsome. It was comprised of people considerably above average in educational background, breadth of experience, and economic status who often relied on their outstanding staff and lay leadership in decision making. However, they would not allow changes in their traditional decor.

Pope, in his *Essay on Criticism*, wrote:

Be not the first by whom the new are tried.
Nor yet the last to lay the old aside.

In your church you will likely have those who seem determined to be the last to lay the old aside. On the other hand, there may be some who, although not avant-garde, are out front in their willingness to change when they feel change is for the better. The issue at which these two groups find themselves at odds may be no more crucial than moving a picture on the wall of the narthex or slightly altering the order of worship; yet such trivia may produce serious discord and strife and may even result in alienation and schism if left unchecked.

Be aware of difficult changes

To be sure, some changes are extremely difficult to bring about in almost any setting. Church leaders should be conscious of the magnitude and ramifications of such changes before attempting them, however essential and justified they may be.

Moving to another location. Many members will be attached to the old building and site, regardless of the rationale for moving. Memorials, stained-glass windows, and other objects about which people are particularly sentimental only compound the problem. Members sentimentally attached to an edifice have been known to stick with the building even though their own congregation had moved out and a congregation affiliated with a radically different denomination had occupied the old building.

Merging with another congregation. A merger is difficult to accomplish even if it involves two congregations of the same denomination; it is particularly intricate and exacting if congregations of different denominations are considering union. Mergers may involve radical changes in name, location, building, organizational structure, leadership, and program.

Starting a building program. Any building program by a congregation requires consummate management skill to avoid disruptive conflicts. The decision to build, the method of financing, the choice of the architect and the architecture, the letting of contracts, and the selection of furnishings and colors are just some of the decisions that may cause serious problems if not handled skillfully.

Redecorating or refurbishing the sanctuary. Redecorating an existing sanctuary may pose as many problems as building a new church. The acceptance of a change in the color of the wall may be trying enough, but the rearrangement of chancel furniture or changes in the pews can be traumatic for many. One church changed the color of the walls in spite of strenuous objections; later when they changed the walls back to the original color, the same people objected again. Such objectors may simply find it difficult to accept change in almost any form.

Displacing an entrenched volunteer. Removing from office a volunteer of long standing can be a perilous action. The worker may be a greeter, a Sunday school superintendent, or a Sunday school teacher. One dare not assume that a volunteer worker, particularly of long tenure, wants to be replaced, even if she or he volunteers to step aside.

Changing worship or Sunday school schedules. Any change in the Sunday morning schedule will prove disruptive for some. One proposed change may be advantageous for parents and disadvantageous for couples without children, or vice versa. Another proposed change may be attractive for those interested only in worship on Sunday morning. Some families may prefer Sunday school and worship scheduled simultaneously so that the parents can be in church while their children are in Sunday school, but others may find such a schedule objectionable because the parents want to attend Sunday school as well as worship, and they want their children to do both.

Revising the worship liturgy. People grow accustomed to an order of worship. One church in my city hasn't made a perceptible change in its liturgy for twenty-five years. Another congregation, seeking to "get with it" a few years ago, decided to overhaul its order of worship to achieve freshness and make it more appealing, but after a short time it went back to the old way because the congregation felt uncomfortable with the changes. Innovative happenings can make worship more exciting. Nevertheless, worshipers tend to feel more secure when surrounded by the familiar, and changes in liturgy are usually hard to bring about without unrest and strenuous opposition.

Replacing any items that have been given by particular families in the church. Items such as an organ, piano, cross, picture, Communion trays, or paraments are difficult to replace without destructive conflict if they have been donated by particular church members or families, even if replacement is badly needed. The donors, their families, and their friends are likely to oppose any change that would replace any article with which they are historically or emotionally identified.

The list could be almost endless, but the above changes are among those most difficult to make. I list them not to discourage you from seeking change if change is needed, but to emphasize how difficult such changes are to bring about. If you try, do it with your eyes wide open and with every skill you can command.

Here are several things you can do that might facilitate change:

Know the local tradition

Whenever a new minister is called to a pulpit, traditions are inevitably upset. Even if the new minister resolves to make no changes in the church for some time, members may sense the uprooting of tradition because the new leader differs from previous ministers. For this reason it is vitally important for a minister to know about his or her predecessors.

A minister may find out what style of leadership has been embraced and employed in the church. Did any predecessors have a personality cult, relying largely on charisma and charm? Were they guardians of traditions and preservers of the status quo? Were they autocratic, insistent on calling the signals and "running" the church? Did they involve staff and laypeople in the decision-making process?

Of course, a new minister can give too much attention to a church's history. One should not *evaluate* people on the basis of how they related to previous ministers. The vigorous opponents of one minister may be staunch supporters of another. The peripheral members of one administration may become a part of the church's nucleus under different leadership. One should never allow oneself to be victimized into inaction by old feuds, old scars, and old problems.

Because traditions are difficult to break without stubborn resistance and travail, ministers and laypersons are sometimes attracted to embryonic congregations in order to avoid the idolatry of sacred cows and the stifling words "We've never done it that way before." True, starting from scratch can more likely satisfy the itch of pioneer spirits to be daring and innovative. But even though churches with virtually no history are not as bound by the past as old ones, the new churches are far from entirely free from the restraints of tradition. Members can bring prejudices and traditions into the newly created fellowship. Some will want to do it the way it was done in their old home church, however inept that church may have been.

Evaluate the congregation

Make the church aware through an educational process that other churches do it differently (if this is the case) and that a change, therefore, would not be as radical as some might surmise. To accomplish this, one might survey other churches by means of a questionnaire. Or one might suggest that members visit other churches to see for themselves how well new approaches have worked.

The educational approach will not work in every instance. Sometimes the reluctance to change has such an emotional basis that members will not even be open to an educational process. Nevertheless, it can prove helpful in some circumstances or in concert with other strategies.

Change in stages

If possible, make the change slowly or on a temporary basis at first. For example, if a church has been accustomed to having business suits in the pulpit, and the new minister prefers to wear a robe, the minister is likely to provoke substantial opposition if he or she begins wearing a robe at each worship service. However, if the minister begins wearing a robe at weddings and funerals held in the church's chapel, and then wears it in the sanctuary only at the worship service on Higher Education Sunday, the changes may produce little opposition or controversy. The minister may be able to make the transition so gradually that the congregation is scarcely aware. Business firms under new management often use such a strategy. The old name of the firm gets smaller and smaller as time passes while the new name looms ever larger. The public may be scarcely aware that the change in ownership and name is being made until it is a *fait accompli*. By then the public may have thoroughly accepted the new name.

Cultivate the traditionalists

Be sure to give attention to those whose egos are wrapped up in the status quo or who are particularly resistant to change. If your church has an old organ that needs to be replaced, don't assume that the donation of a new organ by some generous family or group will cause all the faithful to rise and sing the doxology as one. Some may be offended, even if changing from a small electronic organ to a four-manual pipe organ. They would be offended because they gave some or all of the money that bought that old organ in honor of their late husband.

If someone in your church wants to give a large sum of money for a cross to be designed by an outstanding artist to replace a wooden cross made by a retired carpenter, don't assume that the congregation will welcome that change. The retired carpenter may be much beloved, and many may have grown accustomed to the simplicity and starkness of that wooden cross.

A thoughtful visit may cause those who would otherwise oppose a change to be cooperative and supportive because their feelings were considered and heard prior to a decision. At the least such a visit may prevent their vigorous opposition; it may even elicit their enthusiastic support by involving them in the process for change.

If those who are likely to object to a change are persuaded in advance of the vote to support it, who then will block or oppose the change?

A minister became convinced that additional educational space was essential to the continued growth of the church he was serving. He felt that the congregation would for the most part enthusiastically support the program. He could think of only two board members who would be likely to oppose the building project. He did not foresee their opposition as hard-line or intransigent, but he did believe that the immediate reaction of these two conservatives in board meeting, when the building committee made its report, would be, "I'm against it; we can't afford it."

The minister decided to call on the two men to brief them on developments to that point. The two viewed the plans with keen interest. When the board meeting was held to vote on the question of erecting additional educational space, these two men vied for the floor to make a motion to approve the building project.

The longer a church goes without making any changes in policy, program, facilities, accouterments, or tradition, the more difficult it is to make changes. It's like creasing a hat. When a hat is relatively new, it is easy to change the location of the crease, but after that crease has been in place for months, it is difficult to create a new one.

If you are in a church that has not been innovative, concentrate at first on changes that are least likely to provoke heated opposition. Don't make a change just for the change's sake, but recognize that the more you are able to change, the more you are likely to be able to change.

20

Nine Options in a Changing Neighborhood

Churches in changing neighborhoods must choose their destiny.
—DAVID TRUMBLE

Consider a church similar to mine—white and middle class—that has served the people of its community faithfully for years. Then gradually, almost without notice, members begin moving away, some only a few miles, others long distances.

People begin talking about the new black or Hispanic family who just moved in down the block. The new folks seem nice, but they are different. Members dutifully stop by and invite their new neighbors to church. But becoming close friends seems a mutually low priority.

Soon, membership and attendance dip. Members begin to worry excessively and, ironically, become less active at reaching out to the community. When a few of the new neighbors actually visit, some members feel threatened: "If too many of those people join this church, I'm leaving!" Then again, some members enthusiastically open their arms to the newcomers.

As more minorities move into the neighborhood, church leaders are torn between embracing them, and thus changing the nature of the church, and excluding them, and thus retaining the church's identity but placing the future of the church in jeopardy.

Yet, rarely do many newcomers join the church.

Soon the exodus of old-timers becomes a stream. The leaders then decide that the Bible calls them to welcome the new ethnics. Some members begin to argue, "This is our church, and we're going to keep it that way," while others respond, "Prejudice is a sin!" and "God invites everyone into his family." It's still clear, however, that any newcomers must accept the prevailing ministry style.

Hope for better days starts to sink under a flood of fears. When several new ethnic members finally do join the church, a block of established members makes an exodus. Finally, in near desperation, church leaders begin seeking answers to their complex problems. Alternatives come slowly, and each option bears difficulties.

Our church, located in south suburban Chicago, declined by more than 40 percent before the other leaders and I were able to sort our options. Nine alternatives emerged: (1) maintaining the status quo, (2) relocating, (3) developing a metropolitan-style ministry, (4) renting out facilities, (5) integrating, (6) undergoing transition, (7) merging with another church, (8) planting a new ethnic ministry, or (9) dissolving the church—dying.

As we looked at each of these options, we learned something about our church and its future.

Maintaining the status quo

Perhaps the most desirable alternative is to stay as we are. The church holds precious memories for members. David, a former elder, often talks about a teenage music group we had. "They were loud and sometimes off-key," he recalls, "but everybody loved it when those four boys got up to sing." They also remember church picnics, Bible classes, baptisms, weddings, funerals, and mortgage burnings. Certainly these kinds of memories are worth cherishing.

But what can the church realistically expect for its future? It seems apparent that membership and attendance will continue to decline and eventually lead to financial difficulties that dictate closure.

Paterson Christian Church in Paterson, New Jersey, followed this route for more than fifteen years while the Italian community changed to Hispanic. The church maintained its traditional fellowship but moved from a full-time pastorate to part-time. Later it depended on supply preachers sent from a Bible college.

At one point the parsonage was sold to meet church expenses. Maintenance was deferred, and the facilities fell into dangerous disrepair. Finally the eight remaining members closed the church. Assets reverted to a Bible college, which planted a church to serve the new ethnic community.

When the members' needs take priority over the needs of the local community, ministry gradually declines. Careful conservation of resources can enable a church to continue meeting the needs of remaining members for several years. But it can be frustrating to watch one's own church decline while believing in the desirability of growth.

While I preached on the Great Commission and the desperate needs of people outside the church, Hillcrest members quietly resisted outreach efforts. One year the leaders and I instituted a plan to contact every nearby home by phone and direct mail. I even raised the needed funds outside of regular offerings. But once the campaign started, general offerings dropped.

Four weeks into the ten-week program, the treasurer came into my office and declared, "If you don't stop this program, it will kill our church!" While angry and hurt, I couldn't ignore reality. People's words kept ringing in my ears: "We like our church just the way it is. Why do you have to change it?"

For some churches, patterns are so entrenched that no alternative to the status quo is pursued.

Relocating to greener pastures

Sometimes churches seek to maintain the institution by relocating to a neighborhood in which members now live. This approach emphasizes the church as the people of God rather than the building in which they gather.

Our church leaders, many of whom already had relocated, geographically charted the current membership and recent transfers. The emerging pattern revealed a mass exodus from our area. In 1984, 71 percent of our members lived within two miles of the church. In 1989, only 14 percent remained within the same radius.

In some churches, many of the relocated members cluster in a new location. The church purchases property there and constructs a new building. Often the new building isn't as large as the old one, but the church moves and attempts to sell its old building.

The move usually isn't easy, however. Two primary issues engender strong emotional resistance. First, some cannot separate the church family from the church building; it's a place that holds many memories. Second, those evangelistically inclined feel the church is unjustly abandoning lost souls in the old location.

East 38th Street Christian Church in Indianapolis realized its community had changed and only a handful of members remained locally. The church purchased property and constructed a new building. But when it was time to relocate, a block of frustrated members refused to attend at the new site. Attendance dropped by nearly 50 percent from the already thinned number. All together, the congregation dropped from a high of 2,500 to an attendance of 350 by the time of relocation.

Nonetheless, the heritage of the old church continues at the new location, and a new opportunity for growth has been secured.

As attractive as this option may be for many suburban and urban churches, two conditions must exist for it to become viable: (1) the church must have the financial resources to invest in new property and construction, and (2) a significant portion of the members must live within the target community.

We found that if our congregation moved in any one direction, we would lose nearly three-fourths of our members. The thought of abandoning these loved ones was unbearable.

Thus, relocating entails unique costs, in money and in members who feel left behind. Still, relocation remains the best option for many churches.

Developing a metropolitan style

Many churches focus on the worship service for their corporate identity, and smaller groupings such as Sunday school remain secondary points of contact. Paul Cho of Seoul, Korea, takes a different approach. His congregation derives its primary identity from its cell groups and places secondary emphasis on the worship services. Each neighborhood, each corporate office, each high-rise apartment building, each place where people meet together, offers opportunity for small fellowship cells.

A church in a changing community may want to reorganize its ministry along these lines. While the worship service remains important, primary identity is shifted to the Bible-study groups located where people live. The people drive to the church building on Sundays for a rousing celebration with dozens of other subgroups. A church then can draw from a wide geographic area while maintaining its original location.

Boston Church of Christ had declined severely when it decided to try this strategy. It called a new minister trained in this style, and the church reorganized. At first only two or three groups could be formed, but gradually more were created. Today the celebration service runs in the thousands and the church enjoys fellowship with member groups from all over the Boston area.

Success for the cell-group approach hinges on developing an effective system of accountability. Personal discipling, group allegiance and activity, and loyalty to the mother church need to be balanced.

Many members involved in our church's Bible groups no longer felt it necessary to attend worship. One woman, after joining a women's group, started missing worship regularly. The pattern was gradual but unmistakable. When I inquired about her absence, she replied, "My ladies' group is my church."

In addition, although our leaders favored Bible studies, not all liked personal accountability. One elder declared, "No one can stand between me and God! If this is the kind of church you want, I'll leave."

In a small group, one man said, "I don't care what the Bible says. I'll do what I darn well please!" Fearful of such incidents recurring, several members refused to return.

New churches that start with this system often fare better than established churches attempting to reorganize, perhaps because the newly converted remain more teachable. Long-term church members usually have already defined their comfort zones spiritually and resist change. When I asked one faithful deacon why he didn't attend a Bible group, he said, "For thirty years I've come to church without needing a Bible group, and I don't need one now."

Those considering this option need to evaluate how open members are to the changes required, the potential leadership pool, and the overall ability of members to reach out while ministering to one another. Cho's model is one a church in a changing community might well use. But it is a highly demanding ministry for lay members.

Renting out facilities

Many churches use their buildings only a few hours a week, so renting out their office space, recreational areas, and meeting rooms can generate substantial revenue as well as touch the community.

One Mennonite church struggled to serve its changing community. Expenses kept growing while membership and attendance declined. One of the members asked for permission to move her child-care service into the church. Within a year the child-care center served more than one hundred children of the new ethnic families, at a monthly profit to the church of $500. Office space was leased to a lawyer for $200 a month. The church also owned two small houses, and their rental brought in another $400 monthly.

Ten years later, membership continues in the low fifties. The community's ethnicity has stabilized, and the church remains financially solvent. It even provides a reasonable salary for its full-time minister.

Renting out space may extend the life of a congregation, but there are costs.

1. Making full use of the facility increases expenses in utilities, general maintenance, and unexpected repair. And unexpected tax consequences need to be considered before renting to for-profit groups.

2. Renting requires releasing some control. Scheduling may become critical; conflicts add stress and pressure. Possessive members sometimes resent having to share their facility with outsiders.

3. A church may discover a lack of desirable candidates. My church has been approached by a Jehovah's Witnesses congregation, a rock music teen center, and the high school all-night party committee. We chose not to pursue these options.

Acceptable groups however might include community clubs, recreation groups, service groups, office-based businesses, or even a congregation of a different denomination.

We've enjoyed sharing our facility as a polling place—that is, most of us. One deacon suggested "the church is for worship, not politics." It's important to consider members' feelings about the facilities when considering the landlord option.

Integrating the church

Many voices herald integrating various ethnic groups into one congregation. Yet numerous church-growth experts, including Lyle Schaller, observe that in spite of all the talk and promotion, very few integrated churches exist.

Perhaps ethnic preferences partially explain this. For example, Blue Island Church began as an Anglo congregation in the 1950s. When the area began changing into a Hispanic community in the 1970s, the church attempted to assimilate its new neighbors. A small group of Hispanics joined the church, but generally the new residents preferred a more emotionally expressive service than Blue Island offered.

One woman, newly arrived from Mexico, visited the church with her son. She sat nervously through the service. At one point she started to raise her hands with the music, but her son quickly took her wrist and shook his head. Later a member asked, "How did you enjoy our service?"

The woman was quiet for a moment and then murmured, "No hablo ingles." The family didn't return.

Once a thriving group of three hundred, the church today gathers less than fifty to its Anglo-styled services. It considers itself integrated. The problem: to the church, integration means that newcomers will adopt established mores.

An exception is Westlane Christian Church in Indianapolis, which started in the 1960s with a specific commitment to integrate Anglos and blacks. Although its first ten years convulsed with great struggles, the church gradually developed a style of worship that included a quiet reverence and devotional climate as well as more expressive elements. Variety in music helped both groups feel good about the services. Today the church continues to offer a balanced, integrated environment.

Blending cultures and styles may offer great possibilities for churches in changing communities, but some members will feel threatened. When this option came up among the elders at Hillcrest, one immediately replied, "This will make the church go all black."

Many of us feared losing control. Perhaps part of that fear came from underlying prejudice.

Our elders prayed seriously about integrating our church and initially considered it God's design. They went to dynamic black churches and talked with their leaders. The result was polite but definite discouragement, although one pastor offered to take over our facilities!

The elders and I then discussed the possibilities with several member families. Some responded guardedly, but one stated clearly, "If you change our worship, we'll leave, and so will most of the others." Seeing that integration would precipitate the loss of members and the collapse of the church, we considered this option closed.

"Will it work?" remains the most crucial question for the integration option. Unless the current members feel great love and determination to "become all things to all people," the task is impossible.

Changing intentionally

I asked our director of women's ministry what future she saw for our church. She responded, "I see the church as either a struggling, declining white church or a growing black church."

Logically our church should replace the former members with the new residents. After all, the black believers need a place to worship, and initially no black churches were serving our area.

The task, however, is neither simple in concept nor easy in execution. The black immigrants resist attending an all-white church like ours. And resistant whites agonize over blacks eventually taking over their church.

How can a church established to serve one ethnic group change gradually to serve a new one? Six strategy steps prove helpful:

Hire ethnic leadership to evangelize the new people group.

Develop Bible-study groups in the homes of new residents.

Provide high visibility for ethnic members in church activities.

Develop cross-cultural ministries seeking to bridge gaps in relationships. These might include hosting musical, political, or social events and programs.

Build a worship style to attract the new families.

Finally, turn the church facilities over to leaders of the new ethnic group.

Of course, these are more easily listed than accomplished. We mailed many invitations and contacted personally more than one hundred new residents, inviting them to attend a six-week Bible study in the home of one of our black members. Three women showed up the first evening. The study went well, but before the group closed, one of the guests said, "I'm a deaconess at Daniel's Chapel (a large, city church) and I'd love to take you all to church with me on Sunday morning." The other two women, who'd heard of the well-known church, decided to attend with her.

The intentionally changing church must make the necessary adjustments to attract and meet the needs of the new ethnics in the neighborhood. Gradually, the original style, ministry, and members give way to the new wave of people serving and worshiping God.

Merging with another church

In many denominations, merging two or more congregations remains popular. Commonly two congregations agree to sell one facility (or sometimes both) and meet together as one church. Initially, attendance and membership appear large, and the new church receives a sizable capital gain from the sale of the vacated property. However, it doesn't solve all problems.

A congregation I'll call North Fletcher Church declined from the mid–four hundreds to slightly more than one hundred during the early 1970s as the neighborhood changed from middle-class white to lower-class black. Members gradually moved away, many to a new subdivision northeast of the former neighborhood. The pastor attempted to reach out to the new residents, but resistance within the church brought pressure on him to leave. Finally the economic, ethnic, and cultural differences of the community made the leaders realize, as one deacon put it, "We ain't gonna do any good for them no matter how hard we try."

A small sister congregation, also struggling financially, was located at the center of the new subdivision into which many North Fletcher members had moved. Leaders of the two churches decided to sell the old North Fletcher facilities and invest the funds in the merged church. The congregations then chose a new name—Franklin Circle Church—to help form a joint identity.

The old church building sold for $200,000, and half the money was set aside as a contingency fund. The other half financed building renovation and expansion at the newly united Franklin Circle Church, where worship services had become full. As one woman said, "It's great to see so many people praising God together every Sunday!" The old North Fletcher building continued to serve the neighborhood residents through another denomination.

However, many of the members from the old North Fletcher Church never joined Franklin Circle. "We just don't belong," they said. And several members of the "overrun" church in the subdivision felt dispossessed by the influx of outsiders. Gradually, attendance at Franklin Circle declined. Within the first year, attendance dipped to just slightly more than former attendance at the North Fletcher congregation. Giving also leveled off near the former single-congregation level. After five years Franklin Circle Church continues to serve its community, but at an attendance and membership level far below expected.

Our elders and I talked at length about Hillcrest merging with one or more sister churches. I even expressed willingness to step aside, if necessary, to effect a merger. Finally one elder said, "No matter which church we choose, most of our people won't go along. They're attached to this building."

Another elder asked, "What if they don't like us or we don't like them?" When we queried neighboring churches, we got a mixture of responses, further muddying the waters. The potential for financial stability appeared attractive, but the possibility of great conflicts remained.

First Christian Church in Harvey, Illinois, merged successfully with the United Christian Church in Country Club Hills after a three-year process. They set up a plan to sell one property, hold fellowship gatherings to forge closer ties, call a new pastor for the merged group (following the resignation of both present pastors), and form new boards. Now, the congregation functions as if it has always been one. As a former elder puts it, "We used to feel like a small family, but now we're just a bit larger family, and I like it."

To ensure success, great care must be taken to develop a workable framework for the long haul. Then, to help the members merge into a single body of believers, the leaders must teach, sell, counsel, and prod unity in every possible way.

Planting a new ethnic ministry

Tetsunao Yamamori with the Institute for American Church Growth describes a strategy of planting an ethnically specific fellowship in a church's facilities. This group is founded with its own leadership and worship style. The new fellowship understands that it is free to seek its own facilities and form a separate church as it grows.

The planted congregation can also remain autonomous but connected to the sponsoring church. Gerry Appleby, pastor of Bresee Nazarene Church in Pasadena, California, leads a church with Armenian, Arabic, Spanish, and Anglo congregations all using the original Anglo facilities. The growth of this heterogeneous ministry illustrates the powerful possibilities for churches in a changing community.

When Hillcrest Church began as an Anglo congregation in the early 1970s, we were adjacent to a largely Jewish neighborhood. Over the years, however, little outreach touched that neighborhood. Then a revolutionary concept emerged out of our extensive discussions about our neighborhood's transition: we decided we would hire ethnic leaders and assist them in planting not one but two ethnically specific fellowships.

We met with Asher Carl, a Jewish believer and evangelist, who was enthusiastic about leading our church-planting effort among local Jews. He formed a Bible study, and that group grew large enough to provide a nucleus for the new Beth Emeth Congregation.

We're currently working to launch an aggressive outreach to the emerging black community. We've called an evangelist to develop a new congregation using telemarketing, new-resident visitation, Bible studies, and rallies. This ministry will enjoy a contemporary, gospel-style worship service, and preaching will combine our denominational distinctives, biblical truths, and ethnic issues.

We plan for the three autonomous ethnic congregations to operate under the umbrella church. Each fellowship eventually will enjoy its own pastor, lay leaders, and outreach and nurture ministries.

Jointly, the churches will participate in mission projects, benevolent ministries, facility care, finances, and occasional gatherings. Each congregation will send delegates to serve on the joint governing board, which will coordinate activities, maintenance, joint ventures, basic doctrinal integrity, and other concerns.

I recently asked Avie, a charter member deeply committed to retaining an Anglo feel to our church, what he believed our purpose should be now. He answered, "Unless we serve the people who live here, we won't even have a church."

He's joined by Sue, who moved from Hazel Crest four years ago but still attends regularly and serves on our evangelism team. Her response to this new plan also grasps this fundamental issue: "If I don't have to change my worship, I'll do anything I can to reach people for Jesus."

Of course, unless we're willing to share our facility and the decision-making processes, we'll not be successful. Our job is to maintain ethnic identity and expression within the context of the unity of all believers. It will be difficult, but nobody said death—the last alternative—is any easier.

Death, the final option

In August 1989, I visited the remaining members of our troubled church. I wanted to better understand their concerns about our situation and their ideas for our future. At one home I listened to the pained worries one stalwart widow, a member of long-standing. "The only thing I don't want to see," she told me, "is our church closed down."

This most painful alternative is the one we most avoid. No one wants a church to die. Members who move away feel guilty, and those who remain and see the doors closed feel defeated, helpless, lost.

Theorists, however, argue that the death of a congregation is a part of the logical life cycle of a church. Birth always leads eventually to death in other spheres. But can there be a good death for a church?

Little is written about the demise of a church, partly because it's such a painful event. Yet an estimated six thousand churches close their doors each year in the United States. As many as three to four thousand of these were facing a changing community.

How do you close a church? Often a denominational executive or committee handles the disposition of properties. A date is set to hold a final worship service. The pastor is reassigned. Members are encouraged to seek membership in nearby churches. These parts are inevitable.

But beyond property disposition and other routine matters, we also should remember the hopes and dreams, memories and triumphs, now put to rest in a shuttered church. Great care needs to be taken to provide ample guidance and emotional and spiritual support for displaced members, many of whom often are elderly. These faithful believers need to be embraced by another caring fellowship nearby.

The hard questions and strong challenges racial change poses vary from community to community. The right choice for one church may well be unworkable for another. So each option must be thoroughly explored by any given congregation.

At Hillcrest Church, we invested a full arduous year of study, research, and consultation before we made our choice: a multicongregational structure to reach all kinds of people for Jesus. Through the power of Christ, we believe a long and fruitful ministry to many peoples is possible, and we're committed to making it happen.

Churches in changing neighborhoods must choose their destiny, as we've done. It's good to know death isn't the only option.

21

When Not to Build

When pastor and people properly see buildings as tools
for God's work, then it is time to build.

—Ray Bowman with Eddy Hall

When a young, growing church in suburban Philadelphia asked me to design them a thousand-seat sanctuary, that's exactly what I expected to do. They had called me for the usual reasons: their sanctuary was full and they were running out of Sunday school space. They reasoned it was time to build.

My wife, Sally, and I, working as a team, met with the church board for four hours on a Saturday morning to get all the information we could. During the next several days we scrutinized the church's facility usage, finances, and ministries. With additional input from the church growth committee, we developed a comprehensive plan to accommodate the church's growth.

The next Saturday, we presented our report to the board. Sally and I were no less surprised by our recommendation than they must have been. "What you really need to build," I announced, "is a storage building."

Had the church invited me a year earlier, I would have designed a thousand-seat sanctuary and cheered them on. "The building will bring more people to Christ," I'd likely have said. "Its beauty will draw you closer to God. People will notice that you're here and that you're an important part of the community."

During twenty-three years of designing church buildings, I had heard these statements from pastors and church boards. For twenty-three years, I'd seen no reason not to accept the assumption that bigger buildings translate into greater ministry.

But then Sally and I began church consulting. It was this new hat I was wearing—consultant rather than architect—that made the difference. As consultants, we had studied this fast-growing church through new eyes and had arrived at a startling conclusion: a major building program at that time would in all likelihood stop the church's growth and create financial bondage for years to come.

There is, we had been forced to see, a time *not* to build.

As we've consulted with scores of churches in the six years following our Philadelphia trip, we have identified factors that indicate whether construction will help or hinder a church in carrying out its mission. They fall into three categories.

Seek other alternatives

A church should not build when a better alternative is available.

As Sally and I studied the Philadelphia church, we agreed at once that it had a space problem. At its rate of growth, the congregation would soon outgrow the worship space. Between Sunday school and the Christian school, the educational space was full. The church had no room for additional staff offices. Construction appeared to be the obvious solution.

But it was also the wrong one.

"I found a room filled with missionary boxes," I told the board. "Those boxes don't need heat, lighting, windows, or carpeting." We recommended they store the boxes in a low-cost storage and maintenance building to free up that space for educational use.

"This barn on your property is a historic structure worth preserving," I also told them, "but you're not getting the best use out of it." Then we discussed how they could remodel it into a gymnasium and add a kitchen and educational space at half the cost of a comparable new structure.

"You can meet your worship needs for years to come," I went

on, "without the tremendous cost of a new sanctuary." The wall between the existing sanctuary and foyer could be removed to enlarge their worship area. A modest addition could provide a new, larger foyer, one that would make it practical to hold two Sunday morning services. That immediately doubled their worship seating capacity. The new addition could also house the office space they would soon need for their growing staff.

Finally, we suggested they replace the fixed pews with movable seating. For the comparatively low cost of new seating, the church could use the largest single space in the building for a wide range of activities, space that would otherwise lie useless for all but a few hours a week.

The church accepted the suggestions, completing their remodeling and modest construction projects within a couple of years. From 350 people at the time of our visit, the church has kept reaching the unchurched, and now, six years later, is running 850.

What would have happened had the church gone ahead with their building plans six years ago? The growth histories of other churches suggest the answer.

A burgeoning church launches a major building program to create space for more growth, taking on heavy debt. Though not by design, the building program becomes the congregation's focus. People give correspondingly less attention to the outreach ministries that have been producing growth. Church attendance peaks, drops slightly, and levels off. With their mind-set now changed from growth to maintenance, the church may continue for decades with no significant growth.

Whenever the church seeks creative alternatives to building prematurely, however, "people ministry" can continue uninterrupted, and growth continues. Later, when growth requires still more space, a well-planned building that will be fully utilized can be built without interfering with the work of the church.

Many churches call consultants because they believe they need a new building; few actually do. What most need is a way to use their existing buildings more effectively.

A church doesn't need more space until it is fully using the space it already has. Full utilization almost always means multipurpose use of space. This may call for such moderate-cost alternatives as remodeling, refurnishing, or making modest additions. In many cases, though, it requires no money; only a willingness to do things differently.

Minimize debt

A church should not build when building would increase the risk of financial bondage.

When the Philadelphia church commissioned our study, it was still indebted for the existing building. The congregation planned to borrow most of the money for their new one, but the loan payment would have been larger than their existing congregation could have met. Their ability to repay the loan depended on growth.

To build, the church would have been forced to redirect to the building fund much of the money then being used for needs within the body, local outreach, and missions. The congregation lacked the financial strength to maintain, much less expand, their present level of people ministry while constructing a building. Building, far from furthering the church's work, would have crippled its ministry.

We recommended that this congregation convert their finances to a provision plan, paying as God provided. This meant they would first pay off their existing mortgage. Then they would do the necessary remodeling and build their modest additions on a cash basis.

Operating on provision would mean setting aside regularly for future building needs so the congregation could pay cash or borrow substantially less for their next building. The many thousands of dollars saved on interest would be freed for the church's true work—ministering to people.

The church followed this plan, paying off their debt and expanding the facilities on a cash basis. They also began setting aside funds regularly so they could pay cash for an anticipated building program in five years.

Because they are not saddled with debt, they have been free to invest increasing amounts in ministry to people—their Christian school, an inner-city mission in a nearby neighborhood. By not building at the wrong time, the congregation enjoys a financial freedom that allows them to minister to more people than ever before.

Today, six years after our study, the right time to build has come. The church is building—and without pulling funds away from its essential work.

Scrutinize motivations

A church should not build if its reasons for building are wrong.

Richard Foster describes the first building program he was involved in: "It was actually a rather small project—an educational unit that was to double as a day-care center. We had all the right reasons for needing such a facility. We had gone through all the appropriate committees. We had the architect's drawings and had even launched a fund drive."

A congregational meeting was called to pray for God's guidance on the decision. "I went into the meeting thinking that probably we should build, and left certain that we should not," Foster writes. "The crucial turning point came when I saw the driving force behind my desiring that building to be my unarticulated feeling that a building program was the sign of a successful pastor. Theologically and philosophically, I did not believe that, but as we worshiped the Lord, the true condition of my heart was revealed. Eventually, we decided against building, a decision now validated by hindsight."

Years ago a church of about 150 people in Arkansas hired me as architect to design a new sanctuary. When I saw their building, I was puzzled. Though the building was older, its location was good and the congregation had never filled it.

Finally, I asked the pastor, "Why do you want a new building?"

"These people haven't done anything significant for twenty-five years," he answered. "This is a way to get them to do something significant. Second, the people aren't giving at anywhere near the level they could or should be. A building program will motivate them to give more. Third, a building program will unite the people behind a common goal."

I could understand his concerns, but this pastor was looking to a building program as a substitute for the spiritual work of the church. He was trying to do something that never works: solve nonbuilding problems with a building.

A congregation of about 175 on the West Coast brought us in as consultants, but only after they had put up the shell of their new building. Someone had offered the church a piece of land visible from the interstate at a bargain price. The church had jumped at it.

Confident that an attractive, highly visible building would stimulate growth, they were building a luxurious thousand-seat sanctuary. "We didn't want the inconvenience of building in phases," the pastor explained, "so we built it all at once. I believe that if we just have the faith and the vision, God will provide the money."

By the time we arrived, the church, for all practical purposes, was bankrupt. All we could do was commiserate with the congregation and sadly recommend they board up the unfinished shell, keep using their old building, and wait until future developments enabled them to complete their move.

In a bigger-is-better world, the church is not immune to the temptation to see church buildings as signs of success or statements to the community or substitutes for ministry. For the most part, buildings are tools. When a church wants to build for reasons short of providing a fitting and functional tool to facilitate ministry, it is time not to build.

When to build

But there is a time to build.

When a growing church is so fully utilizing its facilities that it can find no alternative to building that is less costly in time, energy, and money, it passes the need test.

When a church is living within the income God has provided and can build without dipping into funds needed for people ministry, the church passes the readiness test.

And having passed these tests, when pastor and people properly see buildings as tools for God's work, then it is time to build.

The church in Philadelphia has grown faster than we projected and so has had to launch its building program a year earlier than originally planned. Although the building will cost $1.1 million, the congregation is paying cash for it. And this building is not even a sanctuary; it's an education and fellowship center. Why? Because that's what the people need.

The design plans for their new thousand-seat worship space (now called a ministering center rather than a sanctuary) are ready and waiting. When the time is right, they will build it. But first, a couple of things need to happen. Sometime in the next year or two, the church will slip over from two worship services and Sunday schools to three. Then, over the next few years, probably all three hours will fill. Only then will they need more space. Until then, the church keeps setting aside funds for building.

Some day, probably five to seven years from now, Lord willing, the church will get out the design plans, dust them off, and hire a contractor.

Then, it will be time to build.

PART 7

Helping People Change

22

Granting Permission to Succeed

The measurement of success is simply the ratio of talents used to talents received.

—FRED SMITH

The minister had just returned from a missions trip.

"What did you accomplish?" I asked.

"Well, the most important thing I did with the small churches in difficult situations," he said, "was give them permission to succeed."

That was an interesting thought. He must have sensed they saw themselves as losers. Their ministry was supposed to be tough, and they couldn't expect more than meager results. He realized they needed to raise their sights, to see the opportunities for success.

His remark brought to mind a story about one of the gifted golfers on the LPGA tour. This woman, a Christian, possessed enormous talent but couldn't get in the win column. In frustration, she went to a Christian counselor who discovered a surprising thing: subconsciously she didn't think of Christians as winners. She had been raised in a strict home where she was taught that Christians are passive; they lose more comfortably than they win; they're volunteer martyrs. As a result, she wasn't free to win.

After the counseling, she quickly started winning. All the counselor did was give her permission to succeed.

Why we're afraid to succeed

There are several reasons Christians are afraid to succeed.

An incorrect concept of God. Last year while I was speaking at a seminary, a young man walked up and said, "God's got me right where he wants me."

I asked, "Where's that?"

"Broke."

"I have a son," I said, "and it would disturb me if my son were to say to some friend, 'My dad's got me right where he wants me —broke.' He and I would have to have a talk about his wrong concept of my feelings and desires for him."

An incorrect concept of how God works. Sometimes we hear, "Ask, and God will work a miracle." Normally, that isn't the way he works. God is the one who brought cause and effect into being, so usually right results come from right actions.

You have a right to expect pay when you work because "the worker deserves his wages" (Luke 10:7 NIV). In the same way, you have a right to expect results when you diligently and intelligently use the talent he's given you.

Many years ago in Palm Springs, a businessman asked if he could talk with me about a problem in his business. We met at six the next morning, and from the figures, I saw quickly that I was either missing his problem or looking at a most successful business. So I asked, "Am I getting the right picture? Is this as successful as it looks?"

He said, "It is." I stopped talking for a minute to try to intuit what he might see as a problem because it certainly didn't show in the figures. On a hunch I asked, "What's your religious background?"

"The Plain People," he said, naming one of the Mennonite or Amish groups.

"You're having trouble with success, aren't you?" I asked. "You're feeling guilty."

He nodded. We closed the books and talked no more about the business but about his concept of God, and how the loving heavenly Father would be happy for him to succeed—in the right way, with the right motive, while sharing his success.

A hesitancy to accept plaudits for abilities. Before speaking at a meeting of one of the very strict denominations, I was preceded by a young woman who sang beautifully. Afterward I said, "You have a lovely voice."

She hung her head and said, "Don't give me the glory. Give the glory to the Lord."

I said, "My dear, I didn't make a theological statement. I simply gave you a compliment from somebody who tried to sing and was not able to, and yet who recognizes that you can. Since I believe you have nothing except what you've received, any comments I make after that are within the scope of giving God glory."

I remembered a much healthier response from a charming woman I'd met years before. After having dinner with her and her husband, I said to her, "I believe you are one of the most gracious people I have ever met."

She smiled and said, "Thank you for noticing, Fred. I've dedicated it to Christ."

She didn't deny her graciousness; she confirmed it. Oswald Chambers said that worship is when you give your best to God. This was her best, and so she gave it to God as worship.

The issue, at its heart, is *accepting a "worm theology."* Scripture makes many statements about our human condition, both complimentary and critical. The problem is that we are quick to accept the negative. We have a harder time accepting the positive, that God made man only "a little lower than the heavenly beings and crowned him with glory and honor" (Ps. 8:5 NIV). Those who are most comfortable losing readily picture themselves not as children of a great God, but as worms. Now, compared to God, we are worms, but that's not the way *he* sees us. He made us from the dust but didn't intend for us to live there.

As Christian leaders, we have the good news that breaks this psychological barrier and gives our people the freedom to enjoy success achieved with integrity.

What is success?

Before we go any further, let's define *success*. Many people have the wrong understanding of it.

For Christians, success can never be measured by money. When people say to me, "That man's worth ten million dollars," that tells me he's wealthy, but it doesn't prove he's successful. In some cases, it could mean the opposite. For instance, if Mother Teresa, whom I consider a tremendous success, confessed she was hoarding a million dollars, I'd think she was a hypocrite. Money would prove her a fraud, not a success.

Second, success can never be measured by numbers—regardless of what the numbers are. Some churches gauge success by the attendance or budget numbers. Some pastors measure their success by the number of "preacher boys" they have sent to the seminary from their congregation. If the statistic I've heard is true—that 40 percent of seminarians are there because they're trying to find the will of God—I have to believe many of these students have been misdirected by people who were measuring success by a number.

The measurement of success is simply the ratio of talents used to talents received. What you are doing with what you've got, plus who you are becoming. Are you a growing, maturing Christian? Whether you work in business, or in Christian work, or as a day laborer, professional, or academic, if you are a maturing Christian, using a large percentage of your talents, you are successful. Be glad.

Some of us tend to think, *I could have been a success, but I never had the opportunity* or *I wasn't born into the right family* or *I didn't have the money to go to the best school.* But when we measure success by the extent we're using what we've received, it eliminates that frustration. I've known many Christians who had limited opportunities, but they made the most of what they had. They had a great sense of responsibility, a love for God and other people, and out of that flowed a tremendous use of talents.

When I worked for Genesco, I promoted a young man from operating a machine into a lower-managerial role because we wanted to test his capability. Shortly afterward, he was killed in an automobile accident near Lewisburg, Tennessee. Maxey Jarman, Genesco's chairman, wanted to go to the funeral. We drove seventy-five miles to the funeral, and on the way back Maxey said, "I believe Bill was one of the most successful men we have had in the company."

I said, "He was an hourly employee and was just promoted to a small managerial job. Why would you say that?"

"Because he used what he had."

The person doing the most with what he's got is truly successful. Not the one who becomes the richest or most famous, but the one who has the closest ratio of talents received to talents used.

An unsuccessful person, on the other hand, is one who didn't use the chances he or she had. He could have developed himself, he could have made a contribution to life, he could have become a mature Christian, but he didn't. It is my challenge as a leader to keep this from happening, and giving permission to succeed is a good starting place. The Bible says that to whom much has been given, much will be required.

Encourage your people to measure success only by potential, not by what others are doing. One of the prominent Realtors in Dallas came to me a few years ago after the bottom fell out of the housing market. He was very concerned, almost depressed, because business was down 40 percent, and he didn't know how to get it up. We talked a little, and then I said to him, "Why don't you change your goals this year?"

"What do you mean?"

"Why not measure success by *survival* this year? With the current condition of the real estate market in Dallas, anyone who survives is a success."

I saw him two or three months later, and he was smiling. "Fred," he said, "I'm going to survive, and for me right now, that's success. I can't beat last year, but I can beat failure."

Another thing we often forget: being a success doesn't mean everything in our lives has turned out well. We can be successful in coming back from a fall. I have a friend who got into an immoral situation. He genuinely repented and accepted God's forgiveness and moved forward. To me, that was success.

I know a woman who fought severe depression—and won. That's true success. I've seen women lose their husbands to an affair, yet come through that great rejection and reestablish their lives. They have demonstrated the power of God in a human life. They've become successes. Our privilege as leaders is to commend their success!

Who can give permission to succeed?

Only a person in authority can give convincing permission. Anybody can encourage. But permission to succeed comes only from an authority figure—parent, boss, pastor. Permission from such a person dispels doubt and gives assurance this is right.

When my pastor friend went on that missions trip and gave those struggling churches permission to succeed, he was able to do that. As the pastor of a healthy, growing church, he is seen by the people as an authority because he came from where they were. Had he been, say, one of the members of those churches, he could have given encouragement, but not the same permission to succeed.

Many years ago I spoke at Baylor University and met a young woman with unusual character and ability. Toward the end of my stay, I told her, "I believe you could do almost anything you want to do."

She became a missionary. Thirty years later, she called me. "I'm back in the States," she said, "and I want you to know that when the going really got rough in Japan, I would say to myself, *I know there's one big-time businessman back in the States who believes in me.* That sustained me many times—just that one person believing."

All I'd said was one simple sentence, but it was more than encouragement because she saw me as vice president of a large corporation, and so to her I had authority. She accepted the permission to succeed.

Experiences like this have taught me it's not only a leader's privilege, but also a responsibility, to give permission to succeed.

According to management experts, a manager's number one

responsibility is to establish a vision for the company. I think this is also true with a church. And one of the ways you establish the vision is to give people a belief in what they can do.

What's the alternative? If you don't give people permission to succeed, you draw artificial boundaries for them. You say, "You can't go beyond this fence." PBS aired a documentary on children who fail. A great many of these children, studies have found, are verbally abused by their parents: "I hate you. I wish I'd never had you. You'll never amount to anything. You'll never accomplish anything." Yes, a tiny percentage of those people will, in rebellion against that, accomplish a great deal; we hear about those. But we won't hear about the thousands who live mediocre, even criminal lives. A prophecy of failure is wrong. Permission to succeed is right.

As a leader I have great opportunity—the great responsibility —to say, "You have permission to succeed, provided you succeed correctly, by using the right principles in the right way in the right time." In fact, this is one of the thrills of being a leader: to recognize in other people talents they don't know they have and then give them permission to enjoy their success.

What giving permission to succeed is not

Often when I bring up this topic, someone will say, "But, Fred, that sounds like prosperity theology or possibility thinking." It's not. There's nothing I oppose more than prosperity theology. I think it's disrespectful to our intelligence and to our God.

Prosperity theology says, in effect, that because God likes me, he makes me rich. Not at all. The Bible says God gives opportunities and the ability to be faithful. He doesn't work some formula for favorites. Personal success is possible, not divinely guaranteed. There is no automatic prospering here, no putting God under obligation.

But the key difference is in the definition of *prosper*. It doesn't mean you'll be better known than other people or richer. The biblical definition is that you'll mature as a Christian and use a greater portion of the talents God has given you. That is true prosperity, true success.

And possibility thinking? I believe in keeping a positive attitude and seeing possibilities, if realistic. I do not accept thinking that says I can do anything I think I can do. That is unreal. And if something is unreal, it is not divine because if there is anything God is, it's real.

When I gave that Baylor student permission to succeed, I wasn't telling her, "The whole world is yours; you can do whatever you think you can do." I was simply saying that, based on my hours of observation and interaction, I believed she had the ability to excel at her chosen profession. It was a positive statement but rooted in a realistic assessment of her abilities.

A second problem with overly optimistic thinking is that it can be rooted in egotism or in greed or in exploitation. I believe positive thinking, to be Christian, must be rooted in gratitude to God. You can think positively, for example, about your possibilities on Wall Street. But if your success is built on insider trading, you cannot thank God for that.

Four ways to give permission

Permission to succeed is miles from these two unrealistic views. I'd like to offer four ways to give your people the genuine article.

1. Verbalize it. For some reason, many people find it difficult to tell people they have permission to succeed. It's easier to do the opposite, to talk in a negative way. Quite often I hear people say to their organizations, "Now, we can't expect to do miracles here. I mean, we're just a little organization; we're just a band of believers."

But if the people in our organizations are going to reach their God-granted potential, it will usually require leaders saying, "You've got it. God hasn't fenced you in capriciously. The psychological barriers you might have of how important you are or where your family comes from or your education—they'll limit you only if you let them. You have the permission, my permission, to go as far as you can go."

It doesn't need to be said in a hyped-up way. A simple, matter-of-fact statement is powerful enough. When I was three years old, I fell on a Mason jar and badly cut my right hand. The cut became infected. The infection grew worse, and soon there was a question whether I'd lose the hand.

My parents took me to a surgeon in the city, who operated. My father was deeply concerned, but the surgeon told him, "This boy has something in him that he can thrive even without that hand." As it turned out, my hand was saved, though I did lose major function in it. My father told me that story when I was five or six years old, and only two or three times after. He never told it in an inspirational way. He just repeated what the doctor said before the operation. But I felt that this was a form of permission. The surgeon, an authority, was saying, "He is a survivor." That long-ago statement still motivates me.

2. Reinforce it constantly. One of the most powerful reinforcements is telling stories of people who are successful.

I once walked into a plant to meet the president for lunch. He was a pragmatic, engineer type, a noninspirational sort. I knew it was uncharacteristic of him to verbalize his belief in people, and I wondered, *How does he give his people the permission to succeed?*

Then I saw on the wall a chart that showed the company's production and sales for the past five years. The figures started at $200,000 and this year reached $5,000,000. With that chart, he's saying, "Every year we have grown. Every year we've been more successful. Next year we expect to be more successful." He's giving the permission.

Recognizing individuals who have succeeded is another way we confirm the permission to succeed. If you see someone perform in an exemplary way, call attention to it. Some people are willing for you to accomplish only if you don't feel successful. But to be honest, we have to give people the right to enjoy the feeling of success.

Consider the apostle Paul. He said, "There's a crown waiting for me," and in another place, "Only the winner gets the crown." Paul is saying, "I plan to succeed! I'm a winner!" You catch the flavor: "I have paid the price of being successful, and I'm also feeling the joy of being successful."

As I recognize success, I try to stretch people's horizons. I might say, "That was terrific!" but I don't stop there. Tomorrow I might return, repeat the compliment, and say, "Last year, would you have believed you could do that? You may be surprised at what you can accomplish next year."

3. Implement it. Then we need to give people opportunities. In Worcester, Massachusetts, I created a task force of managers but put on it an hourly employee who hadn't been recognized. That assignment gave him the opportunity to run in a different league, and he sprinted! I knew he would; he had the talent and simply needed the opportunity.

One year we all watched the same thing happen with the NFL replacement teams. When the professionals went on strike, hundreds of unknown football players, who had been scrimmaging on YMCA fields, got the opportunity to be professionals. In that environment, several succeeded. Even when the strike ended, certain players were kept because the owners and coaches said, "Look at that Zendejas kick! That ol' boy's got it; we just didn't recognize it before."

That's what I mean by implementing it—you give people opportunities to succeed.

4. Demand it. You don't start by saying, "It's your responsibility to be successful," because you'll overwhelm a person. You start by saying, "You have the permission to be successful." That fuels his desire, and if he has the drive and desire to succeed, he will.

But after the person has become successful, you switch from giving permission to making it a responsibility. You say, "God's given you something to develop. It's your responsibility to take that and do as much as you can with it."

Toscanini, for example, demanded near perfection from his musicians. Robert Merrill told once about singing under Toscanini's direction and repeatedly missing the syncopation in a particular short passage. Toscanini kept bringing him back to it. Finally he walked over and with his baton tapped the beat lightly on Merrill's head. Ever after, Merrill said, whenever he sang that phrase, he could feel Toscanini's baton on his head. Toscanini demanded greatness, and he produced it.

Demanding success may sound harsh, but when done in the right way, and while there are still time and opportunities for the person, it's one of the most caring things we can do. Let me be more specific about what it means to demand success.

First, demanding success means keeping people off dead-end streets. One young woman in our office was not a particularly capable clerk because she was enthralled with the idea of becoming an actress, and finally she went to New York to make it big. There someone was kind enough to say to her, "You are not an actress." She decided to get her MBA instead. She failed in the theater but now has become vice president of one of the large international investment companies. She is a genius in finance, but she needed somebody to say that, for her, acting was a dead end.

Second, demanding success means keeping people from irresponsibility. I once had breakfast with the chairman of the board of a corporation. He said, "Fred, the thing I need most is the accountability of Christian friends. I want someone to ask me, 'Are you really being a good chairman of the board? Are you working as hard as you did twenty years ago? Are you arrogant?' " We all need leaders and friends who will see irresponsibility and point it out. How else can we be successful?

Third, demanding success means keeping people focused on results, not effort. A mediocre leader thanks people for effort without realizing that unsuccessful effort is a great waste. The time to thank people is when they've produced results. I had a boss once who taught this to me in a dramatic way. I didn't have good results to show for a certain project, so I was telling about how hard I'd worked on it. Finally, he said, "Fred, show me the baby; don't tell me about the labor pains." He was right: what we're here for is the baby. And he helped me become more successful by teaching me to focus on results.

I find it difficult as a leader to give permission that I've not received myself. Sometimes people say, "But, Fred, I didn't receive a lot of permission to succeed in my family or at seminary or in my first church."

To them I say, "Keep opening the vista. If you've been able to see a little farther than where you are, it may be possible for you to see a great deal farther than where you are. Yes, everyone has a limit, but most of us and our organizations are so far from that limit that we really don't have to worry about that. It will be a long time before we bump against the limit."

In many instances, that seems to give them permission. And those who feel they have received permission to succeed are always best equipped to give it.

23

Harnessing People Power

Running over people may produce short gains, but you'll pay the price down the road.

—DONALD SEIBERT

Pastoring a congregation is sometimes like refereeing a set of Golden Gloves matches. Fighting begins with the preliminary scraps: music committee versus choir, nursery workers versus Sunday school superintendent, Christian education board versus youth pastor. And then the championship bout: elders versus trustees.

You may not see any knockouts; few wild haymakers ever land solidly. But the infighting can be brutal. Participants can be sore for weeks.

Once I was involved in a church that had a strong commitment to foreign missions—a high-profile missions conference and large missions budget. A few years after I joined, the pastor was succeeded by another man who shared the commitment to missions but also felt that our church's involvement in local ministries was not what it should be.

So he tried to motivate us in the direction of local ministries, but his effort was completely misunderstood as a denunciation of foreign missions. Communication broke down.

I faced similar challenges when I served as chairman and chief executive officer of J. C. Penney. It is often said, "You can't run a church like a business," and in many ways that's true. Some business practices should *not* be brought into the church. But sound management and leadership can often overcome misunderstanding. Here are a few principles that can help harness the gifts and abilities of people.

Foster communication

There are some similarities between the pastor of a church and the CEO of a corporation, but the two positions are not parallel. Like the CEO of a corporation, pastors have the obligation to articulate direction clearly—to educate the church on what they're trying to do and how they want to do it. At J. C. Penney, whenever our management team prepared to issue a statement, whether a press release or an internal memo, we asked ourselves two questions: (1) Is this easily understood? and (2) Can this be misunderstood?

These questions are quite different, and often our original statement failed the second test and needed to be completely rewritten.

We used a number of techniques to test the effectiveness of our communication: attitude surveys, informal visits by members of the senior management committee, discussions with people at different company levels. If you take time to ask questions, you find out quickly what your people understand and do not understand.

All this sounds rather basic, but communication skills are based on common sense. Often they're so simple you ignore them.

Be a manager and a leader

There's a distinction between *management* and *leadership*. Management is the process of assuring that the programs and objectives we have set are implemented through effective administration. Leadership, on the other hand, has to do with motivating people.

Both management and leadership are strategic skills.

Leadership. In this unique role, the pastor has to be the initiator of clearly defined, easily understood spiritual goals. I don't expect him to develop all the programs to accomplish these goals, but he has to initiate them.

Over the years, some of the pastors I have worked with have succeeded at this, but not all of them. In some places I was never sure not only of what I was expected to do in the church but of where the church was going in general.

Most leaders would benefit if they distributed three-by-five cards in the weekly bulletin and asked members to write down in twenty-five words or less their church's purpose. (Participants would want to know later how the survey came out, and if the results were not good, you might have to acknowledge publicly that the church is not together in its mission. But if you didn't reveal the results, people would be cool to later surveys.) An easier way might be to survey verbally a small sample of your most committed people.

If a pastor is not strong in motivating, he can enlist key people who have demonstrated over time they have influence with others. If you can identify these people and get them committed to your objectives, they can help sell your programs and motivate others to put them into effect.

Management. Every pastor needs to know what he has to work with before any work can get done. This means taking inventory of resources—noting where they're placed, and eliminating structural impediments. These are basic management tools.

The buck stops with the pastor, who must assume final responsibility for the way the church is administered. That's not to say every pastor is a good administrator. You have other functions to perform, and you'd probably like to spend more time on sermon preparation and counseling, for instance. But regardless, you have to be accountable for how the church is run. You can delegate administration, but you can't delegate accountability. The big danger in delegating administration—if you then walk away from it—is that the wrong administrator can gradually change the whole program of your church.

But that doesn't mean a pastor must supervise each ministry of the church. I feel I've been a more effective leader when others have actually done the work. And I want everyone to know who accomplished what. It's the same with pastors. The feeling that you can do the job better yourself makes delegation difficult. But delegation is a must in any organization.

Many pastors feel unnecessarily threatened by people in their congregations who have greater expertise in certain skills. I think it's a given that the pastor will not be the most skilled person in the church at everything. Otherwise he'd be leading the choir, singing the solos, and running the air conditioning. In my company, I can find someone who is better than I am at performing almost every function. Marketing, advertising, writing product specifications—you name it, someone can do it better.

But a symphony conductor is not usually the best French horn player, and he or she doesn't feel threatened. The conductor's role is to make the whole orchestra function to its potential. You should not feel threatened by an individual with greater administrative skills. Use him; help him realize his potential within the church.

Of course, you wouldn't want the best French horn player in the world if all he wanted to do was play solo. Participatory leadership may encourage some people to try to exert too much influence. But when a number of people participate in leadership and administration, *they* help deal with the would-be soloist. The responsibility doesn't rest entirely on *your* shoulders. Furthermore, in my church experience, most problems of this nature spring from deeper spiritual problems within the individual —not the result of management styles.

Shared goals

In business, tensions arise when the chief executive's objectives somehow differ from those of longstanding workers in the business. In the church, the same tensions arise when the senior pastor wants to do one thing, and some of the church pillars— Sunday school superintendent, chairman of the board of elders —want to do something else. But the tensions are further compounded by misunderstandings about where the church is really heading.

Let's suppose a pastor communicates to a church that God's purpose is for them to live holy lives and preach the gospel to the world. Based on that purpose, they decide on the specific goals of sending out x number of missionaries and building new Sunday school facilities. What should they do next?

First, as the pastor, I would want to know exactly how equipped I am to handle these ministry goals. I must find out how financially able the church is to meet these goals and whether we have the potential to raise the money. I ask specific things like, Is labor available in the church? Will we have to hire outside help?

Then I ask some more difficult questions: How many people are committed to these broad ministry objectives? Where is the support going to come from? If I don't have a lot of people behind me right off the bat, it would be foolish to go ahead with a building program. Instead, the first objective would be to spend a whole year doing nothing but gaining support and developing understanding for the programs within the church.

The point is, it's critical to know you and your people are together in your goals and objectives!

Finally, goals need to be kept simple and within reason. I've worked with several volunteer choirs, for example, and found that a group of amateur singers may not be able to do justice to some of Handel's music, but if you select material within their level of competence, they sound magnificent. It may take lots of time and effort, but you can gradually raise their level of competence. Perhaps in a few years, you'll be able to come back and have these people sing Handel.

Team planning

Conflict often arises in the local church because leaders overlook an important management principle: the need to agree not only on goals but on a plan.

In the churches I've attended, one of the biggest conflicts has been between lay stewardship leaders and lay spiritual leaders—typically the trustees versus the elders. Ideally, trustees raise and manage money and tangible resources; elders provide spiritual leadership. These two functions aren't mutually exclusive, but too often laypeople can't see how their goals and objectives have anything in common. It's a chronic problem.

Here's how we solved a similar problem at Penney's. We used to agree on our main objectives and then turn each division loose to plan: the retail division produced a plan; the buyers produced a plan; marketing produced a plan. Even though we were all working from the same objective, things didn't mesh. And when the results weren't productive, we had a lot of finger pointing as to whose plan failed.

A few years ago, we moved to a team management approach. We gathered the leaders from each division into a room and said, "Don't come out until you've produced one harmonious plan." Not only did we start to get good results, but the finger pointing stopped because each leader was coauthor of the plan.

I don't want to oversimplify, but is there any reason why the same principle can't work in the church? The elders and trustees, for instance, could put together leaders from both boards and produce one good plan. Of course, for the plan to work, *all* board members must fully understand the plan and be sold on it. Again, communication must prevent misunderstanding.

As is obvious by now, I believe in a democratic rather than autocratic leadership style. Running over people in any kind of situation, church or business, is not only questionable morally, but it's counterproductive. You may produce short gains that way, but you'll pay the price down the road in alienated and departed parishioners. True, many organizations prosper under an autocratic leader. But in those places, you'll also find a lot of unhappy people. When they find they just can't work in that kind of environment, they leave. You don't want that to happen in your church.

What's more, in large churches that have autocratic leaders, a significant part of the congregation becomes so dependent on this type of leader that when he steps down, he's almost impossible to replace. One of the principle responsibilities of a CEO is to assure his company that an appropriate successor is ready to step in if something happens. There can be no interruption of the company's growth. That is hard to pull off in companies led by an autocratic leader. In a sense, it is much better if my organization depends not on me as an individual but on my part in the long-range, goal-setting process. And when I leave, this process must go on.

Learning continuously

Fred Boyce surveyed 1,022 pastors in sixteen denominations about the frequency with which they encounter twelve kinds of management problems. They ranked them as follows:

1. Development of lay leaders.
2. Recruiting and motivating volunteers.
3. Motivating church members to accept needed changes.
4. Budgets for operations, buildings and equipment, cash flow, and appeals.
5. Maintenance of membership and financial records.
6. Planning and controlling effective use of my own time.
7. Fund-raising for the church.
8. Church property management—maintenance, repairs, insurance, taxes, or payments in lieu of taxes.
9. Construction of new facilities.
10. Employee relations—recruitment, supervision, compensation.
11. Purchasing of materials, supplies, and services.
12. Investment of church funds—long- and short-term.

Forty percent of the respondents indicated they had no prior education or experience for church-management problems. Eighty-seven percent thought that theological schools should offer a course in church management, preferably using the case-study method. Some commented that the courses and material now available are too general and/or theoretical. Other felt that most material is addressed to pastors of large churches.

If pastors sense they don't have a good understanding of management skills, they can still have a significant ministry. But they need to recognize that management does need to happen in their church. You can have a great sense of mission, but if you don't understand how to accomplish it, you've failed yourself and God. And just because you've never worked with management principles and tools doesn't mean you can't learn.

I believe a lot more pastors would surprise themselves by discovering what good administrators and managers they really are. A pastor could have the gift of administration and not even know it. We all know people who became good golfers past the age of fifty. They never knew they had the talent. My formal education was not in business administration, and I know other highly successful businesspeople who have degrees in music, English, and philosophy. Administrative skills were picked up along the way.

But we all desperately need to keep ourselves current in our fields. If a person feels weak in management, I suggest that he or she read a lot, listen a lot, and go to seminars tailored especially to the ministry.

In summary, I offer the following action list:

- Understand your own objectives, your own sense of mission and goals.
- Clearly articulate those objectives to your lay leaders, and try to get some feedback as to how well they understand them.
- Exercise patience, realizing that it will take time before you have enough of your parishioners behind you so you can turn objectives into working programs.
- Take an inventory of your personal resources and those available within your congregation.
- If you find you're lacking in personal resources and know-how, resolve to acquire management or leadership skills through continuing education.

24

High-Stakes Gamble

Before making a change, confronting a member, or launching a new program, the pastor needs to figure out if there are enough chips to lose and live.

—LEITH ANDERSON

Pastoring a church is like playing a game of poker (although I must admit I've never known a real poker-playing parson).

Like poker, pastoring is an exercise that combines skill and providence to sort out winners and losers, often with frighteningly high stakes.

Your initial stake

Just a desire to play and win never got anyone a seat at a poker table. A poker player needs chips to enter the game—a stake. When a new pastor is called to a church, a pile of chips is normally stacked up for use as the pastor chooses. They represent the good favor and support of the church people. They may be saved for a rainy day or risked in the first hand of play.

Many complex factors contribute to the number of invisible chips provided the new pastor. If the vote to call was 99 percent affirmative, it's usually good for ninety-nine chips. However, a squeaker vote of exactly 66 2/3 percent is seldom worth more than twenty-five chips. There is already a built-in doubt about the new pastor's ability to lead the congregation.

Even here lie some subtleties only the most experienced players recognize:

The reason is more important than the number. Suppose the call is only 75 percent affirmative because 25 percent felt the selection was hurried after the accidental death of the previous pastor. In other words, 100 percent of the members liked the candidate, but some voted no for procedural reasons. In this case, the new pastor will probably still receive a full pile of one hundred chips.

On the other hand, even a unanimous vote can mean trouble. After being turned down by three consecutive candidates, one church began to wonder if it would ever get another pastor. The fourth candidate made it clear he would come only if he received a 100 percent call. Members who disliked him and held major reservations about his qualifications felt intimidated into voting yes. He received only thirty-five chips to begin his ministry, even though he thought his pile counted one hundred.

Smart candidates give much closer attention to the interpretation of the vote than to the numbers.

The pastoral candidate is often not what's being voted on. The naive would surmise that when a congregation is voting on a new pastor, it is voting on a new pastor. Seldom so!

The church members know comparatively little about the candidate. They may have read a résumé, heard a sermon, and met the family in a receiving line. That is hardly sufficient basis for most members to determine whether this is the right person to lead the church for years to come.

So, instead of voting on the candidate, the congregation votes on the search committee. Everyone knows these individuals. Their likes and dislikes, spirituality and sins, wisdom and foolishness have all been well observed. If the pulpit committee members are well-known and highly respected, it will be assumed they are presenting a worthy candidate. The members vote yes, and the new pastor gets a big pile of unearned chips. On the other hand, a committee disliked by many members in a divided congregation will generate a lot of negative votes and a small initial supply of chips for the pastor.

This is not to say the church will never vote on its pastor. That comes later when an assistant-pastor candidate or a new budget is presented. People may not know much about the proposed assistant or understand the proposed budget, but they have definitely reached a decision about the pastor pushing these recommendations. The pastor's sermons, visitation, clothes, spouse, and children may all be factors in voting yes or no on the proposals.

To the bewilderment of a nixed assistant candidate, the vote may have had absolutely nothing to do with anything he said or did. The church only appeared to be voting on what it was voting on; it was really voting on the senior pastor.

Aside from the vote at the time of call, other factors determine how many initial chips a new pastor receives:

1. Age and experience are often worth up to one hundred extra chips. The pastor with some gray hair and at least one successful pastorate is assumed to bring wisdom and knowledge to the new job. However, the recent seminary graduate or the older pastor closing in on retirement may be docked initial chips for being too young or too old.

2. The previous pastor sometimes unintentionally makes the biggest difference of all. Long-term pastors are hard to follow; they often seem to take most of the chips with them. Long-term pastors who died in the church are particularly unfollowable. And if the previous pastor died in the pulpit preaching a superb sermon after fifty years in that same church, *all* the chips will be gone!

In contrast are those marvelous predecessors who prepare the way. They teach the congregation to love and support the next pastor "no matter who." They even make a special point to endorse their successors and thereby confer hundreds (maybe thousands) of their own chips.

3. Church health can affect the chips either way. Particularly healthy churches may be anxious to grow, so they intuitively stake the new pastoral leadership with the chips necessary to lead. Particularly sick churches often do the same. Like ambulance cases in an emergency room who are hardly in a position to check the physician's medical-school grades, they, out of desperation, give all the chips they have to the new pastor.

But watch out for those arrogant churches too cocky to advance chips. They expect pastors to earn their own. And beware of those churches so ill that they have no chips left. They may be too depleted to survive, much less follow a new leader.

Any good poker player determines his stake at the start of the game. So does the smart pastor.

Gaining chips

Some churches are anxious to add to the pastor's pile of chips, even granting new chips just for being pastor, since they have such high regard for the position. But most chips are won slowly over years of meaningful ministry.

Every good sermon is worth at least one chip. Pastors who preach both Sunday morning and evening can double their rate of accumulation. Scintillating sermons on special occasions like Mother's Day and Christmas win double chips because they not only minister to the regular attender but win accolades from visiting relatives and friends. Church members like it when their guests are impressed with their pastor's preaching.

Individual ministry is a slow but sure chip builder. Every counseling session, home visit, phone call, birthday card, and hospital call is another opportunity for a pastor to add to the pile.

Sometimes new pastors become angry when they don't immediately receive the acceptance and honor afforded their predecessor. It becomes an irritant every time the previous pastor's sermons, visits, and sayings are mentioned. But such reverence was won over years of love, care, and individual attention, and there is seldom any way to hurry the transfer process. Criticizing the prior pastor doesn't help. If anything, such criticism subtracts from the newcomer's stack of chips.

Then there are the chip builders that come from individual style. One recent seminary graduate candidated at a church while his young wife was nearly nine months pregnant. When the lay leader invited her to join her husband on the platform, the candidate quickly went to help her up the steps. Everyone thought he was wonderful. They gave him more chips for helping his wife up the steps than most pastors get for a year of first-class sermons.

In *The Small Church Is Different*, Lyle Schaller compares the expectations of the smaller church and the larger church. Although some professional competence and personal relationships are necessary in both, the smaller the church, the greater the expectation of function. Churches of fifty are more interested in a pastor who relates well to every member, even if the sermons are marginal. Churches of five thousand expect super sermons whether everyone knows the pastor or not.

This is important to remember in winning chips. The pastor of a small church may be perplexed why so much study and so many profound sermons generate so few chips. Likewise, the pastor of a large church may work endlessly to build relationships and get few chips in return because the preaching doesn't measure up.

None of this is to say a pastor should consciously measure every action in terms of its chip-producing potential. That in itself would probably be counterproductive. Pastors must minister as they are able in accord with their call. But they must also be sensitive to the credibility they have in the church, credibility determined by the number of chips accumulated.

Losing chips

In poker, as in pastoring, every hand is also a potential chip loser. Every Sunday morning can add a chip with a good sermon, but every Sunday morning can also deplete the pile with a yawner. Home calling will win a chip if all goes well but lose a chip if the family is offended.

The old advice "Don't change anything in your first year at a church" recognizes the danger of losing chips too fast and too soon. Something as seemingly simple as changing the order of worship may cost a new pastor half his starting chips the first Sunday and create a misimpression of arrogance, insensitivity, and pushiness. It may take a year of sermons and hospital visits just to get back even.

Some pastors seem amazingly fortunate. They move into new churches and risk all their chips in the first month . . . and win. Some even bluff, gambling ten times the number of chips they have on account, and they still win! One pastor led his church to change the constitution, replace staff, and undertake a multimillion-dollar building program shortly after his arrival. There was no upheaval: the church responded with enthusiasm, grew with amazing speed, and did everything he asked. He raked in the chips.

It doesn't usually work that way. More often, the new pastor who risks more chips than he has loses big and folds. A pastor with a chip deficit cannot lead a church for long. Of course, no one will say, "You gambled and lost. You'll have to leave the table." In fact, a year or more may pass before the pastor senses "a call to another ministry" or the church says, "God wants you someplace else," but it all goes back to that day the pastor gambled away his chips.

One New Jersey pastor forgot a funeral. It wasn't that he was neglecting ministry; he was in a restaurant counseling a man from the congregation. He lost track of time and simply forgot he was supposed to be at the mortuary chapel. After trying to reach him by phone, the funeral director recruited another minister from a different denomination who was a complete stranger to the family.

When the pastor discovered his mistake, he immediately went to the home to explain and apologize. The family rejected his apology, refused to forgive his offense, and left the church. To their reckoning, no number of chips could pay for such an affront. Did he survive in the church? Yes. He survived because he had been there many years and had a huge backlog of chips from the rest of the congregation. But the error certainly cost him.

Jesus' counsel to "count the cost" (Luke 14:28–32 NKJV) can be applied to pastoral risks. Before making a change, confronting a member, or launching a new program, the pastor needs to figure out if there are enough chips to lose and live. It hardly seems worth losing a potentially productive pastorate by a bet that could have been avoided or at least delayed until more chips were accumulated.

Assessing your play

Early in my ministry I wanted to move out of the church-owned parsonage and buy a house. During the inflationary years of the early 1970s, it seemed like a now-or-never proposition.

The trustees agreed to sell the parsonage and add a housing allowance to my salary. It was insufficient, but we pressed ahead. A builder in the church helped us find a lot and offered to build for his cost. When a plumber lent his services for cost, it looked like our dream was about to come true. We only needed a final church vote to sell the parsonage and provide the housing allowance.

Although the eventual vote tallied 85 percent in favor, a vocal minority remained highly critical: "The pastor is being selfish. He wants to get rich at church expense. We can't afford it."

Conflicting counsel confused my twenty-six-year-old mind. I didn't understand about chips, but I sensed this decision might affect my whole future at that church. So, after seemingly endless prayers with God and conversations with my wife, I decided it wasn't worth the risk. We dumped the plans and stayed in the parsonage.

Even this cost a few chips, because I was accused of letting the minority rule. But, all told, the church perceived I was more concerned about others than myself, and they piled on more chips. Those were needed some years later when the church relocated, built a new building, and sold the parsonage for the equity. Everybody came out a winner.

How do you assess your standing?

Keep track of your chips. Pastors usually have a sense of their standing in the church. We know how many visits we've made and have a hunch how our sermons are being received. We remember the last episode when chips were lost and how severe the losses were.

A daily journal and an annual review provide two additional practical ways to keep track of chips. Writing a journal is a helpful way to record the ups and downs of everyday pastoral ministry. If an honest journal reveals more defeats than victories, suspect a chip decline and proceed cautiously. If reading the journal shows mostly victories, estimate a chip surplus and be open to greater risk.

A formal performance review by the governing board or a pastoral-relations committee not only communicates how ministry is going but helps tabulate the current number of chips in the pastor's account.

Count the cost. After a while we estimate everyday risks without thinking about them. If Mrs. Folkers isn't visited this week, she won't like it, but we can sustain the minor chip loss in order to use the time to keep a more strategic evangelistic appointment. We accept the inevitable loss without much thought.

A major building program, staff addition, or other significant change demands a conscious effort to estimate the potential losses and gains. Usually there will be some of both.

For example, we may need a new building. However, such an undertaking would probably split the church, and a third of the people would leave. If that happened, we wouldn't need the new building. It seems obvious not to build. On the other hand, the catharsis of losing that third and the construction of the new building might result in greater effectiveness and substantial growth.

A firm calculation of potential losses and gains is impossible, since all of the data for any close decision can never be gathered. Neither life nor ministry is that precise. Nevertheless, we can adequately estimate many risks in advance, so that wise choices result. The time to count the cost is in advance.

Know your priorities. Very few issues necessitate splitting a church or losing a job. Such issues reside in the realm of major doctrinal, moral, and ethical stands.

Beyond those few black-and-white choices (which may be comparatively easy to make because they are so clear), most questions are matters of priorities. We learn to prioritize church growth, evangelism, pastoral care, harmony within the body, happiness of old-timers, receptivity to newcomers, and other concerns.

Some experts say that in order to grow, "a church must want to grow and be willing to pay the price." If that is the top priority, losing some faithful members because of changes may be a painful but necessary price to pay.

Whatever the priorities, they should be known and spelled out as a necessary step before undertaking a significant risk.

Trust the Lord. Fortunately, mortals are unable to get all the facts and make perfect choices. We must trust God. It's better that way.

I have often counted the chips, determined the risk, and then laid it all out (sometimes in writing) before the Lord. Since it's his church and I'm his servant, the ultimate decision is his and not mine—win or lose. Most often this leads to a preliminary decision and a prayer: "Lord, I'll proceed privately as if that's the way to go. If I'm right, keep me going. If I'm wrong, stop me before I lose all my chips!"

Decide. In a poker game there comes a time to play or fold. After the chips have been counted, the stakes calculated, and the hopes dreamed, a decision must be made. The player must toss his chips in the pot . . . or get out of the game.

So we decide. Not hastily, not carelessly, but carefully, prayerfully, wisely. We place our cards on the table—our ministries on the line.

PART 8

Coping with Personal Change

25

Getting Older and Wiser

The young minister and the seasoned pastor each face unique frustrations and temptations—and each has unique opportunities

—R. KENT HUGHES

Our youth pastor, Dennis, came to me recently. "I want to rappel off the church," he said, "off the fourth story!" It was to be a scene for a youth video he was making, he explained.

I could have easily said no. First, it was dangerous. (I like to give my staff room to fail, but this gave a whole new meaning to the idea.) Furthermore, people could justifiably criticize me for allowing such crazy activities. But I decided the risk was worth it. Dennis is a creative guy. He relates well to the kids, and his idea was a culturally hot item. In addition, he was young and capable of the feat.

"Just check with the custodian," I said, "to make sure the rope won't come loose and the building won't be damaged."

So he did it. With a Santa Claus hat on his head, he backed off the roof of our four-story building and rappelled to the ground. The video was outrageous, and the kids loved it.

Rappelling off buildings, however, would not exactly impress the main people I minister to. That's how it should be. The young minister and the seasoned pastor are, in some ways, worlds apart in their view of the church and practice of ministry —and that's okay. Each faces unique frustrations and temptations, and each has unique opportunities to minister effectively to God's people.

I see my own ministry as falling into two basic stages: early ministry, where I did youth work and then planted a church, and ministry now as head of staff. Here are the insights I've gleaned about the hazards and opportunities of each stage of pastoral life.

Phase frustrations

Although my ministry has been fulfilling at each stage, I see that each period also brings with it unique frustrations that, in the end, we simply have to learn to live with.

Lack of respect. When I was a youth pastor, I longed for congregational respect. I used to say I was more zookeeper than pastor: as long as none of the animals got out of their cages, everybody was happy. That didn't do much for my self-esteem, and I felt alienated, like I was off in a corner with no significant role in the church.

That, in turn, nurtured a sort of reverse elitism: *The future of the church lies with the youth,* I'd think. *This is where it's happening. Everybody else is out of it!* That attitude, of course, didn't do much to get me the respect I longed for.

In fact, one advantage of early ministry aggravated the issue of respect. As a young pastor I enjoyed being close to people. I had considerable one-to-one contact, especially with youth and youth sponsors. But sometimes that very closeness diminished my profile as a pastor. When I became only "Hey you!" to people, they didn't perceive me as one having authoritative answers.

And it wasn't only the elders who didn't respect me. Often it was the kids I spent the most time with. At one youth gathering, I found myself under playful attack. "Hey! Let's try to drown the youth pastor!" was their gleeful battle cry. I spent much of the afternoon happily wrestling with some of my guys in the pool.

A few days later, though, I tried to speak with one of the boys I'd been wrestling with. He had been misbehaving in the youth group, and I had to confront him about it. But he wouldn't listen to me.

"I don't think you're so good," he said disrespectfully. "You're not a good husband to your wife or a good father to your kids.

So get off my case!" I believe he spoke to me that way because I had become a little too familiar with him.

Another signal of lack of respect was the relatively meager administrative support I received. During my early years, I either had no secretary or one who merely worked part-time, and I had to rely on old office equipment (or no equipment at all). That hampered my ability to administrate my work efficiently, and it raised my frustration level considerably some days.

The advantage of being a "junior pastor," of course, is that the buck doesn't stop at your desk. If the deacons became testy about a rappelling stunt or whatever, I just ducked. The criticism would fly by and land on my boss's desk. But during my early years of ministry, that plus didn't mitigate my frustration.

Administrative hassles. Now that I'm farther down the time line, I have a vast arsenal of administrative tools at my disposal, but I also find the pace of change is frustratingly slow.

My youth group—and even my first church—responded well and rapidly to change. They didn't ask all the what-if questions: "What if this happens? What if that doesn't work? What if we run out of money?" They were ready to get involved and take risks.

If I challenged them with, "All the heathen are lost," they would consider the matter seriously, saying, "Then I should change my life. I should join Operation Mobilization."

When presented with a challenge to change, the people I work with now are more likely to say, "But that's never been done here before," or "How much did you say that was going to cost?"

Motivating an established church with an elaborate structure and a long, rich history can be like turning the *Queen Mary* around. You can turn a speedboat around on a dime. But it takes seven miles at sea to get an ocean liner headed in the opposite direction. And the older we become, the more likely we are to pastor ships instead of speedboats.

The time and energy that administration extracts from me also tend to separate me from my people. My maturity and leadership now give me the opportunity to make a large difference in many people's lives, but only if I'm willing to stay at the helm of the ship. Frankly, I'd like to be on the deck more often, chatting with the crew.

The varied pacing of ministry

How we pace our ministries also changes over the years.

A holy impatience. When we're young, it's easier to be direct. We see clearly the problems of the church, and we have few qualms about telling people what ought to be done. We think, *This is right, and I know it's right. It's biblical, and this church needs it. So I'm not going to let anyone stand in my way.* So we barge through the front doors, trying to make change happen immediately.

Yes, sometimes we're brash and less than diplomatic. But it's that youthful impatience—especially if it's directed by biblical goals—that can often win the day.

In 1970 I became convinced that the one great thing our youth needed was involvement in missions. At that time short-term summer missions was not a common opportunity, especially for high schoolers. So I wrote missionaries and mission boards on every continent and compiled "103 Opportunities" that I grandly and with much fanfare presented to my kids.

The result? Fifty-five of them spent the summer of 1970 doing missionary work, and they were spread over five continents. It was a spiritual springtime for the church, although not the one great answer I had envisioned!

Younger ministers can get away with that type of holy drive, partly because congregations expect that from us when we're young. But as we mature in ministry, other character traits must emerge.

A godly patience. The more at home I've become in the ministry, the more I use the back door. Instead of barging through the front door, guns blazing, I slip in quietly, unnoticed. I'll take someone out to lunch, listen respectfully, and in the process introduce my ideas in a noncombative mode, allowing others time for thought.

I'm also more comfortable with the fact that my plans won't

get accepted immediately. Getting College Church into a major building program without sinking the church has been a huge exercise in patience. I didn't just stand up one day and announce that we needed to build a $6.5-million structure. I had to lay the groundwork for years.

It began, in fact, when the congregation held a meeting to discuss air conditioning. Many people were saying, "Why should we install air conditioning? It's unbearable only ten Sundays out of the year. We'll still come to church." I had to remind them that a restaurant operating that way would go out of business.

In time I got them to see that we were trying to reach others besides the already committed. Patience paid off. We got the air conditioning, and now, years later, we're building new facilities.

I may have to settle for accomplishing only a small part of the plan at the beginning of a new venture. But if it moves the church in the right direction, in a year or two the whole program can be in place.

Temptations in time

In each stage of ministry, my spiritual life has been tested differently.

Vulnerability to flattery. I didn't get to preach much as a youth pastor. But if someone came up after my sermon and said, "That was great! Do you know what we need around here? We need to hear more of you," I tended to believe her.

Yeah, you're right, I'd think. *That is exactly what this church needs: more of me.* When young, we're more vulnerable to such flattery.

Now I know the difference between compliments and flattery. If a long-time member tells me, "Pastor, that was a good sermon Sunday," that's one thing. But it's another when someone who's been attending but three weeks says, "Boy! That was the best sermon I have ever heard!" Then my red flag goes up. It could be that he has never heard good preaching, but more likely he is flattering me to get my attention.

I've learned, then, to be cautious over the years. Experience has shown me the truth of what Solomon says—to be wary of flatterers.

Vulnerability to security. As one gets on in ministry, I've witnessed an increasing temptation to play it safe, to become vulnerable to the need for security, to see risk as a young man's game. The more one achieves professionally, the more one has to lose and the greater the instinct to play it safe. That's why some pastors are tempted to pad their boards with supportive yes-people and hire staff who don't threaten them.

I have consciously fought this instinct by surrounding myself with superior people, many with abilities exceeding mine. I invite them to push and ask hard questions. I allow them to spread their wings, to try new programs and fresh ideas. And when they fly, I fly—and flying is risky business!

Pastoral care in two dimensions

The essence of ministry—pastoral interaction with people—also changes with the years. The same ministry gets done, but in two different ways.

Pastoral contact. As a youth pastor, my phone rang constantly. I was available all the time. When I became the pastor of a small church, I involved myself in everything: Sunday school, the youth program, evangelism. Since I worked closely with members, they all knew me. We built the new church building together; we cleaned toilets together. People had no compunctions about calling me at any time.

Because of that close contact with people, I could invest myself into individual lives with great energy and good results.

In my early pastorate, I coached a soccer team, The Awesome Aztecs, and some of my players came from Jewish, Mormon, and Hindu homes. We had a great time together all season. To thank me for my efforts, the team along with their parents came to church one Sunday, and they all sat on the front row.

Pastoral oversight. When I came to College Church, I suddenly had ten times more people to pastor, but I received only a third of the phone calls. The older minister usually has more responsibility, so people say, "Well, we shouldn't call the pastor at home. We should wait till tomorrow morning." And sometimes they simply don't trouble me with their problems. It's sad, but some people no longer consider me approachable.

Then again, even when people do ask for pastoral attention, my varied responsibilities force me to weigh my response. A woman recently asked me, "My husband and I are having trouble. Would you counsel us regularly?"

"I can counsel you a couple of times, but then I will have to refer you," I explained. "And if you need some financial assistance, we can help with the first five or six sessions."

I know that if I take even two or three people on for regular counseling, it will demand my full attention. I still counsel people, but not as much as I used to.

I simply no longer have the luxury of being involved with as many people. If I were to do so, I wouldn't administrate well; I wouldn't adequately prepare sermons. As an older pastor with more responsibility, I have to work through other people.

The irony is that although I personally give less pastoral care, more people receive individual attention. I administrate staff people who visit hospitals, counsel, and make calls into homes. Our church also offers courses that train laypeople to give pastoral care to one another.

So although I'm frustrated by administration, my frustration is tempered by the fact that I can oversee the pastoral care of hundreds of people.

Learning to preach

One of the greatest challenges of ministry is to communicate the good news to people. It's a complex task, and not every part of it can be perfected at once. In fact, we should not burden ourselves trying to do at twenty-five what others are doing at fifty-five. I've noticed that different stages of ministry lend themselves to mastering different parts of the preaching process.

Learning to be relevant. When I got out of seminary, I entered ministry armed with all kinds of theological words. I was self-consciously bookish.

But that didn't compute into the world of youth ministry. Kids may be the most challenging group to relate to. They're a demanding audience. They're not going to let you get away with being irrelevant. They want fast-paced, graphic, honest dialogue. You can get away with boring adults, but kids won't tolerate it.

I had to learn, then, to relate to kids on their level. My wife says my vocabulary went through a complete transformation in about a month. So I spent my early ministry years learning how to translate the gospel into contemporary terms.

In fact, I've come to believe that youth ministry is the best place to learn how to do that. If you can communicate with teenagers, you can communicate with anybody. As a youth pastor, I learned many speaking techniques that I still draw on today.

Crafting and precision. In recent years my homiletical style has evolved even further. With collegians I could sit on the floor and dialogue from notes written on the margins of my Bible. When I pastored a small church, I began to construct outlines with greater substance and structure. Now I write out a complete manuscript, even if I don't use it in the pulpit. My people understand more nuances of biblical truth, and I must be clear and precise about how I communicate.

So in this stage of ministry, I'm constantly learning how to craft my sermons. I'm much more fastidious about exegesis and even the use of language. This is not something I had time to do when I was younger. Even if I did have time, I'm not sure it would have been worth the effort. Now it is, not only because I've already learned to be relevant but because my people expect it.

The changing focus

How I give my energies to ministry has also changed over the years.

A singular passion. When I first started out, I thought I could change the world with my youth program. During the 1960s we sat on the floor for Bible studies, strummed guitars, and sang Jesus songs. We thought that was the answer for the whole church. If people would just sit on the floor and sing Jesus songs, they'd became like the church God intended.

That single-issue focus stayed with me into my early years as a pastor. I'd say to myself, *If I can get Evangelism Explosion going, then the church will turn around.* I'd preach with confident zeal, imagining one great sermon alone would affect my people for life. As a young minister, I would often devote myself fully to one thing, hoping it would make a big difference.

Early in ministry, we have the luxury and opportunity to have a narrow focus. That focus allows us to give programs the detailed attention and energy they need—especially if they are being created ex nihilo. And although my grandiose hopes for each program may have been misplaced, each in its own way made a difference.

For example, in my first pastorate, I instituted an intern program for those considering going into the ministry. This provided interested people with ministry opportunities; they also received a modest amount of instruction in practical theology, which I taught weekly. The program continued for more than a decade after I moved on.

A concern for complexity. As my responsibilities in ministry changed, I began to see another dimension: the church wasn't one thing but many, and it was the coordination of the many that would, over the long run, make for effective ministry. Even after great sermons, I found myself realizing, *That may have been one of the best sermons I've ever preached, but alone it won't make any major difference. I've got to keep paying attention to all the other parts of the church's life as well.*

To put it another way, I no longer can evaluate rappelling off the church only in terms of what it can do for the youth. I also must consider how it might affect the ladies' missionary guild or the church's insurance coverage.

Complexities can clutter the big picture and make ministry decisions much harder. Then again, learning to look beyond the single ministry focus has also lowered my fear of failure. I've discovered that just as one sermon will not change history, one mistake will not collapse the kingdom of God. One bad program will not sabotage the church or destroy my ministry.

Rewards at every stage

On my dresser, where I can see it every morning, sits a picture of five guys, with sunglasses and slicked-back hair, on a 1968 Colorado River trip. That picture reminds me of what happened the next day, when four of them prayed with me to receive Christ. And it didn't end there.

One of those guys, Rick Hicks, went on to direct Forest Home, a Christian conference center in southern California, and he recently received a Ph.D. To know that something I did as a youth pastor had lasting impact, to know that more than twenty years later those guys are still committed, pursuing ministries themselves and changing lives for Christ—that is wonderful. Seasons may change, as do pastors, but the rewards are essentially the same.

The rewards, of course, continue to unfold. Recently, I received this note from a junior high girl:

> Dear Pastor Hughes,
> After listening to your sermon today, I recommitted myself to our Lord. I have recently discovered myself just "going through the motions." I have since done devotions and witnessing to people. Your sermon spoke to me. Normally, I must confess, I don't listen very well. Today I did and you had a lot to say. I'm sure you spoke to many nonbelievers in our congregation. I have decided, if possible, to become a member of College Church (although I am only 13 years old and the only one in my family to go to this church).

If you would like to get in touch sometime, my number is . . .
Thanks for your time.

Your sister in Christ,
Elizabeth

As Ecclesiastes puts it, there is a time for every season under heaven. That's certainly been true of my ministry. Each season of ministry has its liabilities and opportunities, but in each season God has been faithful, and his work has moved forward.

26

Growing Pains

Church growth always demands social growth.
Especially for the pastor.

—Calvin Miller

In that long ago, faraway book *The Peter Principle* lies the doctrine of my insecurity. The book states that climbers on the ladder of life are promoted rung by rung until they eventually reach a level they're not equipped to handle. Thus, by doing well, a person arrives at a plateau beyond his real capabilities and successfully "out-succeeds" himself. I have often been haunted by the fear that my church will one day outgrow my ability.

Only one word can prohibit this imagined debacle: *adjustment.* Not my adjustment to the crisis moments of ministry. Such moments belong to every pastor. Not my adjustment to wrenching business meetings or to those lonely nights that follow the hectic days when it seems that, for all my acquaintances, I haven't got a friend in the world.

No, the adjustment required is the ability to relate in different ways to the congregation as the membership expands. This difficult adjustment, I believe, is the reason many church planters cannot grow a church from inception to supercongregation. How does one relate to church members at the difficult plateaus of growth?

One church-growth expert said that because of personal inclinations, there are some "fifty-member pastors," some "two-hundred-member pastors," some "five-hundred-member pastors," and some "two-thousand-member pastors." I'm not sure his statement is altogether true. But if it is, I find myself wondering which is my own magic number of competency. I only know that congregational vitality is somehow related to my ability to lead, and I don't want my church to lose its vitality as it grows.

The whole subject makes me paranoid. Year after year, I cannot escape the dread feeling that I'm not growing as fast as the church. How do I keep adjusting—to keep from stifling my church's growth and yet keep my church from outgrowing me?

I find certain questions accompanied my fears:

Why do I react when someone accuses me of not knowing what's going on in church administration?

Do I sometimes lash out when anyone implies I have taken too much time for myself?

Was the anger on my face obvious to the committee when I confessed to forgetting one appointment on a day I had fifteen scheduled?

Why do I sometimes feel I have created a busy church that's all legs and no heart?

Why do I spend the first six days of every ten-day vacation feeling guilty that I'm living in caprice while hundreds of problems remain unsolved back home?

Was I always plagued by such self-recrimination? Yes. For years I have lived in the double bind of wanting my church to grow but fearing my competency would not suffice if it did.

I want to avoid statistical arrogance, but the truth is, our church has grown in the past two decades. Twenty-one years ago I arrived in Omaha and, with five other families, began the work. My wife and I became members eleven and twelve of what was little more than a Bible study. Now the church has a weekly attendance that would have seemed impossible back then. We aren't one of the top ten great churches of America, but we've added an average of three new members a week for the last ten years. We have just finished what seems to us a huge sanctuary, and the church, at least to me, seems to be exploding in size.

At each stage of growth, I've had to change, and change is as hard for preachers as it is for parishioners. Yet change is the central task of pastors who commit themselves to growing churches. Failure to adjust to the church's new stage of development is a sure way to prevent any further growth.

Let me walk you through the stages as I've seen them.

You get the pizza; I'll bring the guitar

The first is what I call the "Joe, You Pick Up the Pizza and I'll Bring the Guitar" stage of church life. Those who plant churches often begin with this pizza-clique kind of fellowship. At this stage, things depend purely on the pastor's ability to be colloquial.

I confess I graduated from seminary a little too Brunneresque. I began a small church with the false assumption that everyone who walked into our clique was just dying to find out whatever happened to the Socinians. Like most seminarians, I hadn't been prepared to build relationships in ordinary ways. But nobody learns what *down-to-earth* means any faster than a pastor who wants to plant a church.

Churches begin as colloquiums where it's important that we can talk about little things. At this stage, there will be no talk of the Sistine Chapel or Reformation theology. Instead, the conversation will bounce from Jesus to the latest wave of public school chicken pox. Working out the exact date of the Second Coming isn't as important as the next "all-church" picnic.

For our church, this stage was warm and clinging, delightful and close. All six families left our Sunday evening study group and reassembled for fellowship at someone's home for pizza. We were all reluctant to break off our Sunday togetherness.

But we were little only in size, not in vision. The near global idealism of our six families produced a zealous togetherness. We knew at the outset that God was about to use his clique of conquistadors to raise the gospel flag, citadel-fashion, over Omaha. Our group rarely voiced this dream, for, spoken out loud, it seemed a delusion of grandeur. Plus, there's always the superstitious feeling that saying anything out loud breaks the magic. Dreams should hatch silently, incubated by workers who don't talk away the glory.

So our ministry lived in prayer, pizza, and partisan enterprise. We laughed and sang, never talking in grandiose ways about our conquest. But touching each other and being together, we nevertheless kept the dream alive.

My wife and I quite often fed the whole church five loaves and an unmultiplied fish or two. We didn't talk much about saving the world (though we never doubted it could be done). Our themes were generally too intimate to apply the shepherd metaphor, which doesn't seem to fit when the flock is small. We were all shepherds or all sheep or all neither. We were just a clique with a large conscience.

The information flow in our fledgling church was universal, and guilt was the one tool we used to keep each other in line. If Joe wanted to go to Kansas City for a weekend, we wanted to know it well ahead of time. He wouldn't dare just wander off without scheduling it with us. If he did, we all called right after he missed church to chirp, "We missed you!" But Joe knew it wasn't so much a condolence as a threat dipped in guilt and fired at close range by all of us who didn't go to Kansas City.

All in all, we sought unanimity. We were few, and it was important that we felt alike. Each of us would regularly lick an index finger and hold it up to the group, and in such unsophisticated theological tests we measured which way the wind blew:

"Yes, we believe in eternal security."

"No, divorced men can't be deacons."

"What, Joe, you let your kids play Dungeons and Dragons?"

"Dobson was great today, wasn't he?"

"David C. Cook material is optimum."

"The Living Bible is slangy and giddy and not to be given place alongside the NASB. "

A politburo of concord we were, yet we didn't do it to be coercive, but to protect the dream we didn't talk about but never forgot.

Best of all, this closeness hatched fifty-two weeks of Christmas every year. My sermons weren't glorious, but I was somehow key, at the hub of most relationships, so I was rewarded—if not for being brilliant, at least for being central.

But are they members?

The next stage I'll call the "Should We Let People Sing in Our Choir if They're Not Members?" plateau. Little groups are protective of their togetherness. The congregation, like me, wanted the church to grow, but we wanted it to grow without widening the "we feeling" we so enjoyed.

As an artist, I have noticed I can freehand a pretty good circle —as long as the circumference is small. But if the circle is large, I cannot hold the radius equal around the more and more remote center. The effort grows eccentric.

Further, simple geometry ordains that it's harder to see the center of the circle from a wider circumference. So the real tension of this second stage is hidden in this desire: "Let's keep this circle perfect." The corollary is that the circle must therefore remain small.

I began to discover as pastor that it was next to impossible to have over all the "old members" and, at the same time, to have over all the "new potential members." Though the number of either wasn't large, it was still too large to allow my wife and me to fit them all into our small home. As soon as we began to limit "attendance" at the parsonage get-togethers, we began to hear rumblings from those not included.

We also noticed for the first time that we had inadvertently become the sole "entertainers" of our small fellowship. We hadn't meant to be virtually the only family showing hospitality on a group scale, but we had become just that. People seemed to see this as our responsibility. They clung ever more tightly to the small circle, despite their philosophical commitment to widening the scope of our fellowship.

I began to hear the "first circle" criticizing the newcomers: "These (new) people don't love this church like we do." A protective exclusivism was born: "Should we let people sing in our choir if they're not members of the church?" It was an institutional question that sought to protect their own place in the church without being really honest. I remember that the first time I heard the question, I was struck that our choir was so small—we had one man and three women.

At this stage, the number of members and adherents began to grow so numerous that lines of communication, which once had intersected with me at the hub of the circle, now began to bypass me. My self-importance suffered as I often felt I was in the dark about what was going on.

My worst adjustments came in trying to reach out to charter members who seemed to grow intentionally aloof. Were they psychologically retaliating because they weren't the "in crowd" they once had been? Even though I tried to tell them that I, too, was experiencing these feelings, they were unconvinced. In most cases, the pain I felt was sponsored by the spiritualized criticism of those who left.

None of them quit the church for the real reason of psychological insecurity. But some of them found other reasons for leaving, like: "Your sermons don't feed us anymore!" (though I hadn't consciously changed my preaching from when it *had* been feeding them). Others wanted a "truly compassionate" pastor; others wanted one who would "preach the whole counsel of God." Still others left because we weren't being true to the "historic traditions" of our denomination. Many of these people moved about six miles away and started a church that would offer the customary programs of our denomination.

All this was traumatic for me. I learned at great emotional expense that it's okay to lose members. Indeed, I later learned that not every potential member of the church has needs that our congregation can best meet. Still, I had never lost a family without guilt and pain.

Oops, I didn't know we had a softball team

Shortly after we had gathered three hundred resident members and had hired our first full-time staff person, we reached a stage where the lines of communication became sketchy. That summer, I discovered we not only had formed a church softball team but also were doing very well in the city league.

It was the first time I could recall something that "major" being done without my having some role in the decision. My ego was bruised. But the men said that I had been "away" when the crucial decision was made, and they knew I wasn't too "athletic" anyway, so "a group of us got a team together, and we didn't take any church funds to pay the league fees [which is, of course, the acid test in a new church], so we knew you wouldn't mind."

"I don't mind (too much)," I said. "It's just the principle of the thing!" They could tell I was steamed, so they invited me over for pizza after one of the games. There we kissed and made up . . . except that sometimes, late at night, I would pray that they'd lose the championship game.

They didn't, and my administrative grief was compounded by the emergence of huge trophies all over the vestibule—blue-and-gold plastic icons of the decision I never made. Like Zwingli (whose name, I'll admit, isn't cited at many softball banquets) in Reformation Zurich, I had the awfulest urge to sweep through the church smashing softball trophies. But I knew it was simply administrative sour grapes.

In the ensuing years, there would be many decisions made without my counsel. Recently, a square-dance group formed right out in the open "behind my back." Truthfully, square dancing has always looked like fun, but that doesn't change the fact that Baptists have firmly stood against dancing of every sort ever since Herodias did her thing. The group assured me this case was different from John the Baptist's: nobody's head was at stake.

"What about mine when the deacons find out?" I shouted. "Deacons can make Herod look compassionate." They succumbed, and for the most part there was no square dancing, so we were still free from the "obvious sins."

The point is that as churches grow, pastors must be prepared for the fact that they gradually lose some touch with all that's going on. Even though I was removed from the planning of these events, fireworks often exploded because of such uncharted acts. The congregational explosion might have been the first time I realized I was unaware. I often found myself having to patch over the bruised feelings associated with these events.

But you married us, remember?

One element usually associated with growth is long tenure. When a church is small, the pastor knows every member by name. In a small church, the pastor is "in the know," and knowing is a kind of job security, a feeling of control. This relationship is vastly different for the pastor who has such a big congregation he or she can't possibly know each member.

I was the keynote speaker at an Arizona gathering, and when the meeting was concluded, a rather striking man came up to me with two towering, six-foot boys whom he introduced as his sons.

"I'm Roberto Blair," he said.

"Roberto!" I replied. "Nice to meet you."

There was an awkward silence. He waited, apparently to see how long it would take me to remember him. I realized I was in the vise. It was important to him to have me remember his name. I fished desperately. With a name like Roberto, his wife was probably named Rosita or Carlotta, but then, I had once known a Consuela . . . no, she ran the missionary lunchroom in Monterey, didn't she? It was no use. Finally I blurted out, "Have we met before?"

"Aw, come on . . . you baptized me and my boys. You even led us to Christ."

"Of course," I said. "Uh, how long has it been?"

He said the late fifties. I didn't ask if he meant the 1850s or the 1950s. I asked his forgiveness for forgetting and blamed it all on a clogged carotid artery. He seemed at peace, but inwardly I felt bad. I had baptized almost two thousand people in my ministry, and I found it hard to remember all their names.

Once a middle-aged couple visited our church. When I introduced myself, the man asked, "Don't you remember us? You married us seven years ago!" I confessed I didn't remember.

My problem lies in the number of people I meet every week—usually between six and fifteen new families. At Easter and special occasions, we have as many as two hundred new families visit us. Still, I can't help feeling guilty because I feel I should remember everybody I meet and be able to recall the name.

Much of my guilt comes because I was sociologically in control at earlier levels of the church's development.

Now I must adjust to a growing remoteness. I am learning that the pastor of a growing church must somewhere quit memorizing saints and start equipping them. I must challenge the congregation with compassion. Unless members minister to each other, real ministry will die in the growing congregation.

The only answer is that I must stop insisting on the official singularity of the word *minister*. Carlyle Marney says we (*laos* and *cleros* alike) must be all "priests to each other." As pastors, we must equip every Christian to minister, and we must quit wallpapering our offices with degrees that insist that we alone are certified ministers.

George Bernard Shaw once said that every profession is a conspiracy against the laity. God help us if that should be true of pastors. We are on the side of the laity, one with the laity. We are calling them to be ministers so that the number of members on a church roll exactly equals the number of ministers. Canadian pastor Paul Stevens is both sensible and theologically correct when he writes: "I keep the official record of it, my ordinational certificate, over my desk partly to remind me of what I am not. I am not the only commissioned minister of my church. I am not the only called person. I am not the only person who should be called a minister. If the institution of ordination perpetuates a practical heresy in the church by slighting the nonprofessional minister and favoring the professional, then it should be abolished."

Hear, hear! Listen to the wisdom and the accountability of a growing church. There's no room in the authentic, growing church for pastors insisting on their right to stardom in the ministry. My role is one of equipage and not empire.

Sheldon and Davy Van Auken called it "creeping separateness" and spoke of it as a danger in their marriage. A growing church also has a sense of creeping separateness. The task of trying to be intimate friends with everyone in the church drives me crazy. There are always new names and faces. At the same time, loneliness stalks the madness. On any given Saturday night, when the various bowling leagues or bridge cliques are playing, my wife will feel alone. Are we driving ourselves neurotic trying to be friends with the whole congregation?

We're not complaining, mind you. We are so often tired that an evening alone is a rare gift that sometimes comes to refresh us and gives us the feeling that life can be managed. Yet in the fishbowl of a large church, our thoughts are ever on the newcomers.

The danger is that one of the "newcomers" will surprise you with a bit of history. "Mr. New, I presume? Not new? Really? I married you and what's-her-name a brisk five years and six thousand handshakes ago?"

If the flag is flying . . .

Finally, our church has arrived at what Lyle Schaller calls the "minidenominational stage."

I will never forget seeing Windsor Castle for the first time. As we walked about the spacious gardens and walkways, I asked if the queen were at home. The answer I received in crisp British was, "If the flag is flying, the queen is in residence."

I remember a long breathing spell in the middle of a racquetball game, when one of my very finest friends told me he had been a member of the church long enough to see my role changing.

When I told him his words were cryptic, he simply said, "I have seen you pass from a doer to a symbol in our congregation." He went on to say that pastors in larger churches cannot possibly touch individual lives as frequently as they might in smaller churches.

"You're my pastor," he said, "but many others now provide me spiritual counsel and insight. While you're central in my understanding of how the Word of God is ministered, you're more the model than the mode of my counsel."

His words both blessed and rebuked. As a church grows, the pastor's role does become one of focus and symbol.

I still make about twenty visits a week, as do the other pastors on the staff, but at this snail's pace, I could never visit all the families in the church in a year. The church's need is now wider than my stamina and time. Still, visitation is important so that my ministry can have relevance *to me*, if not to them. If I were to cease making calls, something in my evangelistic impetus would die, something I need to keep Aristotle's pathos (sensitivity and feeling) in my sermons. Without a strong sense of pathos, I might never find the verve I need to convince others (as well as myself) of the priority of seeking the kingdom of God in life.

Still, I must fit all my personal ministry into a schedule laden with student rallies, staff meetings, family life, church growth, and Bible conferences. For me, the big-church syndrome means I have to work harder than ever to maintain the necessary home-base feeling. I cannot feel authentically pastoral otherwise.

My resolve is bound up in my desire to *be* a pastor and to *be thought of* that way. This is an important symbol in our congregation. They need to see me as someone who is always available. So when they say to me, "If the flag is flying, the king is in residence," I want them to say it with a smile. Made in a good-natured way, the comment says, "I understand the church has grown, and growth is our calling as a church." I hope they also see that it means they are obligated to minister to each other.

Social growth: a painful necessity

Growing can be painful. Who needs it? Wouldn't it be better to settle down in warm, containable settings?

No, because we have met Christ, who told us to win the whole world, or as much of it as we can. Hence, as I see it, not every great church is a big church, but every great church is a growing, changing church. I realize the statement has some limitations in dying rural situations or hard-locked urban districts. Still, great churches are busy increasing either their numbers or their vision.

Whichever is the case, relationships must also widen to create room for such visions. Joseph Aldrich, president of Multnomah Bible College, said we should visualize the Spirit of God hovering over our neighborhood. It is this vision that calls the church to integrate the new. Ours cannot be the greatest problem; remember how twice early in Acts thousands of people were swept into the church on single occasions. There was little question that the Holy Spirit was hovering over their urgency. As he hovers over Omaha, my own adjustment must continue.

If, as the shepherd, I am not continually growing, changing, and developing my own relationship skills, there is little hope for greatness in this flock.

The number one response to all change is anger. I have known the resentment of seeing close friends push me perimeter-wards in their growing circle of relationships. I have sometimes been angry because I wasn't invited to some soiree where I knew laughter and good times were going to swell. I have felt hurt because the very family that I prayed with through thirty hospital visits had a prayer retreat in their home a year later and invited an Episcopal rector to direct it. I have been angry because my best friend's daughter didn't ask me to do her wedding ceremony, picking one of my associates. But my anger lives only till I kneel in prayer and ask God to bring to my remembrance the right of everyone to be free in the fellowship. Then I see that they're only doing what I must do so often in my own complex world of relationships. They are picking and choosing, and they can't all choose me all the time.

Then, too, it's really all for Christ. And yet, when I'm honest, I wonder how much of the spotlight I would shine on Christ if some of the "edge-light" wasn't always spilling on me. It keeps my best spiritual moments smudged with doubt about my dedication.

All I know is that I love them. As Paul said, they are "my joy and crown" (Phil. 4:1). I am blessed to be their shepherd, however heavy the task.

As shepherd and flock, we all have to allow for some diminishing of closeness. In a sense, this is born of self-denial. We are creating space so that all those not yet born again may also come to know Christ.

In lessening our grip on relationships, we set others free, and we also free ourselves. It takes courage to stand without clinging, but only as we release our grip are we free to stand straight and self-sufficient before our world. Is it not heresy to know Christ and call ourselves self-sufficient? Yes, of course, but the self-sufficient Christian finds sufficiency in Christ and not in clinging to another. At the heart of all relationships in a growing church is the strength of Christ.

Church growth always demands social growth. Especially for the pastor.

27

Making the Right Moves

In the Bible I find a lot more promises from God indicating that
he'll shepherd me than commands to find his specific will.

—Knute Larson

The candidating process for becoming pastor of The Chapel took fourteen months.

During the drawn-out ordeal, I slipped into a low-grade depression I couldn't shake, losing nineteen pounds. I felt guilty for even considering the idea of leaving my church in Ashland. After fifteen good years, I wondered if I were "deserting" that church. It felt like divorce.

Feeling discouraged and confused one day, I threw down what I knew to be a silly and desperate challenge before God: "Lord, I'm going to turn on the car radio. Whatever this radio preacher says will be what you are saying to me."

I clicked on the dial, and the first words I heard were, "Go, I am sending you, and I will give you courage and what to say."

At first I laughed. Then I cried. Naturally, I wasn't going to let this "coincidence" or the voice of John MacArthur determine my future, but it did make me fidget.

A month later, still in depression, I put out another such unorthodox fleece. Late one evening, my wife and I were discussing the pros and cons of moving when I said, "Jeanine, I'm going to turn on *Haven of Rest*. Whatever is on the program tonight will give us the answer."

She smiled. (I would have said, "Baloney," if *she* had proposed it.)

I turned on the radio program only to hear the program's associate director explain why he was resigning and moving on to a new ministry.

"I have struggled with the issue of my indispensability," I recall him saying. "But I've come to the conclusion that God can replace me in this ministry. The work here will go on, so I must take this next step in my life."

We sat a few moments in silence, prayed, and tried to figure out if God or the enemy or coincidence was behind this.

I finally did accept the position at The Chapel, though not on the basis of those two happenstance radio messages (though they did play a role, I have to admit). Other factors, like the match between the church's needs and my gifts, the enthusiastic support of my family, and finally, my own desire to go, were the key factors.

The thought of moving can play havoc with our emotions, surging from paralysis to impatience. We know the decision to move has far-reaching consequences, perhaps for good, perhaps for ill. In fact, it's one of the toughest decisions pastors make. Here are some principles that have helped me think more clearly about such times.

When leaving is wrong

A variety of things can stir up discontent in our present ministries, but no single problem is usually reason enough to leave a church. Here are some common frustrations that shouldn't necessarily point us down the road.

First, we shouldn't leave just because things aren't going well. Ray and Anne Ortlund give some excellent advice along these lines. Speaking to a gathering of pastors at The Chapel, they warned of the dangers of the ABZ Syndrome.

A pastor arrives at a church and enjoys a honeymoon period— stage A. But inevitably the day comes when the honeymoon relationship sours. When the criticism starts, disillusionment can set in —stage B. Pastors are then faced with the dilemma: "Do I stay and pray and gut it out?" or "Do I begin sending out my résumé?"

The Ortlunds believe that if we stay and endure the pain of stage B, we can eventually move into stage C, where energy and enthusiasm for the ministry return. As a result, we may even reenter stage A, finding great contentment in our setting. It's possible to go through stages A, B, and C several times in one church.

However, those who find stage B too uncomfortable often move directly into mode Z. They decide staying is useless, pack their belongings, and do it over again in another setting. Unfortunately for many pastors, life is a series of ABZ experiences. They miss the joy of seeing God strengthen them through their trials and thus achieving genuine peace.

Second, we shouldn't leave just because we have to deal with an obstinate person or problem in the church. I remember a young pastor, a former intern with our church, telling me that he had decided to leave his church after only a year. The board chairman was unbearably aggravating.

"He won't allow me to lead the board in devotions before our meetings," the young pastor complained. "He's put me on notice that he's the board leader and that I'm the spiritual leader. Deciding who will give devotions, he says, is his responsibility."

"How often do you meet one-on-one with the chairman?" I asked.

"Well, ah, we don't meet," he replied.

I encouraged the young pastor to get together with his chairman once a month, even twice a month if possible, to nurture a more personal relationship.

The pastor followed through on my advice. Soon, he was giving devotions at the board meetings. Through their times together, the pastor communicated to the chairman he was interested not in power but in genuine spiritual leadership.

Third, we can be tempted to move on because we're restless; we don't feel challenged. After eight years at my previous church, I felt some of this. While the church was growing stronger, I was growing restless.

Instead of looking for another ministry, though, I was able to assume responsibilities with our denominational headquarters.

That additional challenge was all I needed to find contentment for seven more years.

For many pastors, simply adding another challenge such as writing or volunteering in the community can meet a need for personal growth and development. Restlessness seems to be a normal characteristic of ambitious people, but finding another arena to stretch our muscles often can be done without resigning the present situation.

When it's time to go

So what is a legitimate reason for leaving? Here are three good reasons for considering a change of scenery.

Holy ambition. During the time I was deciding whether or not to come to Akron, a member at Ashland challenged me, asking, "Are you sure this isn't just your move up the corporate ladder?"

"Maybe it is," I replied. I was half-ashamed to say so, even though I think moving up the ladder can be a good thing. Ambition becomes destructive when we try to usurp control from God. Or when it drives us to walk over people or use churches. Or when ministry decisions degenerate into self-serving schemes and carefully manipulated calculations. In such cases ambition becomes another word for pride and rebellion.

I'm impressed with the parable of the talents, in which Christ rewarded those who took their talents and wisely invested them. To me, using our gifts to minister to more people or in a more receptive setting can be simply good stewardship, though numbers can never be the main consideration.

A special calling. Some pastors have the unique skills of a church pioneer, who can build a church from the ground up. Others have proven to be specialists at interim pastorates, serving angry or hurting churches. (Some denominations insist that a church call an interim pastor following a long-term leader or in the midst of congregational turmoil.)

Others may not be as well equipped to take a church to the next stage, though they may have been successful up to a certain point, so they move on.

Loss of vision. When I'm asked the question, "When is it time to leave my church?" I usually reply, "When you lose your vision for the church and can't get it back again."

Losing vision can be traced to a sense of failure or fatigue brought on by conflict. Or it can be the result of completing the work you set out to do: the church has been successfully planted, the building program completed, or the transition from one era to another finished. If your original vision has been fulfilled, and another doesn't take its place, the time to leave may be near.

I would add this caveat: There's a difference between losing vision and failing to confront frustrating issues with wisdom or patience. Some matters take time to be resolved. Pastors generally leave too soon rather than stay too long.

The heat is on

As we consider moves, some fear is to be expected and desired; it helps us weight such important decisions. But letting fear have its way can paralyze us.

While wrestling with the move to Akron, I was preparing to run in a five-mile race. I had trained for months with a friend. We developed a good-natured rivalry and routinely sent each other anonymous notes, trying to "psych out" the other person before the big day. He signed his notes "Mercury"; I used "The Streak."

Just before race day, my friend presented me with a tee shirt that said, "The Streak." On the back of the shirt was a large yellow stripe running down the spine.

Little did he know how close he had come to the truth about my feelings. The decision facing me whether to stay at Ashland or move to The Chapel had partially paralyzed me. I was terrified I might make the wrong choice, hurting the people I loved the most in the world. I thought I might be committing spiritual adultery! They had been loyal and loving. How could I consider abandoning them?

I gradually realized, though, that leaving a congregation is no more abandonment than a man or woman leaving family to get married. There is a time to stay and a time to move on. I had to learn to reframe my central question: not "Am I deserting these people?" but "What is the best way I can glorify God and help people, making the best use of my abilities?"

That, of course, elicited another fear—that I would not live in the center of God's will. I got over that fear once I realized that I didn't agree with the "dot theory" of God's will: God has a specific town, place, and address he desires to send us to; our challenge is to locate that dot on the map; until we locate it, we shouldn't go anywhere.

I suggest that for many decisions, some of them very important, God has not given us special instructions. Instead, he's given us latitude to make a decision, within the moral and spiritual boundaries set by Scripture. I'm to use my God-given wisdom to decide between alternatives, weighing such things as family concerns, the church's vision, and my own gifts. With many decisions, as long as I'm seeking to live faithfully, there may be two or three "godly" outcomes, ones God would approve of.

The nicest thing anyone said to me during that decision-making year was, "You can't make a mistake." My good friend George had said that, wanting me to realize that because I really wanted God's input and wanted to be used by God in this decision, I would be successful in God's eyes, no matter which path I took.

I now repeat that assurance frequently when I talk to others considering a similar change.

We have to contend not only with our fears but also with our egos. While I was waiting for my present church to conclude their search, a church on the West Coast, convinced I was the right man to pastor their congregation (though I have never candidated there), voted unanimously to pursue me, telling me that coming there was God's will.

During the fourteen months I was talking with Akron, this California church continued to court me, calling, writing, and even visiting me.

"I can't go any further with you," I told them repeatedly, "until the Akron situation is resolved." But when things began to drag a bit in Ohio (I had not heard anything for months), I finally agreed to travel to their church and speak—with the understanding I was not a candidate.

That was a mistake.

As soon as I arrived, I fell in love with the church. That week we went through several quasi-interviews, always qualifying our meetings with the statement, "But of course, this isn't an official interview."

Looking back, I regret ever having become involved with another church while the process in Akron was still up in the air. Obviously, I eventually decided against it, but in the meantime, it only confused matters for everyone. Frankly, it's nice to be courted, and it's hard to say no.

Now when I get a phone call or letter to consider a church, knowing I should be here, I say, "No, thank you," rather quickly so there is no hint of starting what cannot be finished.

A third temptation is to fail to do one's homework.

After seminary and two years as an associate, I had agreed to candidate at a church I knew little about. After only a brief meeting with their committee, I consented to a candidating weekend. I arrived on a Friday evening, and within ten minutes, I knew I had made a mistake.

The people were great, but I sensed we spoke different languages, especially when they talked about church evangelism and a few areas of practical theology.

I hung around through Sunday morning, but as it approached, I grew increasingly uncomfortable. During the service, a down-home gospel group sang the special music, which symbolized to me our deep differences. I prefer classical, traditional, or contemporary music. Well, this number never seemed to end.

Afterward a church trustee invited me to his home for lunch. During the meal, he said, "The people like you." I nodded weakly.

After the meal, he stood up and said, "I've got a surprise for you." He put on an album by the group that had performed the special music.

"How do you like their music?" he asked with a big grin.

I groped for words. My wife, obviously interested in my predicament, emerged from their kitchen just to see how I would handle the question. I finally mumbled something bland like, "They obviously enjoy their ministry." I could have saved myself a lot of awkwardness had I investigated the church more thoroughly before agreeing to candidate.

The downside of moving up

Life is a series of trade-offs. Though most of us think of moving up to churches with larger staffs and more ministry opportunities, moving to a larger congregation may not be for everyone. Several considerations should be kept in mind when contemplating such a move.

The pastor-Peter principle. Lyle Schaller has identified the different roles a pastor must play as a church gets larger. Pastors, for example, may find themselves moving from being a "gardener" (keeping the place weeded) to becoming a "rancher" (supervising the work on two thousand acres).

The disconcerting news, to some anyway, is that good gardeners don't necessarily do well at managing a ranch. Thus if we're not honest about our strengths and weaknesses, we may find ourselves in a place that doesn't match our abilities. That will only hurt us and the church.

Three roles in one. When I took on my present church, I discovered I had to become three persons in one. (No comparison to the Trinity intended at all!)

First, I became the president of a large corporation. A great deal of my time is now spent on staff, vision, and business issues. I read financial summaries and check the compass much more than in a small church.

I also became a shepherd of a large flock. I help direct the spiritual lives of a congregation where I don't know everyone by name. When I pastored a smaller church, I knew everyone I visited in the hospital. Now, many people are anonymous to me. Sometimes that feels uncomfortable to them and me because a part of me wants to shepherd people one by one.

Furthermore, the larger the church, the more specialized the people problems tend to be. When I do have pastoral opportunities, I find that I spend much of my time with either "leaders" or "needers." The former are staff people and lay leaders. The latter are people who, because of their highly visceral needs, refuse to talk to anyone else.

Finally, I became a guest speaker to a large fringe group. This is my "Bible conference" and evangelism ministry, which, when a church has more than four or five hundred, becomes part of the pastor's job description. These are people who attend church only occasionally or hear me only when I speak at a civic function.

Most of the time, I enjoy all three roles. Each is a challenge and stretches me, but the combination is not for everyone.

Loss of intimacy. It's hard to stay connected with as many people as I once did. It was much easier to be a "people person" when I pastored a smaller church. In a larger church, I'm forced to surrender much of the shepherding tasks to others in the church. As a result I wind up losing a certain amount of intimacy. I do work closely with many people, but I can't help everyone who asks for help with a special ministry or program.

The myth of perfect peace

Strange as it sounds, seeking complete peace of mind before saying yes to another position is an unwise and unreasonable expectation. We'll never feel peace about some decisions until they are made. The tranquillity often comes after we've made the difficult choice. That was the case when I accepted the call to The Chapel.

The long journey to that peace began one day while I was vacationing in Michigan. While a colleague and I were walking along a beach, I stopped at a phone to pick up my messages. The church secretary informed me I had received a postcard from a church in Akron.

"Do you want me to throw it away?" she asked.

"No," I said. "Keep it until I get back home."

When I returned home, I responded to the postcard and discovered their candidating process involved nine steps. Each step required a unanimous vote from the search committee of eighteen.

During that time, I began keeping a journal. In it I identified some doors that I believed had to open in order for me to accept the call.

One door was a deep desire on my part to go there. I wanted to feel a passion to serve that church if I was going to go through the pain of changing churches. This evolved slowly.

Another door involved persuading a local bank to turn our church's current construction mortgage into a permanent mortgage. The bank president had already informed me that if I left the church, they would not renew the mortgage. But when our board of elders met with the bank directors to discuss the issue, the bank eventually changed its mind. We received a letter from its president saying, "We believe the church is strong, and the leadership is not vested in one man alone." Another door had just swung open.

Still another door was the agreement of my family. As they visited the city and began thinking about the possibility of moving, my kids said, "Dad, you'd be crazy if you didn't take this opportunity." My wife was equally enthusiastic about the idea. She urged me to keep responding to their interest. They regretted a possible move, but they still encouraged me.

During the actual candidating week between two Sundays, I decided to add a final—the eleventh—door to my list.

"I'm not going there unless I get a 94 percent affirmative vote," I told my wife.

She looked at me for a moment and then replied with her first anger about my handling of the moving process: "Knute, I'm afraid you're playing games with God. If you don't want to go, why don't you just admit it?"

I didn't know why I had chosen 94 percent, but I said it, and I thought maybe I meant it! When the church eventually voted on the second Sunday, two church leaders involved in the candidating process stopped by our motel and told us the results: 95.7 percent in favor.

My wife and children cheered. "Well, that settles it," they said. "Here we go!"

But I was still skeptical. "I don't know yet," I replied somberly. "I still don't have peace about it."

I retreated to my bedroom and lay down. After nine different steps, fourteen months, and two weeks of preaching at the church, I still didn't know what to say. But I had told the church chairman I would give him my answer within two hours of his call to me.

For the next two hours, with hands folded like a cadaver, I lay on my bed, trying to decide what to do. I didn't want to make the call, but at five minutes to four, I got up, went to the phone, and dialed the chairman's number.

"We're coming."

My kids applauded, my wife hugged me, but my only emotion was the same old depression I had carried for so long. A part of me knew I had made the right decision. But it certainly didn't feel right. Immediately we drove back to our home church, and I delivered my resignation at the end of the evening service.

(The church knew where we were because I had chosen to announce the candidating one month before, knowing people hate surprises; in addition, I sought their prayers for wisdom.)

Five weeks later, our last day at the church, the congregation held a farewell reception. We stood in line for nearly two hours, hugging and crying with the people. My depression still had not lifted.

During the sixty-five-minute drive from our old church to Akron, a remarkable thing happened. My depression lifted like a cloud. When we pulled into the driveway of our temporary new home, I had the wonderful feeling of being my old self again. I don't know if the healing was directly from God or if it was just that the ordeal of deciding was finally over. But I finally found the peace I had been seeking.

Although I never received a direct call to go to Akron in the form of a theophany, God did work through the long, slow, and deliberate process (including a couple of radio messages!) to convince me to accept the call from The Chapel. In the end, common sense, good counsel, hours of prayer, and numerous green lights encouraged me to move.

I now rest in the fact that in the Bible I find a lot more promises from God indicating that he'll shepherd me than commands to find his specific will! Our main call is to keep our hearts pure and open to him, wherever we go.

28

Following a Beloved Predecessor

God's call to leadership is not a call to privilege and displays of power but a call to servanthood and humility.

—LEM TUCKER

One afternoon in 1981, John Perkins, founder and president of Voice of Calvary, called my wife and me over to his home. I had some idea of what he might say. The last few years, John had made several overtures about resigning but hadn't carried through.

This time, however, it was different.

"Lem," he began, "I'm going to resign, and I want you to think about becoming president of Voice of Calvary."

Eleanor and I were poles apart in our reactions. She was scared, and I was excited. I was sure this was a chance to take a significant, nationally recognized community development ministry into the promised land. I was ready to fly; I had no intention of putting on the brakes. It took me only half a day to decide.

Eleanor, however, saw nothing but loose ends, problems, and entanglements. She figured I was buying a $100 ticket on the *Titanic* for $5 and boasting about the great deal I'd gotten.

As Eleanor and I talked and prayed, I tried to calm her misgivings. In my naiveté, I didn't think her concerns were that large. And in the end, Eleanor agreed to support me in the move.

Looking back, I realize there was no real contemplation. And even more important, I didn't consult any mentor who could have warned me of what happens when you try to fill the shoes of a beloved predecessor, not to mention trying to fill everyone else's expectations.

Not every leader, of course, has gone through the trial of transition yet. Chances are, however, that before your ministry is through, you will go through at least one. I offer the lessons I've learned in hopes that they might help you through some rough days.

Taking the heat

Whenever you follow a strong leader, you sometimes find yourself in a no-win situation. On virtually any major decision, if you choose one direction, people will accuse you of being the founder's puppet. If you opt the other way, you can be accused of being disloyal to the dream.

Right before I became president, a highly controversial firing took place. I didn't realize when I accepted the presidency how the fallout from that firing would affect me.

I was out of town when the firing took place. As Voice of Calvary's executive director, I was the one who usually handled hiring and firing. When I returned, a number of staff members came to me and said, "Lem, you've got to tell John to hire this person back."

As executive director, I was committed to carrying out the directives of the founder. I wasn't going to undermine his leadership by bucking him publicly.

When I became president, the pressure to reinstate this person continued. But again, I didn't feel it was appropriate to countermand John's decision. Even today, I still run into people who refer to that incident and say, "You're not a very compassionate leader. That person was run over by a freight train, and you could have helped, but you didn't."

In retrospect, I'll admit I was scared. I don't know whether I was afraid of losing my job or of failing in John's eyes. Perhaps I should have taken a stand. But I felt my responsibility was to continue the direction we were going. I was tempted to demonstrate my independence by reversing the previous decision but knew that was not appropriate. No decision I could have made would have been popular. My wife and I definitely felt the heat.

This incident and others that quickly arose made me realize I'd overlooked a simple biblical mandate when I accepted the new responsibilities: I hadn't counted the cost. This is not to say I would have rejected the position had I fully counted it. I'm still glad I made the decision. But looking back, I see I could have spared my wife and myself a lot of emotional and spiritual anguish had I thought things through a little longer.

I wish now I'd made an honest and unabridged list of all the organizational snags and loose ends I'd be facing. Eleanor and I would have been better prepared mentally for the tensions, for instance, had we noted from the beginning even such minor things as these: though John would hold no official position in the organization, as founder his name would always be identified with the ministry, often more prominently than any current leader's; people inside and outside the organization would continue to invoke his name even when his opinion on an issue was unknown.

It pays to seek wise counsel before accepting such a position —and to take it seriously when you get it. Your spouse, other family members, or mature advisers may be able to bring you down from Mount Sinai for a while and give you a reality check. The first blush of enthusiasm can make you think you've been handed the chance to turn the world around for Jesus. Thank goodness for your spouse or your family, who know you're good —but not that good.

The inevitable comparisons

Most of us won't be as forceful or as charismatic as the previous leader. John Perkins was a hard act to follow. I consider him a prophet. I love and admire him. He forged a new vision for black leadership and a new understanding in the evangelical church of what it means to wed social action and social justice with biblical evangelism and discipleship.

His influence started locally and then spread nationally and internationally. His vision of a racially reconciled biblical community has gained adherents throughout the world. Under his leadership, Voice of Calvary became an international study center for Christian community development. Its influence has spread to interracial communities in Australia and South Africa.

How do you follow an act like that? At first, I became so tired of hearing that I was not enough of a "people person," that I needed to maintain a "higher profile." After overhearing comments like "Lem just doesn't have the same vision" or "I don't know if Lem is going to catch on," my doubts multiplied.

During this time, Genesis 4 became to me the most important passage of Scripture: The Lord comes to Cain, the less favored, and says, "Why has your countenance fallen? [Why are you depressed?] If you do well, will not your countenance be lifted up? And if you do not do well, sin is crouching at the door; and its desire is [to master] you, but you must master it"(vv.6–7 NASB)

That passage taught me a great lesson during those dark days: Despite the temptations and the circumstances, I needed to be willing to put one foot in front of the other. God's warnings to Cain, and Cain's failure, were profitable warnings to me to take care not to stumble.

In the end, Cain wound up lashing out and destroying his brother. The temptation to lash out was sin crouching at my door during my dark days. I didn't want that. Once a leader begins lashing out, it is easier to do it again and again. It's a sure way to failure.

I have great empathy now for the person who said, "Many times, taking just one more step is all anyone can do." As a leader, you can't always see what's down the road. You might not want to know. Getting through the transitions and the comparisons and the accompanying depression is, most of the time, simply the result of taking one step at a time and doing what needs to be done.

But we'll still have to weather the (sometimes hurtful) comparisons.

The urge to purge

During the first few months after John's departure, several staff members made unilateral decisions without consulting me. These were decisions I knew they would definitely have run by John. I felt, rightly or wrongly, that they perceived me as untrustworthy.

I felt like retaliating, to purge the organization of those who weren't eager to follow my direction.

But I'm glad now that I didn't. If you retaliate, you may miss a teaching moment: God may want me to love that hostile person *through* his or her frustration. I coined a saying that helped me get through those days: "He who has the greatest truth must have the greatest love, which is the greatest proof." Anyone who thinks his truth is the higher truth can neither retaliate nor retreat from that truth if he hopes to have any credentials. Had I used my office to retaliate, I would have belied the very truth I asked others to accept.

The leader who follows a strong predecessor will inevitably have to deal with being misunderstood. Reactions will always be mixed.

I may have felt this more intensely than other new leaders because Voice of Calvary is not simply a place where people leave their work at the office. It's a close community consisting of a ministry, a church, and house groups that meet regularly: the people you work with are also the people with whom you live and worship. Personal problems often have more serious ramifications.

I had days when I wished I worked for IBM or any other corporation but Voice of Calvary. At IBM, I imagined, if some employees felt I had done them wrong, they could complain to their family members and sit around and get mad together. They could complain as loudly as they wanted. But their frustration would not rip the very fabric of IBM.

But at Voice of Calvary (and in most churches), there are many overlapping reference points. Problems beget problems; they create a ripple effect in our tight community of work, play, and fellowship. Among a close community, no decision is ever won "hands down."

I had to remind myself that when you follow a beloved leader, almost everyone, at least initially, is involved in the ministry *because* of that leader. People naturally feel continued affection and loyalty.

I learned I needed to make no sudden moves, but instead to anticipate how the complex reactions would develop, in order to get my job done effectively.

Accepting your role

In every organization, there is a founder's phase in which there is a lot of energy, excitement, and charisma. The focus is on the project initiation. If something is overlooked, it's usually in the area of follow-through. The successor's role is to contemplate the next steps and not begin projects unless there is some assurance they can be finished. When I finally understood this, it freed me to be a far more effective leader.

It took a while to accept the fact that my role as successor was different from John's role as founder. Charisma will carry an organization only so far. After that, it takes a good manager and organizer to keep things running.

In many ways, a second-generation leader has a tougher job than the founder. It's my responsibility to take a vision and apply my organizational skills to make it run smoothly. We're always open to charges of stifling the dream because we put an organizational and structural framework around it. We're often viewed as constricting. But that's because we have the conflicting responsibilities of motivating the workers, tending the organizational machinery, and charting the new frontiers for growth.

Voice of Calvary's effectiveness for the first generation came from applying the gospel in new ways to specific community needs. Its effectiveness for the second generation will come from staying in touch with changing needs, trying new ways of meeting them, and blending those with the best aspects of the first generation.

I've had to learn to make decisions based on both the past and the future—to rely on the wisdom of past leadership when it's necessary but to be astute enough to know when the past won't work anymore. Keeping or redefining the vision and scope of an organization is the great challenge of the new leader. Past glories will fade, and new styles of ministry will need to be put in place in order to move forward.

Spiritually and emotionally, I've found this role taxing. Fortunately, I'm a sustainer and a plodder, and I'm durable—three traits that have become perhaps my greatest assets.

Finding emotional support

Finally, I've learned you need to be prepared for an emotional roller coaster when you take over from a founder or a beloved leader. Not only do you suffer the inevitable misunderstandings and comparisons, but some people will, no doubt, leave.

I thank the Lord for my wife, Eleanor, who, despite her hectic and frenzied schedule as a television newscaster, continually gives me her love and concern. We've had times of challenge, but we've seen each other through.

In addition, one of the best moves I made was to get myself a bailout group. Some people call it a support group, but I like the term *bailout* much better because it more accurately describes one's condition during a transition.

This is a group of people I've learned over the years can be trusted; when they see my weaknesses, they don't use them against me. They don't expect an explanation from me every time we get together; I don't have to convince them of my side of the story. I can let them see my discouragement, and they won't worry that the ministry is coming apart. They accept me as I am and can provide meaningful and honest encouragement.

For instance, occasionally I have to make a difficult decision about personnel. Someone's job must be changed, even terminated. When that happens, coworkers normally murmur, divide into factions, and chew on whatever the rumor mill produces. I've often wished I could tell everyone all the factors that went into the decision, but in many cases, some of the information must remain private.

Especially at a time like that, I've appreciated my bailout group. They know the difference between agreement and loyalty. They don't always agree with the decision I've made, but they're willing to stick with me anyway. They're "on my side" not because we always think alike but because we've walked enough paths together that they know my commitment and motivation, and they're willing to give me the benefit of the doubt.

I don't mind taking my share of the arrows that come a leader's direction. But I also deeply appreciate the member of my bailout group who once told me, "Lem, I might have handled things differently, but it's your job to make that decision. I'm with you. I'm convinced you're the leader God has for us at this time."

My bailout group has become a reference point that gives perspective when conflicts and obstacles can so easily preoccupy me.

I've also taken comfort in the thought that many times God's means of keeping a ministry's vision close to himself is to prevent the leaders from getting too self-assured. Sometimes, he gives them thorns in the flesh so that in weakness they can rejoice in the strength God has given. Other times, God may use a failure to prune back pride, or an uncertain future to encourage living by faith.

I'm becoming more and more convinced that God's leader will never be allowed to get too comfortable. Something will always be coming undone; one more thing will be careening out of control. These things continually remind me that God's call to leadership is not a call to privilege and displays of power but a call to servanthood and humility.

29

Picking Up the Pieces

Preaching and visitation are essential in any pastorate, but in a broken church, their need is magnified.

—ED BRATCHER

I was jogging down the street, thinking about my new church (I had arrived in Manassas only a few weeks earlier), when a man I had never seen motioned with his hand for me to stop. I stopped and tried to catch my breath.

"Are you the new pastor of Manassas Baptist?" he asked.

"Yes," I said, smiling.

"I'll never go there again!" he exclaimed heatedly. Then he began an angry tirade about the church's hypocrisy, its control by a few members, its lack of love. Thirty minutes later, he was finished.

I could tell he had been deeply hurt, but I wasn't sure what to say. I only knew this was going to be the most difficult pastorate of my ministry.

Meltdown

The previous pastor at Manassas, whom I'll call Fred Sharpe, had resigned under pressure from charges of sexual indiscretions and aberrant theology. When I had candidated, the pastoral search committee described the problems in general terms, with a note of sadness. "Fred was a man of unusual abilities," they explained.

Before Fred had become pastor, the congregation had been divided on whether to call him, but Fred had been highly recommended and had demonstrated qualities the congregation sought: he was articulate, personable, and young, and he held a reputation for leading churches into growth.

The church grew rapidly under Fred's ministry. Many were attracted to his nontraditional approach to preaching and worship, and soon a second service was started. After about eighteen months, however, a few people started leaving the church, upset primarily by Fred's theology and his practice of drinking beer in public. Rumors of sexual indiscretions flew.

As I had considered the call to Manassas, Fred was still living in the community and had started a "church without walls." The Manassas Baptist Church staff was in disarray: one of the associate pastors had resigned; the other was having serious marital problems. I sensed the church's financial condition was unstable, even though the interim pastor assured me this was not the case. (Time proved him wrong.)

For these reasons, among others, I struggled for three months with whether to go to Manassas. But I accept as a good definition of God's call "a task to be done and the ability to do it." People told me they felt I had the abilities, so after much prayer, I accepted the call.

The rest of the story

I thought I had the full story when I went. But about six months after I arrived, Fred moved in with his girlfriend. Neither was divorced at that time. I learned that Fred's sexual improprieties had been going on for several years, straining his marriage. The search committee had not mentioned the problem; no one knew the extent or severity of it until Fred and his wife separated.

Every member's attitude toward me and the church was in some way colored by these past events, yet each person viewed the events in different ways. It was difficult to get a clear picture of what had happened.

The complexity of the situation can be seen in the different reminiscences of four members:

A strong supporter of Fred: "I'm not sure why I wasn't aware of the moral problems, except that maybe I wasn't in contact with anyone who disagreed with us. Those who agree with an embattled pastor tend to surround him and cut him off from divergent viewpoints. There were a few vague charges brought out at a couple of business meetings, but they were discounted."

A female church leader: "Looking back, I realize Fred was making improper overtures to some of the women. Tales came back to me of such actions taking place at retreats, but they also occurred in the homes of the members."

A deacon who opposed Fred: "My opposition began when Fred preached a sermon on open marriage, the essence of which was biblically and morally unsound. Prior to that sermon, I had become concerned about rumors that Fred, in his home, encouraged young people to experiment with alcoholic beverages (though only in moderation)." When this deacon's opposition became vocal, many members reported to him rumors of Fred's sexual indiscretions. He took these rumors seriously because of the people who reported them. "By the time a vote of confidence was called for, I was convinced Fred was involved in extramarital affairs, and that was the major issue in my mind in seeking Fred's resignation."

One of the staff members who worked with Fred: "I was supportive of Fred's program. I also feel the church leaders shielded me from the conflict. I was still in my twenties, so they didn't want me to get hurt in the crossfire. I was concerned over the problems Fred and his wife were having, and as a result, I probably was not 'hearing' what was being said about Fred."

The iceberg under the tip

Fred's sexual behavior was not the only issue in the controversy, but when Fred moved in with his girlfriend, immorality became *the* problem for members of the church. This public confirmation of their suspicions caused the members who were left at Manassas Baptist to forget the other facets of the problem, and therefore made the healing process more difficult.

Among the other problems, for example, was a power struggle between the old and new members. The rapid influx of new members had made the older leaders concerned over their own loss of power. Many leaders had been upset, for instance, the time Fred asked some older members to withdraw their names from consideration as deacons so newer members could be elected. The older members also resented several new programs pushed through by Fred.

At one of the first business meetings I attended, a conflict erupted over whether a nonmember should teach a Sunday school class. The problem was seen as a clash between those who had caused Fred's resignation and those who had supported him. The debate shed little light but generated much heat.

One of the two major adult Sunday school classes had identified itself as "conservative," and the other considered itself "liberal." The "conservative" class saw its task as combating any remaining influences of Fred's theology and life style. The "liberal" class saw its task as combating the rigidness it identified with the opponents of Fred's ministry.

Meanwhile, Fred and his new church were still in the community. He sent a letter to selected members of Manassas Baptist inviting them to the new church he had started. I called him and questioned the ethics of that practice.

"I don't see anything wrong with it," he replied. "I have many friends at Manassas who would like to know what I'm doing. I won't stop contacting those members or any others I might choose."

Fred's behavior plus these conflicts scattered the leadership at Manassas Baptist. A new Baptist congregation had started in town while Fred was still pastor at Manassas Baptist, and over several months, a number of members saw this as an opportunity to respond to a new challenge (of starting a church) as well as a way out of a difficult situation. In addition, Fred had taken with him many of his followers.

I had the remaining members, many of whom were hurt and disillusioned. Some withdrew from active participation, but the rest became a united remnant committed to praying and working for the rebirth of the congregation.

As a result of these complex and overlapping problems, I learned to accept all reports with a grain of salt. I had to listen with a "third ear" for the feelings and hidden agendas behind each statement.

In many ways I proceeded like Abraham, seeking to follow God's will but not knowing fully where I was going. My age, fifty, was a definite asset. Had I been thirty-five or forty, I doubt if I would have survived. The problems I had gone through in three previous pastorates helped me to listen better and also to retain my hope for a positive resolution.

Leadership strategies

I began by taking some specific steps to rebuild trust in the pastoral office and unity in the church. Here are the principles that guided me through this challenging new pastorate:

Go through the board. Shortly after I arrived at Manassas, I scheduled an overnight retreat with the deacons to deal with whether to keep the two staff members who had survived the conflict. I decided to ask the deacons—rather than the personnel committee—to make the decision. Most of the standing committees were severely weakened by the exodus of trained leaders during the conflict, and therefore, the real power was with the deacons.

I indicated to the deacons that the decision had to be theirs; I was not going to decide for them. One deacon took me aside before the retreat and said, "Ed, the deacons are looking to you for guidance. You must be prepared to share your views." I assured him that I would, but that I wanted the deacons to make the final decision.

The retreat proved exhausting. The first session on Friday evening went until midnight, and many of the deacons continued their discussions until 2:00 or 3:00 A.M.

On Saturday morning after prayer time and a devotional, we

tested for a consensus. There was none. All of us were emotionally drained and discouraged.

So after sharing with the group what the one deacon and I had talked about, I made three specific recommendations: (1) that both the associate pastor and the part-time minister of music remain, because I needed their help, and it was unfair to dismiss them without notice because of the church's financial problems; (2) that the associate pastor and his wife, recently separated, be given our love and support in this difficult time in their lives; and (3) that the position of the associate pastor be reevaluated after one year. These provided the catalyst for further discussion, and we decided unanimously to present these recommendations to the church.

Our recommendations were accepted with little discussion by the congregation. This was to be the pattern at the monthly church business meetings for several years to come. The church members were so tired of fighting, they wouldn't voice opposition or offer suggestions.

To those familiar with congregational meetings, this might appear to be a godsend! It was only in part. We were left without feedback, so it was hard to develop strategies and programs for which the members had any enthusiasm or sense of ownership.

I continued to use the deacons for several years as the primary, if not the only, decision-making group in the church. By the time I left, however, the deacons were primarily concerned with family ministry and spiritual growth. The various committees—finance, personnel, missions, building and grounds, and others—were again functioning well and carrying out their assignments with minimal input from the deacons.

Focus on the basics. At the first deacons' meeting, I outlined my priorities. First, I would spend the greater portion of my time in visitation; specifically, my wife, Marjie, and I planned to visit each deacon. Second, I would focus on my preaching. I stated also that I would not, for the most part, get involved in rebuilding or strengthening church programs.

Preaching and visitation are essential in any pastorate, but in a broken church, their need is magnified. At Manassas, the members needed to hear the good news of God's love and power, to have their hope renewed, and to experience human concern and love. These aims were best achieved through preaching and visitation.

A serendipity of my announcement that Marjie and I would be visiting in the homes of deacons was that many invited us for a meal. This provided the double benefit of giving and receiving love.

Be an encourager. I'm not by nature a glad-hander and an ego builder. I don't make it a practice to announce how great the church is and how wonderful the services have been. My preaching style tends rather to "afflicting the comfortable."

However, four years before going to Manassas, I heard a series of lectures that encouraged pastors to pattern their preaching after Isaiah's words: "Comfort ye, comfort ye my people" (40:1 KJV). At first I rebelled against that suggestion, but at Manassas I turned to it more and more.

Twice, for instance, I preached on Barnabas, "one who encourages," and how he was an example to us. The response was overwhelming; people realized they needed to encourage one another.

To help the church feel it had a viable place in the community, I initiated an annual interchurch conference, to which all the local churches were invited. We brought in major speakers and underwrote the expenses. As the conferences were enthusiastically received by others in the community, people in the church began to feel encouraged that the church was doing something constructive.

I also felt that instilling a spirit of encouragement was also the responsibility of the deacons. I even confronted them once about their discouragement, suggesting that they weren't inviting others to church because they were ashamed of our church. Most agreed I was on target.

Focus outward. A fourth strategy was to encourage the church to focus on missions. Because my parents were missionaries for forty years, I have a strong commitment to missions. In addition, I found the congregation already had several missions interests I was able to nurture.

We invited missionary couples to the church; one spent a

whole week teaching all age groups, including adults, during our vacation Bible school. Local mission needs were identified as well, and Manassas Baptist took the leadership in providing help to an unexpected influx of refugees. These efforts resulted in a dramatic increase in missions giving, not to mention a renewed sense of congregational purpose.

Celebrate the good. A broken church needs to highlight occasions when it can celebrate the blessings of God. We held services in which we focused on God's goodness in the lives of individuals. We took time to express publicly our thanks for the service of various members and staff.

When our church reached its centennial, we held a year-long celebration with the theme: "Thankful for the past and committed to a second century of ministry." The centennial celebration included historical pageants, the writing of the history of the church, a homecoming Sunday, and a banquet.

Survival tactics

In pastoring a hurting church, we expend so much that personal survival tactics become as important as leadership strategies, perhaps more so.

My first survival tactic was a redoubling of my efforts in personal spiritual growth. I had been aware for many years that I was often more concerned about leading worship than in participating in it. Marjie gave me a framed copy of a prayer by Martin Luther that so impressed me, I began praying it before every service:

> O Lord God, Thou hast made me a pastor and teacher in the church. Thou seest how unfit I am to administer rightly this great, responsible office; and had I been without Thy aid and counsel, I would surely have ruined it long ago. Therefore do I invoke Thee. How gladly do I desire to yield and consecrate my heart and mouth to this ministry. I desire to teach the congregation. I, too, desire ever to learn and to keep Thy Word my constant companion and to meditate thereupon earnestly. Use me as Thy instru-

ment in Thy service. Only do not Thou forsake me, for if I am left
to myself, I will certainly bring it all to destruction. Amen.

I asked the deacons to meet with me for prayer prior to the
service. Some saw it as a spiritual crutch and resisted the idea at
first, but eventually, "prayer with the pastor" became an important part of the role of the deacons.

I found myself spending more and more time in prayer—on
prayer retreats, on Saturday evenings in the dark sanctuary. I
was not alone in trying to grow spiritually. One member in writing her recollection of the key events over those difficult years
concluded by saying, "There is now a solid foundation being
built in regard to the spiritual life—prayer, meditation, and Bible
study."

A second strategy was to be more open about asking for help
from church members. My first major attempt at this came at the
time of the marriage of our daughter. She was not known to the
church, because she had already established her own career and
home before we moved to Manassas. I announced that she was
to be married in another state and that Marjie would be gone a
couple of weeks to help with the wedding preparations. I
planned to follow later to perform the ceremony.

I received no response from the congregation. No one seemed
to be interested. I had tried to "rejoice with those who rejoice,
and weep with those who weep" (Rom. 12:15 NKJV), but now it
seemed like those whom I had tried to serve were letting me
down. I felt hurt and angry.

While jogging late one evening, I decided to go to one of the
families in the church and talk about it. The family listened to
me, and they contacted others. By the time I left for the wedding,
there was an outpouring of love through various words and
deeds.

On the Sunday I returned, I preached "Carry One Another's
Burdens." It was to have been just another sermon, but somehow
I was able to confess how hurt I had been, and also how much I
had been helped by their love and support. I stood before the
members of the church at the time of altar call and said, "I need
you, and I thank you for your love."

Many still speak of that worship hour as one of the highlights of my fifteen-year ministry there. "Carry One Another's Burdens" became something of a motto for many in the congregation.

I also gave attention to the many other sources of renewal available to a pastor. Continuing education events helped me not only because I learned new things about ministry, but also because such classes got me away from the stress of the church. Writing a book, teaching classes, speaking to groups, and consulting were outside interests that I learned to pursue—with the encouragement of the congregation. Both Marjie and I, being duty oriented, had to grow in our ability to allow ourselves to enjoy outside interests. We also began traveling and enjoyed it immensely.

Prior to Manassas, as I later realized, I had placed too many burdens on Marjie and my family. Through the sometimes-trying times at Manassas, I learned the value of pastoral peer groups, with whom I could share my deepest feelings. I value such mutual support among pastoral friends.

Also, regular exercise helped me. Strenuous and enjoyable activities such as handball, racquetball, jogging, and swimming worked wonders in my life. Even yard work was a good release, although I do admit to relishing it less than racquetball.

Long view

A while back I showed a written account of those first years to one member and asked for comments. The member said, "Your strategies, conscious or not, worked, but the healing process took far longer than any of us would have thought." The key words are *worked* and *took far longer*.

That my strategies *worked* doesn't mean they were perfect. Some problems continued during my years in Manassas, and when I retired, work yet remained to be done. Many dedicated members did too much and burned out. At times, some members had an Elijah complex: "I alone am left." I know I hurt some members—unintentionally—but still they were hurt. Some members left the church because they felt they couldn't work with me.

But healing did take place, although not in the span of the three or four years I had envisioned. There were two important watersheds in the healing process, at ten and fifteen years after my arrival at Manassas.

During my tenth year, the man who had accosted me while I was jogging joined the church. He immediately became active in worship, Bible study, and service. Also at the ten-year mark, the church planned a celebration for Marjie's ministry as well as mine. Not only did we enjoy it, but it indicated that the leadership could take initiative again, and that they believed there was something to celebrate.

I retired fifteen years after going to Manassas, announcing it several months before it happened. The members' response was a marvel to behold. The leaders formed committees to plan our retirement festivities and to work toward finding interim and continuing pastoral leadership. The church members accepted tasks and provided feedback on what they considered to be the needs of the church. In all, the church spirit was reminiscent of the words of the apostle Paul: "But one thing I do: Forgetting what is behind and straining toward what is ahead, I press on toward the goal" (Phil. 3:13–14 NIV).

Certainly the transition into a church torn by a difficult experience with a previous pastor is not the easiest. But now I understand Paul's statement: "I have worked harder than anyone else. It wasn't I; it was the grace of God."

30

Preparing to Leave

*I've gradually learned how to leave properly so that with the
tension there is also a sense of joy.*

—ROBERT KEMPER

The fable of the race between the tortoise and the hare reminds
me of when I've accepted a new call. It's not so much the unexpected outcome of the race or the moral about tenacity or the
warning about overconfidence that impresses me. It's just that
when I accept a new pastorate, I feel like *both* a tortoise and a
hare.

As he moves, the tortoise carries with him everything he
owns, with the consequent risk that entails. I am amused by the
New Yorker magazine cartoon depicting a turtle with a hung over
look on his face. The caption says, "What a night! Hailstones!"
Such are the complications of self-contained units.

After deciding to move, there comes a moment in the moving
process, whether I am loading a U-Haul trailer or professionals
are filling up a huge Allied van, when I see all my worldly possessions strewn upon my front lawn. To me that's not only a
dramatic symbol of what is taking place in my life, it reminds me
how vulnerable I am at such moments—like the cartoon turtle
in the *New Yorker*.

Then again, after receiving a new call, I also feel like the hare.
The hare, of course, represents speed. Likewise, after taking a
new call, I instantly become future oriented. My whole being
moves toward what will be; the past and present become disproportionately smaller, and the future looms big and bright. I feel a

great rush to get on with the future or, better, to get to the future. The present seems a barrier, an annoying distraction from what is really important to me. "Let's get going," says the rabbit in me.

In spite of such tensions, my three pastoral moves have been glad and celebrative experiences. There's something about closing one chapter of my life and opening myself to a new one that excites me.

Over my three moves, I've gradually learned how to leave properly so that with the tension there is also a sense of joy. Here are some of the principles I've found helpful.

Letting emotions have their way

Watching my daughter get married—that moment was filled with mixed emotions. On the one hand, I was sad that one era of my wife's and my relationship with our daughter was ending. On the other hand, it was the beginning of something fresh and wonderful for our daughter.

There are many experiences in life like that, where two contrary emotions struggle for predominance. Changing churches is one of them. At one moment, I feel terrific—a wonderful church wants me. I look forward to helping the people move ahead in ministry for years to come. Then the next moment my twelve-year-old daughter comes to me in tears, "Daddy, do we *have* to move?" The ecclesiastical hero has become the family villain.

It's difficult to live back and forth between contrary emotions. For one thing, it wears me out. But if I try to fight these emotions, or simply suppress the negative in favor of the positive, I complicate the already complex situation and make myself more exhausted still. Consequently, I've found it better to let such emotions weave their way in my life and let God, in his own time, resolve the tensions.

In particular, I have found great help in being able to talk with a ministerial friend, not just a colleague, but one who speaks my language, who lets me be myself, who often knows intuitively what I'm feeling. I like to talk with another human being without my having to paint the picture or qualify myself. To such a person I can say things aloud I do not really mean but need to say, and I can speak about my ambivalent feelings.

A good good-bye

Moving means having to write a "Dear John" letter. Somehow I have to tell my congregation that I am leaving them for another.

Because it's so difficult, I've been tempted to make a clean break of it: "I hereby resign my pastorate effective December 31." Technically, that is all I have to say.

But then I begin to think of particular people in the parish: my golfing partners, the women at my baby's shower, the person who slipped me extra cash for a getaway vacation, the troubled ones who have trusted me and counted on my support. In addition, special memories crowd into my consciousness: the place my daughter was baptized; the budget battle we fought and won, despite the odds; the addition of a new Sunday school wing.

When such thoughts rush in, I feel as if I'm rejecting friends and renouncing treasured moments. And so that letter becomes harder and harder to write. I'm eager to tell these loved ones about my good news, but my good news will be bad news to them, and to me. At such times it's not unusual for me to wonder, *Am I doing the right thing?*

In composing the letter, I find it helpful to recognize the strong emotions that swirl within. Then exactly how to write the letter becomes easier in one sense: I tell people what's going on with me.

So I not only tell them what is happening, but how I'm struggling. I tell them how hard it is to make this decision, and how painful it is to leave a congregation that has been good to me. To me, that's the proper tone for a pastoral letter of resignation, not because it's the most diplomatic, but because it's the truest.

In addition, I also remind the congregation of the need for changes, that I cannot do everyone's funeral, confirm or baptize every child. I celebrate what has been good between us. I also name high accomplishments we've worked on jointly. Finally, I assure them that the church goes on. Paul used the phrase, "When Timothy comes . . . " I've found that a useful analogy to employ; it helps the congregation get used to the idea of someone succeeding me.

Lyle Schaller also suggests that we include in this letter a variety of reasons for leaving: theological ("It's God's will"), professional ("The new church will use many of my gifts"), and personal ("We'll be within an hour of my wife's parents"), and the like. If we offer multiple reasons, members will surely understand at least one of the reasons we're leaving and so better accept our decision to move.

Ministering until the last

Until my resignation takes effect I am still the incumbent. I still have continuing duties, and in spite of my rabbit impatience to get on, I try to perform these duties with professional competence and integrity.

Special occasions. Some of these routine duties take on a special urgency for the congregation. People want me to baptize a child, marry a daughter, or whatever, before I leave. Although such last-minute requests can crowd my calendar, I try to do as many as I can. They are testimonials to the congregation's regard for me, and I want to honor that.

Administrative urgencies. Elected lay leaders feel a new sense of responsibility for the church when they know I will not be there to counsel them. So they ask many questions of procedure and propriety, sometimes in desperation.

There is a story about a fresh seminary graduate who, shortly after graduation, called the professor of practical theology to ask, "What do you do at a funeral?"

The professor was astounded. "We covered that in class," he said.

"Yes, I remember," said the graduate, "but this guy is *really* dead."

Something of that sort goes on with lay leaders when we resign. They have heard what to do, but faced with the prospect of having to do it themselves, they are in a bit of a panic.

One way I respond to this anxiety is by cranking up the special administrative machinery that will help the church find a pastoral successor. In my denomination that means meeting with our moderator, the chief lay officer of the congregation. I make sure the moderator, other church leaders, and denominational officers responsible for helping churches get in contact with one another.

In our case, the church council must nominate a search committee that, in turn, must be elected by the whole congregation. I often urge the moderator to make sure that many different parts of the congregation be represented on that committee, including youth. In that way people will feel their concerns are addressed in the selection of the new pastor.

Polities differ in how they find successors, of course, but I've followed one piece of advice given in all of them: I give no direction to the selection of a particular person to succeed me. My role is simply to teach them how to find a successor—of their choosing.

Private audiences. Certain people need to meet with me personally and privately. No matter how I communicate my resignation, a few people (some with whom I'm close, others who may feel betrayed, others who are counting on me) are entitled to a private conversation about my move. In such conversations, I try to communicate my decision is not a personal rejection of them.

Reconciliations. Then there are people I've managed to alienate from the church during my tenure. In some cases I have to let bygones be just that. But sometimes one last stab at reconciliation is in order.

In one parish I served, we had a husband and wife who were loyal parishioners and who also loved music. They had wanted our church to purchase a new organ. In what I thought was the best interests of the congregation, I had not supported their idea. They held that against me for the rest of my pastorate.

Before I left the parish, however, I made a call on that couple. I acknowledged they had probably felt hurt and disappointed in me for not supporting their cause. I told them I thought that new ideas had to be good and timely, and that theirs had been good, but the time was not right. I cannot say that they were suddenly enlightened by this explanation, but we parted with a greater mutual respect.

More gracious to receive

Truly, it's more blessed to give, but it's more gracious to receive. So I try to anticipate and accept graciously the parting tributes of my parishioners.

First there are the gifts. People want and need to bid me farewell, and giving gifts is a way they do that. In addition, there is some sort of collective party at which a special gift is given— although I never anticipate exactly what! (When asked what I want at such parties, I simply ask that the occasion be celebrative and not maudlin).

In addition, dinner and luncheon invitations abound. Sometimes I've found all this becomes a bit much. Parting festivities blur into one big mirage; I cannot remember who said what or what I did and did not do.

Nevertheless, the congregation and I *both* need this. The proper word for all these festivities is *closure*. Endings need to be formalized in some way. First, they mark the new chapter in my life. Second, they clear out debris for the church, so it can make a fresh beginning.

In addition, I've found that graciously receiving farewells prepares me to receive new welcomes. For me, tears are part of farewells, even though most of the time I'd rather avoid tears. But when I shed no tears, I fail to acknowledge the permanence of the change. When no permanent change is acknowledged, I have a more difficult time starting up in my new place.

One caveat: when leaving a parish, I do not believe all the nice things said about me. I receive tributes graciously but also with a grain of salt. If I don't, I may wonder why I'm leaving these wonderful people in the first place, and I may convince myself that my new sense of call was nothing but indigestion.

Meanwhile back at the parsonage . . .

When I was ten years old, my father, a pastor, received a new call. I remember my mother gathering a school party for me. My parting gift was an address book. At the party my classmates entered their names and addresses that we might write to each other. It was a memorable gift, symbolically and in fact.

I also remember attending my parents' farewell reception and some dinner parties. In sum, as a ten-year-old, I was not excluded from the family's closure ceremonies. Further, my parents made a special effort to show me pictures and drawings of our new home. As a child, I needed to be assured there was a special place for me in the new and unknown environment.

In various ways, I need to recognize my family's needs at such a time. They need to experience closure too. My wife will have farewells at her work, my children at their school. As often as possible, I like to share these experiences with them as they shared mine with me.

I mentioned that poignant moment when, like the turtle, I see all my worldly possessions strewn out in front of me. Before I get to that moment, however, I'm tempted to vigorously and decisively eliminate some of those possessions: *No sense carrying around things we no longer use,* I think. For me, books especially are a case in point.

However, there is another side to this issue. Books, for example, are my professional tools, too powerful of a symbol to discard lightly. Nor should I be too quick to cast off my children's old toys; children, too, need symbols of continuity in the face of uncertain change. Just before a move, then, may not be the best time to simplify one's life.

"By faith Abraham . . . obeyed and went" forth from Ur of Chaldea (see Heb. 11:8). So he did. Clear. Simple. But the Bible does not say how Sarah felt about it. It does not mention the late-night conversations in the tent about whether to go. It does not show Abraham having to explain to neighbors where he was going and why. We don't see the hassles of changing addresses, negotiating with movers, filling out forms, and making deposits.

We don't hear about the nitty-gritty of moving that can be a pain in the neck, not to mention heart rendering.

Of course, the Bible is right in focusing on the larger events, like the divine call to which we must respond. But moving also contains many little things, little concerns we are wise to attend to. When we do, it makes our dutiful obedience to God's call all the more joyful.